Sailing to the Heart
of
Japan

Sailing to the Heart of *Japan*

A Cruising Adventure and How-To Guide

by

Nicholas Coghlan

SEAWORTHY PUBLICATIONS, INC. • MELBOURNE, FLORIDA

Sailing to the Heart of Japan
A Cruising Adventure and How-To Guide
Copyright ©2024 by Nicholas Coghlan
ISBN 978-1-948494-90-8
Published in the USA by:
Seaworthy Publications, Inc.
6300 N Wickham Rd.
Unit #130-416
Melbourne, FL 32940
Phone 321-389-2506
e-mail orders@seaworthy.com
www.seaworthy.com

All rights reserved. No part of this book may be reproduced, stored in a retrieval system, or transmitted in any form, or by any means, electronic, mechanical, photocopying, recording, or by any storage and retrieval system, without permission in writing from the publisher.

Library of Congress Cataloging-in-Publication Data

Names: Coghlan, Nicholas, 1954- author.
Title: Sailing to the heart of Japan : a cruising adventure and how-to guide / by Nicholas Coghlan.
Description: Melbourne, Florida : Seaworthy Publications, Inc., [2024] | Includes bibliographical references. | Summary: "Sailing to the Heart of Japan is an adventure narrative and how-to guide about a sailing voyage in a 27ft boat from New Zealand to Japan, onward into the Inland Sea, and finally to Alaska. The story of the author and his wife's fifteen-month-long cruise includes wide-ranging commentary on Japanese history and culture, with a focus on how World War II is remembered today. An appendix includes notes on weather and charting, advice on dealing with bureaucracy, detailed harbour information, and GPS positions; as such it will be useful for others thinking about embarking on a similar adventure"-- Provided by publisher.
Identifiers: LCCN 2024003618 (print) | LCCN 2024003619 (ebook) | ISBN 9781948494908 (paperback) | ISBN 9781948494915 (epub)
Subjects: LCSH: Coghlan, Nicholas, 1954---Travel--Japan. | Coastwise navigation--Japan. | Sailing--Japan. | Sailing--South Pacific Ocean. | Sailors--Canada--Biography. | Bosun Bird (Sailboat) | Voyages and travels. | Japan--Description and travel.
Classification: LCC DS812 .C644 2024 (print) | LCC DS812 (ebook) | DDC 910.92 [B]--dc23/eng/20240212
LC record available at https://lccn.loc.gov/2024003618
LC ebook record available at https://lccn.loc.gov/2024003619

Table of Contents

Author's Note vii

Prologue: The Old Tin Trunk (Berkshire, England, 1978) viii

Chapter One: A Nail that Stuck Up (New Zealand, 2010) 1

Chapter Two: Boarded! (Vanuatu and the Solomons) 9

Chapter Three: Into the Rising Sun (Pohnpei, Guam, and the Approach to Japan) 36

Chapter Four: Kagoshima and Kamikazes (Southern Kyushu) 53

Chapter Five: Embarrassing Encounters in the Nude (Sailing the East China Sea) 65

Chapter Six: Dying Islands and Closet Christians (Nagasaki and Goto Retto) 74

Chapter Seven: The Bosun and the Pilot's Brother (Hirado to Fukuoka) 87

Chapter Eight: Through the Barrier Gate (Into the Inland Sea and Hiroshima) 105

Chapter Nine: Of Monks, Prostitutes, and Typhoons (Mitarai and Onomichi) 127

Chapter Ten: The Three Musketeers of Kitagi (Tomo-no-Oura, Kitagi, and Nao Shima) 140

Chapter Eleven: Twenty-Four Eyes (Shodo Shima and Kiba) 152

Chapter Twelve: There at Sumahama (Suma, Kobe) 158

Chapter Thirteen: The Black Ships (Kii Peninsula and Shimoda) 174

Epilogue: Kodiak, Alaska 193

Appendix: Cruising Notes for Japan 199

Acknowledgments 231

About the Author 232

Note: The Japanese kanji ideogram 海, used to separate sections of the narrative within each chapter, means "sea" or "ocean." It is pronounced "umi."

Author's Note

*I*n my career as a Canadian diplomat, an important part of my job was to understand and interpret the issues at play in the foreign country to which I was accredited. I would prepare as well as I could for every face-to-face meeting I held with political players, warlords, and pundits, but I would often find it very useful to play the naive, ignorant foreigner. This would allow me, after begging forgiveness, to pose blunt questions that often provoked surprisingly revealing responses.

In Japan, Jenny and I had no need to act the part of know-nothing foreigners, for we truly were that. We lacked any prior knowledge of the country beyond the most superficial: a few short histories, the novels of popular writers such as James Clavell, Mishima in translation, classic movies such as *Seven Samurai*. We spoke next to no Japanese. I am under no illusion that in the course of our fifteen months in Japan we went on to do anything more than scratch the surface of an ancient, highly sophisticated culture. There are things we no doubt misinterpreted or misunderstood. For this I apologize in advance to the many friends whose kindness and understanding we may have inadvertently abused.

But if we discovered neither the Soul nor the Brain of Japan, I do believe that we found its Heart - not just geographically in the Inland Sea, but in the astounding kindness with which we were met in every conceivable setting. To our many friends in Japan: please forgive this still-ignorant Gaijin his errors.

Prologue:
The Old Tin Trunk
(Berkshire, England, 1978)

The small tin trunk was painted military green. At one time it had probably held ammunition, perhaps mortar rounds. On the lid, carefully hand-painted in fading cream was my father's rank and name: "Capt. J. F. Coghlan." In the bottom right-hand corner, it said: "Not Wanted on Voyage."

The trunk lived in the family garage for years, under flowerpots, rusting pairs of shears, and a moldy yellow parasol. I pulled it out one July day when my wife Jenny and I were in the midst of frenetic packing for our big adventure: marriage, immediately followed by a teaching job in Argentina. It looked as though it might be useful for cramming in a few of the more fragile odds and ends that we hadn't found room for in my two old school trunks, which we were about to send off to Harwich for sea shipment.

"What was that voyage, anyway?" I idly asked my father, who'd come out with me to help find the trunk.

"Japan," he said thoughtfully. "But thank God we never left."

In the summer of 1945, with the European campaign over, he'd been brought back from the British Army in Greece and was on a short leave with my mother in Lincoln, near the military barracks to which he was assigned pending his next posting.

"We'd all heard about Guadalcanal, Guam, Okinawa...the kamikaze attacks. The Japs seemed to be fighting harder all the time. God knows what it would have been like on the home islands. And then..."

He paused and changed tack.

"I can remember it now. It was a beautiful summer's day. We were out walking by the cathedral. I'd seen a headline in the paper that morning. Some kind of a new weapon, but it didn't mean anything to me; we were always reading things like that. Then we got the call to return to barracks immediately. I thought they must have advanced our departure. We all sat in a classroom...

There was nothing dramatic. It was as good as over, we were told. The atomic bomb. It was the best day of my life."

I suppose I must have looked shocked. Dad went on, after a moment:

"We were terrified, you see. All of us. We'd seen what a hell of a time the Yanks were having. We knew it would be much worse than Italy, worse than Germany, probably. They'd fight to the death, defend every inch. Oh, we'd have gone, of course we'd have gone; you had no choice. But we all dreaded it. Your mother more than anyone."

Much later, he'd had opportunities to travel to Japan in the course of his work. But Dad had never taken them up. In fact, he'd point blank refused to go, more than once.

"I should go one day. Everyone says how kind the Japanese are, how beautiful the country is. But I don't think I can bring myself to. It's not because of the way they fought; I suppose you have to admire that. Perhaps I'm still afraid. Or perhaps I'm just afraid I'll find they're perfectly ordinary people, just like all of us."

Chapter One:
A Nail that Stuck Up
(New Zealand, 2010)

Thirty years on. From Argentina, we'd emigrated to Canada; Jenny and I were now balancing my career as a diplomat in the Canadian foreign service with long stints of ocean cruising aboard our little blue cutter-rigged sailboat, *Bosun Bird*. It was an existence that had taken us to work in geo-political hot spots such as Colombia, Sudan, and Pakistan with interludes cruising Namibia, Brazil, the stormy waterways of the Beagle Channel, and the empty expanses of the South Pacific.

The contrast between the two ways of living appealed to me. The life of an expatriate diplomat, however much exotic travel it might involve, is one of constraint and compromise; you are a small cog in a very large machine, an actor whose every public statement must conform with precedent, hierarchy, the rules of the game. The essential skills are tact, caution, preparedness to conform, geniality (however superficial), and a command of language (written and oral). All of the time, even off duty, you are representing your country, for better or for worse.

At sea and in the ports on the cruising circuit, by contrast, you may proudly fly the flag of your country, but you do not officially represent it; you have no particular prestige, your passport is just like anyone else's. Your scope of action is almost literally limitless in that the high seas, for now, are under no nation's remit. You depend on no one but yourself (and your companion if you have one). The skills you must command are practical: reading and understanding the weather, fixing diesel engines, sewing Dacron, working with fiberglass. Caution is still in order, but if you take it to an extreme, you will never leave the dock. Knowing a foreign language is an asset in both worlds, but as we'd discovered when dealing with engine problems in Patagonia, a degree in Spanish literature is not that helpful when you are trying to track down bearings for your defective water pump or negotiating to have the cylinder head re-bored.

For Jenny, I knew, the flip-flopping between the two lifestyles was sometimes trying. With one degree from Cambridge and another from Oxford, she was more professionally qualified than I was. But while I advanced (however slowly) up the ranks of the Canadian diplomatic service, she was obliged to re-invent herself with every foreign posting, taking jobs that ranged from Embassy IT support in Mexico City to editing the Pakistan Journal of American Studies of the University of Islamabad. It didn't get any easier for her once we were at sea. We agreed that you can't sail offshore as a floating democracy; in a crisis there needs to be one person emphatically in charge, and as I had marginally more sailing experience, that fell to me. I liked to think, all the same, that we worked well together. Typically, I had the grand ideas, while she brought me back down to earth, but not all the way.

We came together, too, in seeing that the expat and the cruising lifestyles share one great thing: each offers an opportunity to see and know the world and its people in a way that no amount of tourism allows. Conveniently, the Canadian government cooperated with our plans in that I was permitted, as a civil servant, to take up to five years unpaid leave in the course of my career and still hold down a job.

Most recently, after leaving the boat on dry land for two years in French Polynesia to permit me to take the job of Deputy High Commissioner of Canada in Pakistan, we'd sailed down to New Zealand's North Island. Here, at the historic old whaling town of Opua, we were hunkering down for the duration of the South Pacific cyclone season (November through April) before resuming our slow journey by sea: home to British Columbia, via the Western and North Pacific.

In some ways, it would have been easier to return to Canada by taking the long route: west over the top of Australia, onwards to South Africa, across the South Atlantic to the Caribbean and the Panama Canal, then a loop out to Hawaii and back to British Columbia. The weather patterns of the world are such that this would have taken us downwind nearly all the way. By going north instead, we'd have the wind on the beam (the side) of the boat for much of the time, and it would only swing behind us once we reached Japan and turned to the east, over the top of the high pressure system that dominates the North Pacific every summer. But we'd already taken the round-the-world route once, back in the 1980s on a different boat. The Japan itinerary would be shorter, and it would take us to many new destinations.

I didn't say anything to Jenny, but I'd also thought occasionally about the conversation I'd had all those years ago with my Dad, over the old tin trunk. I was curious about these people he'd both feared and hated more than the men of the Herman Goering division that he'd faced in Italy. What did today's Japanese think about the war (if they thought about it at all)? How different

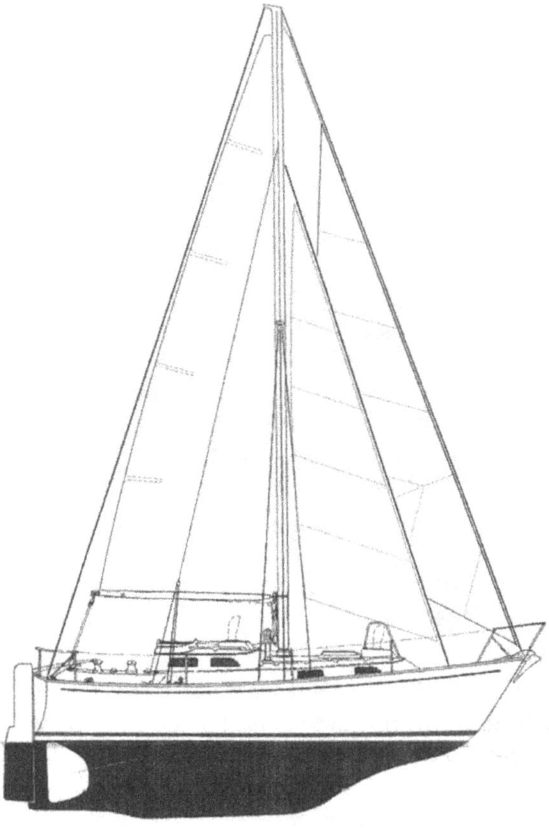

Bosun Bird   Victoria, B.C.

(Vancouver 27)

were they from "people like us" (whatever that meant)? How far would we be able to penetrate this ancient and very foreign-seeming culture? I was doubtful about this last question, but it seemed to me that it might be interesting to try.

As we waited for the cyclone season to pass, we left *Bosun Bird* safe on her moorings at Opua and travelled all over New Zealand. Occasionally, there were intimations of the long sail ahead of us, with Japan as the principal waypoint. At Cape Reinga, as far north as you can go, we walked the beach where Maori

Cape Reinga, New Zealand

spirits make their final departure from the Earth and had our photographs taken at the lighthouse. A bright yellow sign pointing out to sea told us it was 8,475 kilometers to Tokyo.

Christchurch, on the South Island, we found intensely English. You can rent a punt on the River Avon and have yourself poled around by a young man in a boater and striped blazer; you can peer through the gates of Christ's College where the younger boys wear shorts and ties with horizontal black and white stripes and look like schoolmates of Harry Potter. The Cathedral is filled with brass plaques and Anglican priests glide quietly around in the gloom.

Jenny summoned me over one afternoon to a corner of the Cathedral square, where there was an eclectic display of maps in a bookshop window. "Take a look at this," and she traced her finger from the top of world map vertically downwards, through open blue spaces, down to where you normally find Antarctica.

I squinted in puzzlement for a moment, then realized it was a deliberately quirky upside-down map, with New Zealand in the upper center, the landmass of Asia dominating the lower hemisphere. Together and from this unfamiliar perspective, we plotted the route we hoped to take, from the North Island, straight down to Vanuatu, on to the Solomons—there was the big island of Guadalcanal—across the Equator, diagonally to Guam and finally to the island chain of Japan.

"It's the route they took in the war," I reminded her. "The Americans. These were the stepping stones, one by one, starting after Pearl Harbor, all the way to Okinawa and the four home islands."

And I thought for a moment of the tin trunk again. My dad had been on the front lines in Italy, then working counterinsurgency in Greece as he followed the sketchy news from the distant Pacific with slowly growing concern, suspecting that was where he'd be going next.

One day we took a bus from downtown Christchurch and trekked along a ridge of sun-yellowed grass and baked earth to Godley Head, overlooking the sheltered blue waters of Lyttelton Harbor. On a steep hillside are the foundations of three sets of coastal defenses, each from a different historical period. First a giant Rifled Muzzle Loading (RML) gun—also known as a Disappearing Gun on account of its recoil—was placed here in 1886, when for reasons now largely forgotten, it was Russia's turn to be Enemy Number One of the British Empire. In 1914, it was Germany. Another set of naval guns was installed. Nobody came, either time.

In 1939, the next war scare came and even more heavy guns for Lyttelton. New Zealanders, and Australians volunteered in their thousands and embarked for Europe to defend the old country, just as they had in 1914. But for the troops stationed out here at the battery, the probability of action must have seemed very distant indeed. Until, that is, the shock of Pearl Harbor. Immediately afterwards came the fall of Singapore, and Japan's rapid military reinforcement of the dozens of small Pacific islands that it had been granted as its share of the victors' spoils in 1918. The enemy now seemed to be barely over the horizon. There was a massive bombing attack on Darwin, Australia, that destroyed more ships than had the attack on Pearl Harbor; a Japanese midget submarine made its way through defensive nets right into Sydney Harbor.

The Japanese Imperial Navy was never sighted or engaged from Godley Head. The only time the guns were fired was in October, 1939, when a local fishing boat, the *Dolphin*, failed to identify itself and a warning shot accidentally killed two crewmen.

Back in Opua, as the southern summer faded, we made our preparations to leave. There was a surprisingly hectic social scene, with dozens of other foreign yachts making plans just as we were, and frequent happy hours, some of them sponsored by local yacht chandlers keen to make last-minute sales. One day, as we relaxed over lunch in *Bosun Bird's* cockpit, tied up to the floating breakwater that protects the Opua marina, there was a friendly hail: "Coghran San! Here is Chinami!"

Chinami was a Japanese single hander, balding and bandy-legged, in his early sixties; he sailed a 35-foot sloop named *Kifa*. We'd last seen him back in Tonga. He'd seemed lonely then; he spoke only fragmentary English and had obviously found it hard to break into the sometimes cliquey sailing fraternity. We took it upon ourselves to invite him around and introduce him to others. As cruisers do, we'd broken the ice with him by asking about his recent passages and, as a single hander, about his routine for keeping watch, especially at night. The passages he listed seemed to have taken him an inordinate amount of time, considering their length. But it's rude to say so. Things became clearer when we got to his nighttime routine.

"But I just go to bed," Chinami said, looking puzzled.

"Yes, but for how long? How often do you get up to look around?"

A frown.

"I take sails down so I no need to get up. *Kifa* stops. Then I sleep eight, maybe ten hours, yes? Maybe I need to, how you say, piss, but that all…"

The reason for Chinami's slowness was that he was only sailing sixteen hours out of every day.

"But what if there is a ship coming?"

Now Chinami smiled tolerantly, clearly thinking us rather stupid.

"I never see one ship. I am sleeping."

Chinami San and Jenny

From New Zealand, Chinami was now planning to head east, the way we had come. It was his intention to make for Chile directly. This would be a feasible but daunting sail of over 4,000 nautical miles, almost entirely in the band of cold and windswept seas known as the Roaring Forties. He had an iPad with him. He booted it up immediately, trembling with pent-up enthusiasm, and swiped until an electronic chart of this section of the Southern Ocean came up.

"Here is Opua, I think." And he moved the cursor to the right, drawing a straight and emphatic red line on the screen as he went. "And here is the Cape Horn. What you think?"

Now the common wisdom is that in approaching Chile from the west, the safest strategy is to make for Valdivia or Puerto Montt—1,200 to 1,400 miles north of Cape Horn—then work your way gradually south, in the protected natural waterways known as the Chilean channels. Both ports are well-marked landfalls with no off-lying hazards, and they are north of the band of heaviest weather. They are also the only points on the southern coast where it is legal to enter Chile from the open ocean; the highly efficient Chilean navy enforces this vigorously.

We pointed all this out to Chinami. Either his English was too poor for him to grasp what we were saying, or he had already made his mind up. Either way, after twenty minutes or so, he put away the iPad and we turned to our own plans.

"Ha! I have idea!" he said, pointing at me in childish-seeming glee. "I see Coghran San[1] boat name and now I remember special friend in Japan!"

Later, we'd get used to Japanese friends often ignoring Jenny (the woman in the partnership) on all matters they considered to be of importance; we didn't take offence. But we were both puzzled as to what he could mean, as many English speakers had to have the significance of *Bosun Bird*[2] explained to them. More laughter:

"My friend, he bosun in Japanese navy! I know what is bosun."

Chinami took the paper napkin we'd given him as we ate lunch; he carefully drew a map in pencil, of what he explained, with some difficulty, was a cozy bay on an island off the north coast of Kyushu. He wrote a series of Japanese characters, then spelled them out to us aloud and rendered them carefully in western script. He added, from memory, what seemed to be a phone number. Chinami finally drew five or six squares behind the bay, marked one with an "x" and said:

"Bosun house!"

---

1   "San" is common honorific, used to mean either Mr., Ms., or Ms.
2   Bosun Bird is the familiar name for a Tropicbird, a family of pelagic seabirds distinguished by their streamer-like tail feathers. The birds' call is said to resemble the sound of a bosun's whistle.

He made another careful "x" in the bay.

"And here *Bosun Bird*!"

After we'd bade our friend a cheery goodbye—he bowed in laughing self-parody, his hands clasped together—we tucked the paper napkin away in our logbook and prepared to get back to work. Later, we'd learn how exceptional Chinami was, bucking the huge pressures that Japanese society exerts on non-conformists; at home he'd have been called, scornfully, a nail that sticks up. But for now, we were simply worried. Jenny said:

"I really hope he knows what he's doing."

As we made our way slowly north through Vanuatu, the Solomons, and Micronesia, we'd think often of Chinami San, wondering.

Chapter Two:
Boarded!
(*Vanuatu and the Solomons*)

The sea passage between New Zealand and the tropical Pacific islands to its north has an evil reputation. Among the community of local and international yachts that gather in Opua in the southern autumn, captains and their crew try to outdo each other in telling stories of narrow escapes. Especially popular are those who have gory first-, or even second-hand accounts of sailing disasters:

"There were these friends of ours; they were in the Queen's Birthday storm in '94, and what they reckon is this…"

In twenty or more cockpits, over Steinlagers or gins, every story is mulled. For every storm tactic that one skipper swears by, another says a mate of his drowned doing just that. Over the years, Jenny and I had learned to listen—you might pick up the odd hint—but to be skeptical. We must have sailed through half a dozen stretches of ocean that local cruisers swore were the most dangerous waters in the world. Every country had its Skeleton Coast, its Graveyard of (name your ocean).

At least, we said to ourselves, going north we'd be going from the coolish sub-tropics, with variable weather, to the more predictable and warmer winds of the tropics. The idea was to time things so as to leave just after a front had passed, giving us favorable southwesterly winds all the way up to thirty degrees south, where we'd be safely back in the easterly trade winds. Early May looked good. A front was sweeping across the Tasman from Australia, due to bring in its wake strong southerlies for several days. There was a pesky depression sitting over the warm waters off the Queensland coast, but lows in that neck of the woods are supposed to slide to the southeast then weaken; it shouldn't bother us.

On May 1st a flotilla of nearly fifty yachts left Opua, bound mainly for Tonga and Fiji. In spite of our experience and our mental vows to stand firm, it was hard not to feel that we might be mistaken in hanging back. Could so many people be wrong?

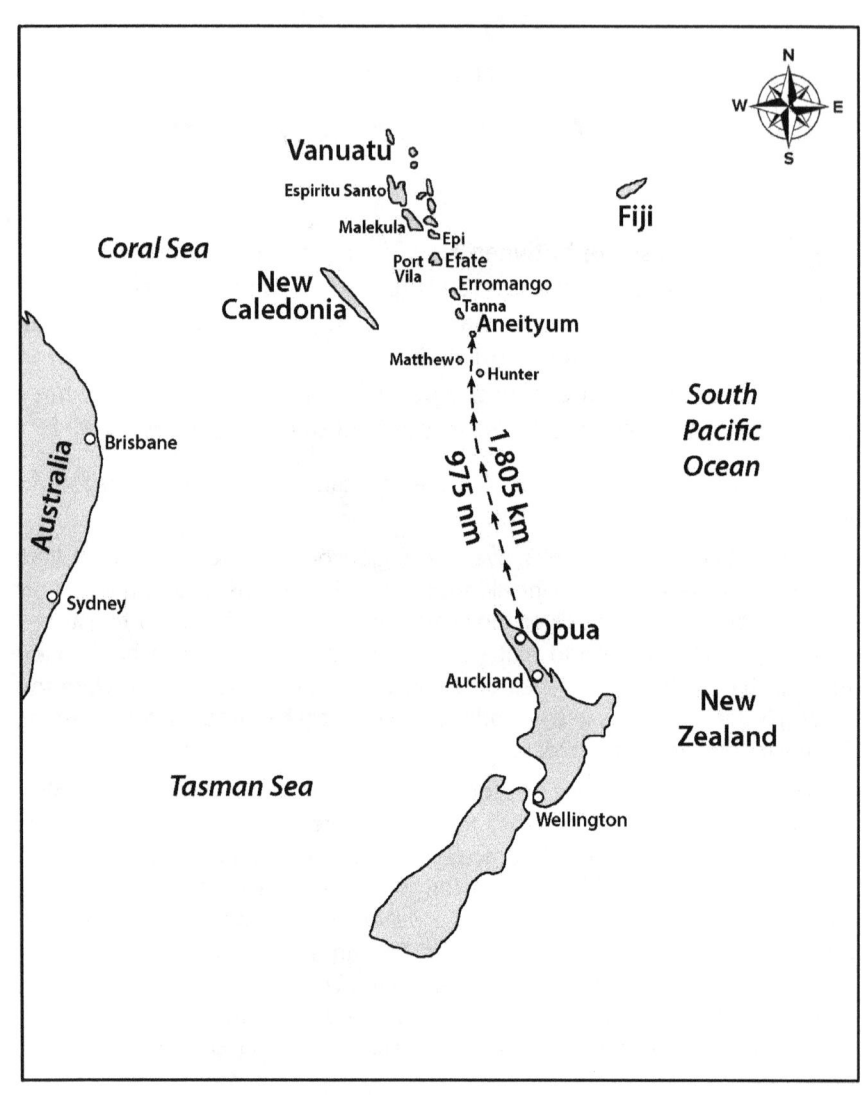

New Zealand to Vanuatu

Jenny reminded me of a moment way back in our earliest days of cruising. We'd been anchored in a remote bay on the west coast of the Baja California peninsula, along with half a dozen of the large fleet of cruising sailboats that makes its way south from San Diego to Mexico every winter. There were mares' tails in the sky—"mares' tails and mackerel scales make lofty ships to carry low sails," goes the saying—and the barometer was dropping. Four boats left together, leaving just ourselves and one other swinging at anchor in the bay. We knew the four were all hoping to spend Christmas together at Cabo San Lucas, where friends were coming down from the USA to meet up. Clearly, they were more worried about missing their rendezvous than the weather.

For an hour we argued between ourselves: should we go, too? Reluctantly, I agreed to wait, though I felt we were being overly cautious. That evening the breeze picked up to gale force and blew hard for two more days. Our anchor line was bar rigid as we careered first one way then the other. But we watched the landmarks on shore carefully, and we didn't drag an inch. Weeks later we learned that one of the four leavers had such a bad time of it that they put their boat up for sale in Cabo and flew home. Peer pressure and deadlines could be just as dangerous to a cruiser as any amount of bad weather.

"Besides," Jenny said now, "we haven't finished our shopping; and there's a half price happy hour at the pub tonight. Why head out straight into a beating?"

We waited another day. The wind duly eased; the skies were clear; the barometer was rising. Then, all in a rush: a quick visit to Customs and Immigration to obtain our clearance papers, a last-minute call at the Opua store to pick up fresh bread and vegetables. At ten in the morning, we were untying from our long-time berth on the breakwater and heading out into the Bay of Islands. It was a bright but cool sunny morning. Out past the Ninepin at the head of the Bay, and by dusk we had the Cavalli Islands abeam, our course north-northeast.

We were quite sad to leave New Zealand. We'd both found it an easy and comfortable place, if not very challenging for anyone of a middle-class Anglo-Saxon upbringing. In another life we would have been very happy to settle here. But there was a nip in the air and new horizons beckoned: Vanuatu, the Solomons, Micronesia, and Japan.

For the first couple of days, we had light but favorable winds and sailed within sight of a large green yacht.

"*Balu, Balu,* this is *Bosun Bird*" we called on the VHF after straining to read the name painted on her bows.

"*Bosun Bird, Balu,*" came back a thick Irish brogue. "Bound for Vanuatu, we are. And you?"

Understanding now that the unfamiliar flag drooping over *Balu's* stern was neither Indian nor Iranian, we agreed to stay in touch as long as we were close. Normally we are more than happy to lose sight of other yachts—we never quite trust their night watch-keeping to be as vigilant as ours—but it's fun to have some company as well, especially on long passages.

One morning as I sat in the cockpit, Jenny called me from below, to take a look at the laptop. On the morning's weather chart, just downloaded through our Iridium satellite phone, there was a black splotch centered on the Queensland coast:

"I don't like the look of that…it's starting to form into a closed system."

The rain-bearing low carried on deepening and, notwithstanding daily predictions, obstinately refused to move southeast. The tell-tale arrows on its circumference now had three, even four feathers, each indicating ten knots of wind. At the back of our minds now was that infamous Queen's Birthday storm that everyone in Opua loved to talk about, and that had wrought havoc on the 1994 cruising fleet. Twenty yachts had been abandoned, three crew drowned and there was a massive rescue operation by several navies combined.

The wind hardened, the sky darkened. By our fourth day out we were close-reaching—the wind at about 60 degrees relative to our direction—into a 30-knot near-gale, with heavier weather forecast. Soon we had three reefs in the mainsail and were flying a tiny storm sail forwards; the motion was wild, the skies scudding. As we ploughed down ever steepening wave fronts, the wooden vane on our Aries self-steering gear flopped back and forth, correcting our steering every few seconds.

"Time to put the wind off," I said.

Checking to see that my tether from my safety harness was securely fastened to the boat, I clambered up onto the rocking and rolling windward quarter of the stern, yanked at our screaming wind-generator so that its blades feathered and secured a small rope loop to stop it turning back into the wind. The lessening of the noise brought instant relief.

That evening the wind built steadily until we were at 40 to 50 knots, with gusts probably ten or fifteen knots higher (approaching hurricane strength); the laptop was now showing the rarely seen diamond symbol (50+), instead of feathers. For the first time since we have owned *Bosun Bird*, we reduced the size of the mainsail to a tiny fourth reef, lowered the storm jib, and hove-to, to ride out the storm. With the mainsail sheeted firmly to the center line, the tiller lashed to leeward, we rocked comfortably enough at fifty or sixty degrees to the wind. This way the bows took most of the shock of the building seas as we slowly drifted off, leaving a slick of smooth water upwind. Once or twice heavy breakers out of sync with the wind caught us broadside on, bursting into the cockpit with a great rush and effortlessly ripping the grommets from the canvas lee-cloths that enclosed the steering space.

Worse than the motion was the noise: a high-pitched shrieking in the rigging, with a background roar of breakers all around in the night. Occasionally foam from breaking seas swept right over the foredeck and coach roof,

Bosun Bird's Aries wind vane at work in heavy weather

scattering winking phosphorescence over us. But apart from those ripped lee cloths everything held up. As we made one violent roll, I heard a thumping crash from below.

"Everything alright?" I yelled down into the darkness.

"I've broken off the galley faucet…" Jenny eventually replied. "I'm going to sleep on the floor now; that way I won't break anything else."

By morning the worst was past. Over the space of an hour or so, the wind dropped from 45 knots to absolutely zero and the sun came out. But there was a chaotic, violent seaway running and, with no wind to position us, we were bucking around violently. We decided we should raise the vulnerable fiberglass paddle that, hanging over the stern, drives our Aries gear.

The Aries wind vane is a Heath Robinson-looking contraption mounted on the stern of the vessel, above and behind the rudder. A lightweight plywood vane is aligned in such a way that, with the boat steering the desired course relative to the wind, it remains vertical, its leading edge angled into the wind. If and when the boat veers off course, the wind will make it flop one way or the other. This motion is transferred by gears to a paddle that trails in the water, rotating it slightly. As the paddle starts to rotate, the force of onward-coming water will drive it up hard to one side or the other. That powerful driving force is transferred by lines to the tiller, which pulls the boat back onto its correct course. It's a lot easier to understand how it works by watching than explaining.

Wind vanes like this have been around since the late nineteen-sixties. They relieve the helmsman of the arduous chore of steering by hand and have the great virtue of drawing no electricity; they are driven only by the wind and the forward motion of the vessel. They are out of fashion these days, as most cruisers prefer electric autopilots: arms that push the tiller one way or another as the boat deviates from its pre-set compass course. We are still firm believers in vanes. On a small boat we have relatively little electrical power on hand and in any case, autopilots can lead you into deep trouble as and when wind direction changes without you noticing.

Our Aries did have one little character quirk. In the middle of the operation of pulling up the steering paddle after the storm, the boat gave a particularly violent lurch and its gears jumped by one tooth. It was nothing catastrophic, but it did mean that until we were able to reengage the gears in their correct place (preferably in a calm location) all the vane settings were off.

After the storm: more frustrations. The wind remained light, and came from all around the clock, meaning we had to change the arrangement of the sails almost every hour, including during the night. We coasted slowly between the remote, uninhabited islets of Matthew Island and Hunter Island, keeping Matthew in sight for three days. These inaccessible mid-ocean rocks held a special fascination. Our Admiralty charts dated from the mid-nineteenth century had told us the islands were discovered in 1788 and 1798 respectively; the Admiralty pilot book (a kind of nautical travel guide put out by the British authorities) added that "jets of sulphurous vapour have been observed." In two hundred years each has seen maybe half a dozen landings.

When Matthew first came into view, I called out to Jenny, "Remember the last time we were here?"

She looked blank for a moment, glanced at the chart, then, "1987, or was it 86? On *Tarka*, en route for Brisbane from Fiji."

Tarka was our previous boat, the same length as *Bosun Bird* but a lot less sturdy. We'd spent the years 1985 to 1989 sailing her around the world; now we were crossing our old track almost at right angles.

Flying fish signaled to us that we were back in the tropics; every morning there would be one or two stranded on deck. Evenings we checked in by radio with a listening station, manned by volunteers in Russell, in the Bay of Islands. Every night, through the crackling ionosphere, New Zealand seemed more distant.

We never really found the steady trade winds that are supposed to predominate north of 30 degrees, but thirteen days out we made our landfall on the southernmost island of Vanuatu: Aneityum. We anchored in clear, calm water, at Port Aneityum—"Surveyed by Captain Denham, *HMS Herald*, 1853," said the chart—on the southwestern tip of this high, lush, and green island. Protecting us from the swell was a horseshoe reef, most of it awash, but a part of it covered in palms: Inyeug Islet.

Regulations (this was not an officially designated port of entry) meant we could not go ashore, but we spent two very peaceful days here swimming in the lagoon and trading with the friendly locals who came to visit us in their dugouts. Two D batteries and a tin of tuna bought us eight enormous Pamplemousses, the oversized grapefruits of the tropics, and a hand of thirty bananas. We also took advantage of the calm water to deploy our satellite phone and hold an email correspondence with the Denmark-based maker of our vane, Peter, and successfully rectify the anomaly that had arisen after the storm.

From Aneityum, it was an overnight sail to the next island, Tanna. In the middle of my off-watch, Jenny woke me:

"You'd better get up. We need to reef. I can hear thunder."

I poked my head out of the cockpit. It was a brilliant starlit night with not a single cloud in sight. But then there was another rumble and a flash lit up the sky ahead. It was Yasur volcano, we ruefully realized, spectacularly active ever since Captain Cook became the first European to see it. As we drew closer, we could see red molten lava being shot high into the sky, and as dawn came up, we could set our course on the thick black smoke belching from an 800-meter cone.

We anchored in historic Port Resolution, a U-shaped cove open to the north, on the windward side of the island. Historic, because this was Cook's first contact with the group he named the New Hebrides, and also his first certain contact with cannibals. The chain went down just after seven o'clock in the morning, among five or so other yachts that were rolling heavily. We were soon exploring ashore, lurching like drunks on the solid land.

As at many villages in Vanuatu, the local community had nominated one person to be the lead contact with yachts, in this case a friendly young Melanesian.

"Hallo 'dere mon, ah'm Stanley...," he said. "Dis de yacht club," and he pointed up the hill to a straw hut overlooking the bay. "You'll be wantin' to go to Lanakel for immigration, I s'pose? An' de volcano? You haf to do dat..."

Jenny took a pick-up ride to clear us into the country of Vanuatu at the small town on the other side of the island, while I watched the boat. We rolled so heavily in Port Resolution that I started to feel sick and was more than happy to join Stanley and Jenny that evening for a trip to Yasur's rim. For an hour we stood awe-inspired as the ground shook and rumbled loudly under us. Great clouds of smoke billowed up and every few minutes firework-like fountains of red lava shot up directly in front. The prevailing wind conveniently ensured that the red-hot rocks landed on the far rim and not on us. The display was all the more impressive in that we went as dusk was coming on, and the red glow from deep inside the crater began to light the underside of the clouds above.

"You see over dere?" asked Stanley, pointing along the rim to a small promontory fifty meters or so away. "Well last year dere was some yachties from France, I tink. An' guess what?"

We looked at him expectantly.

"He was hit by one of 'dem hot rocks," said Stanley. "Splat. Dead, right dere."

Later that evening we drove on to Sulphur Bay, for another unique experience. This is the home of an unusual religion (or cult) known as the Jon Frum movement.

Frum was a mysterious person who appeared from the sea on Tanna in 1936 to some kava drinkers, and said he was related to the God of the Volcano. What ensued is far from clear. According to some he promised that if white Europeans were made to leave Vanuatu, great wealth would ensue. His name may be a corruption of "John from…," but from exactly where is not known. Six years later, nearby Espiritu Santo Island became the principal base for the American effort to dislodge the Japanese from the southwest Pacific (from Guadalcanal in particular). 250,000 American troops passed through Santo in only two years. They brought with them what seemed to the local people massive affluence: Coca Cola, cigarettes, refrigerators, electric fans, earth movers, and so on. Many of the soldiers were black, which was quite astounding to the people of Santo (and the many men from Tanna who went there as local labor). The Ni-Vans[3] had hitherto associated material wealth only with white men, that is to say their British and French masters. The black Americans also brought their own music: rollicking gospel, banjos, and guitars.

In some manner, for the people of Tanna, all this seemed to fit with the prophecies of Jon Frum. His followers now adopted the American flag, held military parades in imitation of the Americans, took on their music. Today, every Friday night representatives from Jon Frum communities all over Tanna— "companies," as they are known in militaristic terms—assemble at Sulphur Bay for twelve hours of music and singing, from dawn to dusk.

Under the light of a single bulb lit by a car battery, we sat for an hour as the celebrations began. A group of five or six men with guitars, one with a drum,

---

3   Ni-Van: a person from Vanuatu.

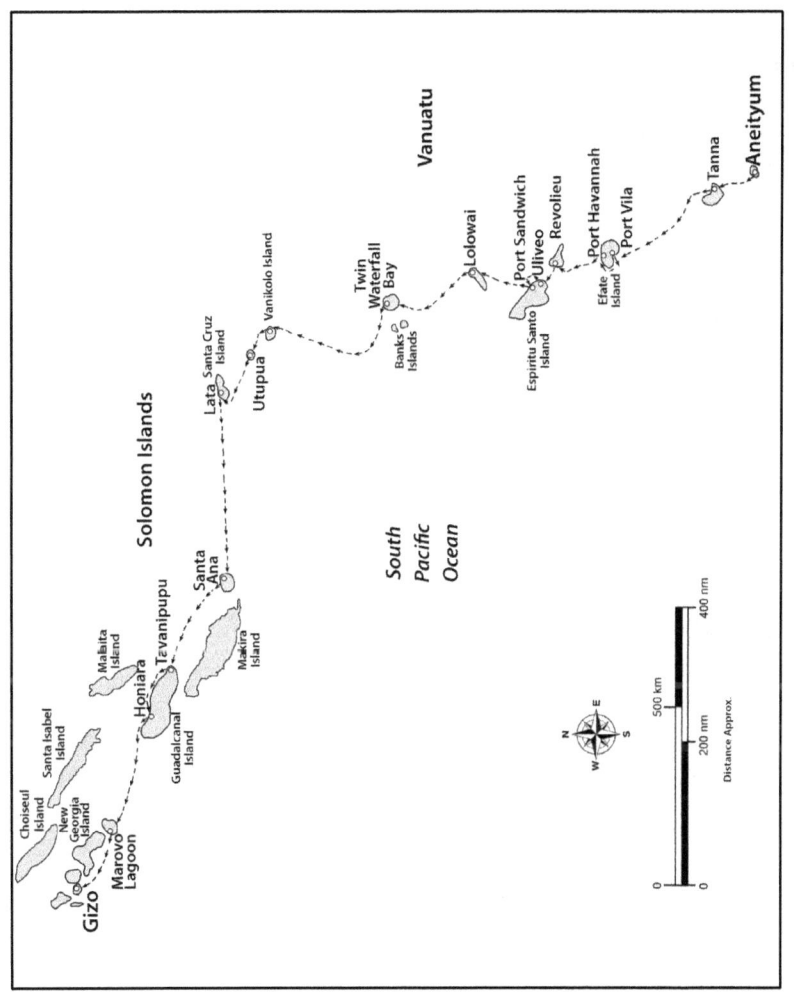

were formally summoned by rhythmic stick beating; they formed a kind of scrum outside the open-sided hut and then in formation shuffled in. As women brightly dressed in their best Mother Hubbards took their places all round, the men sat in a circle on the ground and began a session of ten rousing songs in Tanna-ese. It sounded just like gospel singing and an old man told us that it was, but that the songs had the aim of summoning Jon Frum. Around the hut, in the utter darkness of the tropical forest but with Yasur rumbling eerily in quiet moments, many of the rest of the community jived and moved to the songs. After the session of ten songs was over, there was a pause, more beating of the stick, and another "company," this time from our own community of Port Resolution, took over.

Everyone seems to have a different theory on what it is all about. The red crosses on buildings that distinguish Jon Frum communities from others, for example: for some they are an adaptation of the Christian cross, while others say they date from the war and are in fact the Red Cross, another supplier of great bounty like the USA. The government of today is ambivalent about the movement. Understandably they are particularly uncomfortable with hundreds of young men periodically drilling (albeit with wooden weapons) and saluting the American flag. There are cargo cults in other parts of the southwest Pacific, but Jon Frum is unique to Tanna.

Jon Frum followers meet at Sulphur Bay, Tanna

The night at Sulphur Bay was moving. These are communities where radio, let alone TV, is still unknown. The weekly music sessions brought villagers together in a traditional, ancient way that survives in few other places in the modern world. And as our jeep headlights picked out our route back, through tunnels of thick jungle and gargantuan banyan trees, the volcano rumbled on.

"I think if I'd grown up here," I said to Jenny, "I'd believe a god lived in the volcano. And if a prophet appeared who said I could have wealth like the Americans, then I'd sign up for sure…"

海

Back at Port Resolution, the rollers coming into the bay were starting to make things ever more uncomfortable. More worryingly, strong northeast winds were forecast, and the bay is open to the north. This was one of those occasions when the cautious option is the decisive one. Although we had only been here two days, Jenny and I were sufficiently well-tuned to each other that we didn't need to discuss it when I said that evening:

"This is no place to hang about."

This is one of the frustrations of the cruising lifestyle, I reflected as we readied for departure; the need constantly to watch the weather and the security of your boat means you miss some opportunities. So just after dawn next morning, we were off again, this time bound for the island of Efate, 130 nautical miles to the north-northwest. The only other boat still remaining in the bay, *Nathape* (named after Nathalie and Peter…) came to the same conclusion shortly after we

Bosun Bird running north from Tanna

did. They overtook us mid-morning as we worked up the weather coast of Tanna in strong winds and growing swells. We took pictures of each other, and *Nathape's* photos, when we eventually got to see them, showed us almost lost from sight between the waves.

It was fast sailing until evening, but rain then set in…and then thunderstorms and even heavier rain. In fact, we'd never been out in anything like it. It was like having a fire hose trained on *Bosun Bird's* topsides for fifteen hours straight. Most frightening were the thunder and lightning, topped off by a climactic storm just after dawn. Twenty-four hours out, the wind reached forty knots again with visibility near zero in horizontal rain.

But all things pass. We were soon motoring into the welcoming haven of Port Vila, Vanuatu's quiet and modest capital, and tying to a mooring buoy among a dozen or so other yachts (one of which comfortingly told us that the weather of the last few hours was the worst he'd seen in six months in Vanuatu). 1,200 miles on from Opua in New Zealand, we were back in civilization.

We spent several weeks at Vila, a two or three-street town set along the waterfront. Here there was the usual collection of semi-permanent resident cruising yachts, with transients frequently coming in to rest and stock up for a week or so. Less usually, there was tragedy in this particular sailing community. One of our neighbors, a middle-aged American on a sturdy double-ended fiberglass boat with weeds growing on its waterline, rowed over one morning and we got talking.

"I'm looking for crew," he said, explaining why he had been here so long. "I sailed here with my wife. Took us two years; we were living a dream. About a year ago we went up the islands, headed for the Solomons…" He paused in thought. "She came down with what seemed like malaria. But it wouldn't go away. It kept coming back. I spoke with a couple of the other boats on the radio. One of them recommended a herbal remedy he'd found on the Internet. It took me a couple of weeks, but I finally got some shipped in. She took it… and she died. Almost right away…"

Not everyone's dream turns out well. Dave was drifting, almost literally; he could see no way forward, no way back.

Port Vila has a few relics of the confused colonial period when Britain and France ruled jointly under an arrangement known formally as the Condominium, and more informally as pandemonium. There are two prisons (one French, one English-speaking), one or two classy French restaurants that offer bat in a red wine sauce, French baguettes from a chain of good supermarkets called Au Bon Marché.

There are some reminders, too, of the massive American presence here in World War II. The three main districts of town are known as "Numbawan," "Numbatwo," and "Numbatree" because those were the names of the three US radar stations. Port Vila's airport – Bauerfield - is named after Harry Bauer, a US Navy captain who was killed in action off Guadalcanal in September 1942, when a Japanese destroyer sank his command. The airport was being modernized with funds from the government of Japan.

We picked up some Bislama (the local variety of pidgin). There are many myths about Bislama. Often quoted is the supposed translation of the word helicopter: "Mixmaster blong Jesus Christ." Another is the phrase for a piano: "black fala box we igat black teeth, hemi gat white teeth, you faetem hard I singout." These are sadly fabrications. But there is no lack of real, colorful, and expressive terms: "bagarup," means broken (from buggered up), while "man wiwi" is a Frenchman (a man who says "oui, oui"); a bra is a "basket blong titi." On independence in 1980 the inspired decision was made to enshrine Bislama (rather than English or French) as the official language of the new country. It seemed to us that this had contributed tangibly to a sense of unique identity and national pride, both of which we later found lacking in Vanuatu's otherwise comparable neighbor to the northwest, the Solomon Islands.

Restocked and replenished, we began a leisurely meander northward through the rest of Vanuatu, stopping at many more of the dozens of islands that make up this great sailing destination. First stop was just around the corner on Efate Island: the vast natural harbor of Port Havannah. Named after a Royal Navy ship that explored these waters between 1849 and 1850, this became a key part of Naval Operating Base Efate, which the USA began to build up in March 1942, as part of its strategy to retake the offensive in the Pacific. Just out of range of Japanese bombers in the Solomons and New Guinea, Havannah was the assembly point for the American fleet that fought the Battle of the Coral Sea in May 1942: the first ever engagement between opposing aircraft carriers, and perhaps the first naval battle ever in which neither fleet saw the other.

All around the enclosed and lake-like blue waters of Havannah are overgrown, decaying reminders of those days. There is an eerily abandoned 3,000-foot fighter field (imagine those great, but now deserted expanses of cracked concrete in Yorkshire and Lincolnshire, where the Flying Fortresses took off to bomb Europe, but in a tropical setting). In the undergrowth you can find remains of a pipeline that was built to supply ships' tenders with fresh water. In various locations in the jungle are large concrete structures, all but obscured by great green walls of creeper: kudzu was imported to Vanuatu on account of its fast growth rate and its ability to rapidly conceal strategic assets. In a junk-filled shack under palm trees on the shore an eccentric and enthusiastic local welcomed us in with an exaggerated American twang:

"Welcome, mah frens! Yass, welcome indeed! Come right in! An where y'all from? Now you jus' take a look at this...ain't it sumpin'?"

The war museum, Port Havannah

Ernest proudly showed us a bent propeller blade from a P-38, unidentifiable scraps of aluminum fuselage, two old jeep radiators. But his prize items were in lines on the rickety shelves:

"Now you just take a look at these, if you will! See here…San Francisco, 1943; Cincinnati 1944…" as he thrust one old Coke bottle after another into our hands, the wording molded into the glass base.

At Havannah we were introduced to the pattern of daily shopping that would now be with us for months. Most mornings, a few dugout canoes would pull up alongside, offering coconuts, tomatoes, snake beans, a variety of spinach known unappetizingly as "slimy cabbage," pawpaws, giant Pamplemousses. After some chitchat, we would ask:

"Do you want money or to trade?"

Trading usually involved, on our part, staples not easily available far from shops (sugar, flour) and items such as school exercise books, pens, fishhooks. Locals often asked for reading matter. Once we exchanged a one-year-old copy of *The Economist* for two large mud crabs. It was possible to place orders; in fact, the locals were often on their way to or from their "gardens" (vegetable plots), which could be some distance from their homes, so they could easily pick a few more of some particular item on our behalf. Sometimes the conversation would take an odd turn:

"Ok, I'll give you three pens and an exercise book for two coconuts."

"Make dat four pens, mon…"

"Sorry, no more pens. How about an AA battery?"

"No, no… You got an iPod? Dat be good."

From Port Havannah on Efate, we sailed fifty miles north to Revolieu Bay, Epi Island. Distances like this are awkward; with good winds, we might just be able to leave in the very early morning and arrive before dusk. But we found it safer and more relaxing to make such passages (and there would be many to come) overnight, meaning we would clear land before darkness, and then have a leisurely 24 hours before we needed to be securely anchored again.

A long walk south on the island took us through the remains of what was in the 1920's and 30's one of the largest copra plantations in the islands, at Valesdir. In the 20's this estate even had its own currency, with coins marked "six pence" on one side, "five cents" on the other. On big estates like Valesdir the Ni-Vans were employed virtually as slaves. But this was still a vast improvement over the conditions they had been forced to accept when, over a fifty-year period starting in 1850, Queensland sugar-planters had forcibly recruited and shipped out over half the male population, a practice known as Blackbirding ("blackbird" was Australian slang for the natives of the Pacific islands).

Valesdir was broken up at the time of independence in 1980. Copra is still harvested but only sporadically and according to rises and falls in its international price. We wandered through square kilometers of towering palms that were eerily quiet with only a gentle breeze from the ocean rustling the treetops. At the old estate house there were no signs of life but a woman who was brushing coconut husks into a pile told us that a Frenchman in his nineties still lived there.

To the west and a little north we came to a maze of small islands and channels on the south end of Malekula Island: the Maskelynes, named after an Astronomer Royal in the time of Captain Cook, who pioneered a technique to calculate longitude from observations of the moon. At the one-family village of Awei we were adopted and invited to church.

Missionaries were a blessing and a curse for Vanuatu. Although they were effective in ending inter-island warfare, cannibalism, and Blackbirding, they have left behind them a legacy of inter-church rivalries and practices such as the Adventists' prohibition of eating crustaceans and shellfish, not to speak of drinking tea and coffee. But absolutely everyone belongs to a church of some denomination or other and it is assumed that all white visitors are fervent Christians. In this case, the entire village (Presbyterian, the dominant strain in Vanuatu), having been summoned by a bell made of an old diving canister, was present in their Sunday best. There was much fine singing of old English hymns interspersed with American gospel, and then we all adjourned for a feast, eaten cross-legged on the floor. The principal dish is always laplap, a kind of huge pizza, whose base is made of banana or taro paste, which is baked in an underground oven and then strewn with anything from pieces of fish to vegetables and batwings; the concoction is carved with the family's ceremonial wooden laplap knife.

At Uliveo, another of the Maskelynes, we spent nearly an hour anxiously cruising around in a tight little natural lagoon, looking for the perfect spot to anchor. Once we were snugged down, a small dugout came out:

"Hello there. I am Stuart! Welcome!"

Old friends from another cruising yacht, *Sunstone*, had told us about Stuart, who had befriended them the previous year. We were both touched and a little anxious when Stuart told us that he and his family had been scanning the horizon for our arrival "for many weeks."

Stuart was our guide for ten days and also gave us carefully worded hints on island politics:

"You have to understand that we are three villages on this island; in ours there are good people, but…that man who sold you those eggs that were bad? You remember? Well he is from the other village: you cannot ever trust them."

"And tell us the story of the sailboat mast we saw in someone's garden this morning."

"Ah…" said Stuart. "Those people…they are, what do you call them? Wreckers, that's it, wreckers…"

But most evenings such rivalries seemed to be dispelled when the men would gather for a few "shells"—cups made of coconut shells—of kava (the mildly narcotic root-based brew that is common to Tonga, Fiji, and Vanuatu). Ambon, who ran our nearest kava bar and who had spent several seasons picking fruit in New Zealand as part of an enlightened program sponsored by both governments, was our guide to kava etiquette. Kava "parties" were never disputatious. Every so often, but at gradually lengthening intervals, you would be invited to swill down a draft (which looked and tasted much like lukewarm dishwater) as you sat around, occasionally mumbling some inconsequential phrase. As the evening went on the silences would grow longer and longer until, in the total darkness that reigns at night everywhere outside the two metropolitan centers of Vanuatu, you were not really sure there was anyone still around. After a polite amount of time had passed, Jenny would catch my eye in the gloom, and we'd make our excuses; by which time nobody usually noticed our leaving anyway.

We edged our way north up the east coast of Malekula Island, spending several days at the well-protected natural harbor of Port Sandwich. James Cook (never too confident in the use of capital letters) was here in July 1774:

"About nine o'clock we landed in the face of about 4 or 500 Men who were assembled on the Shore, with Bows and Arrows, Clubs and Spears… The people of this country are in general the most Ugly and ill-proportioned of any I ever saw…"

Cook was fairly sure that the local people practiced cannibalism; he was sadly proved right several times over the next hundred years or so, as successive European missionaries were cooked and eaten.

The high point of Vanuatu's year is Independence Day on July 30st. We participated as honored guests in a whole week of festivities at Ranon, on Ambrym Island. Every day there were "futsal" soccer matches on the sloping field behind the settlement, with fiercely contested games involving the girls; a volleyball tournament; speeches (tending to the long and turgid) by local dignitaries; an "island dress" competition; and a string band contest. Vanuatu string bands are 10 or 12-person outfits whose principal instrument is always a kind of double bass made from a wooden tea-chest, which is accompanied by ukuleles, banjoes, and guitars. The music owes much to the presence of those black American troops in Vanuatu in the war and tended, to our ear, towards the tinny and repetitive. For the Big Day itself, the government had made available to every settlement in Vanuatu a sack of rice and a cow, so we joined the whole village in beef curry for lunch.

You'd think that in a poor country like Vanuatu, for the government to spend money on parties for the people was not the wisest investment. But in hindsight and after spending time in the Solomons, we weren't so sure. These multi-island and multi-ethnic island groupings are at best strained as cohesive nations, and any expenditure that tends to instill a sense of national pride seemed to us to be a sensible one.

From the near-perfectly sheltered natural harbor at Lolowai, on Ambae Island, we made a visit to St Patrick's College, one of a number of boarding schools dotted around the islands. They were all founded by churches (in this case the Anglican Church of Melanesia) and are a response to the huge financial and logistical difficulties that would otherwise be associated with providing secondary education in an island nation with little transport infrastructure. St Patrick's is located in an isolated set of clearings in the jungle, an hour or so's walk from Lolowai. Among its illustrious former pupils was Father Walter Lini, who led Vanuatu to independence. We chatted with Ezekiel, the school chaplain, who was from the Solomons.

"My people," he said, meaning the people of the Solomons, "are extremely Christian…"

He paused.

"But not always in a good way. I think that really the Ni-Vans, the people of these islands, are more truly Christian. There is much violence, thievery in the

Solomon Islands. Even though they all go to church on Sundays. You will need to be very careful when you go there. Yes, very careful."

Ezekiel was not exempt from the inter-church rivalry that still bedevils the entire Pacific.

"Just last week," he told us gleefully, "I converted two boys who had been raised as Seventh Day Adventists. The only problem is that now I must tell their parents when they come for Speech Day."

Ambae is the Bali Hai of James Michener, the author of *Tales of The South Pacific*,[4] the collection of stories published in 1947 that gave rise to the famous musical and movie. He could see its looming whale-like mass from the island of Espiritu Santo, where he was stationed for much of the war, and it was to Santo, as it is universally known, that we sailed next. We bypassed the island's capital, the World War II-vintage collection of decaying Quonsett huts called Luganville where the young army lieutenant was based, because its anchorage is exposed.

At our penultimate port of call in Vanuatu, lovely Twin Waterfall Bay, we were touchingly welcomed by all the inhabitants of the village with their special "Welcome" song to the tune of God Save the Queen. The ladies of the

Water music at Twin Waterfall Bay

---

4   Michener, James. (1984). *Tales of the South Pacific*. New York, NY: Fawcett Publications.

village performed their equally unique version of Handel's water music in the deep and cool pool at the foot of the falls and Chief Karely cajoled all the yachts in the bay into participating in an afternoon-long potluck luncheon in his longhouse. From Esau, Karely's brother-in-law, we commissioned the carving of a Laplap knife in rosewood. It was ready in less than a day, his only tools were an old hacksaw blade, a nail, and a piece of glass.

Esau walked with a peculiar hunch:

"About one year ago I could not get up. My legs would not work. I tried everything. Then I called in the kastom doctor," he said in a matter-of-fact way, referring to the traditional or witch doctor. "He cured me but now I must stay out of the water for exactly five years. No fishing, no swimming. And I must not fall in."

Karely spent an evening on board *Bosun Bird* with us, earnestly wondering whether he should enter political life. He was an honest man of great charm and intelligence, at once worldly but remote from the world.

"You know what?" he asked one evening. "Last month there was an American yacht here. We were talking, like we are now. I asked them: is it true? Is a black man really the President of America? I could not believe it when they said yes. I did not know a black man could become President of the United States."

As Vanuatu's Torres Islands, the last significant island group in the world to be discovered by Europeans, sank into the gloom and we set a course for the Solomons, Jenny said to me:

"Vanuatu is what I'd always hoped the Pacific would be…"

"Yes," I conceded. She was right. "It just took us twenty-five years and fifteen thousand miles of sailing through Polynesia and half of Melanesia to find it."

It was only an overnight sail from the Torres Islands to the first of the Solomons: Vanikolo, in Temotu province. We worked our way through a narrow passage named after an Irish pirate named Dillon, to a lake-like anchorage surrounded by high jungle-clad peaks, with mangroves ringing the water's edge.

Although we had only come a hundred miles and were still in Melanesia, it was soon obvious we were in a new land. The dugouts here were single-hull, not the Polynesian-inspired outriggers of Vanuatu; and when their paddlers opened their mouth, they were stained red as if by blood: betel nut, not kava, is the narcotic of preference in the Solomons. The people were also noticeably less shy. Within minutes of our anchoring, dugouts were heading for us from the nearest village, three or four kilometers away. A woman proudly showed us the tethered heron she used to help her fish. The locals were friendly and wanted only to trade, but hours of constant visits, with canoes lining up to talk to you, while others knock against the hull and chip away at the paint work, can be trying. The Pacific-wide concept of Island Time was just the same.

"My name's Peter," said one man who paddled up to say hello.

"Hi Peter, and where are you from?"

He gestured towards the small village that was barely visible at the head of the bay.

"I'm a policeman. I work in Honiara, the capital… I was supposed to be back there two weeks ago."

"No ship?"

"That's right. And I don't know when the next one will be. Last time I was on leave I waited nine months."

It was a short hop to the next island, Utupua, and another mangrove-lined and well-protected anchorage. Here the pastor was the first to greet us, but with a friendly warning:

"You heard about that Swiss yacht that came here?"

"No…"

"Well, they anchored right here, man and wife, just like you. He wasn't too sure about the anchor, see. So, he decided to dive in and check on it. His wife, she was watching."

We waited for the pastor to go on.

"Well, the crocs, they ate him, didn't they? He still had his mask on when they found his head. His wife, his widow, she sent money, and we built a school. She's been back. What was left of him is buried in the village."

At Temotu's "Big Island" of Santa Cruz (or Ndende), eighty miles onwards, we anchored in a corner of a very large bay called Graciosa. Titus came out to greet us and invite us to his yacht club (a bar…). Titus, who had worked on American-owned fishing boats and who knew Hawaii, Guam, and Pohnpei, blithely assured us:

"Yeah, mon, we got Customs, we got Immigration, we got an ATM: dere's everythin' you could want in town."

After a hot walk of six kilometers, we discovered Titus was being optimistic. Although there was a large and apparently new sign informing us of the opening hours of Customs and Immigration, it had been six years since an officer from either government department had been posted here. Later it was suggested to us that at the time of The Tension (a period of near anarchy and inter-island civil war that lasted from 1999 to 2003), many government officials bought the government housing in which they were living at knockdown prices amounting to only a few US dollars and, after quitting service, had been living in their new homes ever since. There was indeed an ATM but a passing local warned us away, tapping his nose knowingly:

"Dat machine, he no good; he take your card, but see, he got no cash inside…"

We were able to buy a few Solomon dollars from a shop. The owner was a slightly podgy, florid white man.

"Yup, the only white man in the province of Santa Cruz," he said. "And I don't reckon there's too many more, white Solomon Islanders I mean, anywhere…"

Ross' s life story was unusual.

"I came out here with my mum and dad, Tom and Diana, and my twin brother Ben, on a Brixham trawler named the *Arthur Rodgers*. It was 1948. Bill Crealock crewed for us… We stayed on. We've a place on the Reef Islands, Pigeon Island, a few miles offshore from here."

It rang a bell with me. A year or two earlier I'd read a non-fiction work called *Faraway*,[5] by an English writer named Lucy Irvine. She had earlier made her name with *Castaway*,[6] her account of a year as a voluntary castaway on an island in the Torres Strait. *Faraway* was the story of Tom, Diana, and their twin boys Ross and Ben Hepworth; the book was not kind to Tom or Diana, I recalled. So rather than talk about that, we shot the breeze over Crealock, who had gone on to become one of the best-known yacht designers of the century. We were tempted to sail out to Pigeon; it sounded idyllic. But our chart was a very poor one, the anchorage looked iffy. So many choices.

Remote Santa Cruz Island has an interesting history. When the Spaniards were exploring Peru in the early sixteenth century, one of the most pressing questions was the source of the gold used by the Incas in their fabulous ornamentation. In one of the great con-tricks of history, the conquistadors were told that it came from some islands over the horizon. Alvaro de Mendaña was one of a number of sea-captains to take the Incas at their word. He sailed almost the entire width of the Pacific before stumbling on Santa Cruz in 1567. Imagining that this must at least be the site of King Solomon's mines, he gave the islands their modern name. Alas there was no gold.

Later he returned to found a colony here. It failed and all traces of the settlement have long since disappeared. Ross suggested to us that Mendaña's influence lives on in the disproportionate number of island chiefs whose names begin with "M." I was a bit doubtful about that.

Santa Cruz has also given its name to another great naval engagement in World War II. Hoping to break the military stalemate that had existed on Guadalcanal for some weeks, Japan undertook a major land offensive starting October 20, 1942. In support of this attack, and with the hope of drawing away American vessels from besieged Guadalcanal, the Imperial Japanese Navy

---

5   Irvine, Lucy. (2001). *Faraway*. London, UK: Transworld.
6   Irvine, Lucy. (1983). *Castaway*. London, UK: Random House.

sought out their enemy north of Santa Cruz. Like the earlier Battle of the Coral Sea, this was an engagement between aircraft carriers that never saw each other. One American carrier was sunk, and another forced to withdraw, for no comparable Japanese losses. But the Japanese lost so many aircraft and their veteran crews in the engagement, that Japanese carriers thenceforth played no role in the Guadalcanal campaign. Santa Cruz was a pyrrhic victory for Japan.

From Santa Cruz it was a full two days' sail to the main grouping of the Solomon Islands. We began our meander west and north at the tiny but densely populated island of Santa Ana. Here a family with a fascinating pedigree adopted us. Heinrich Kuper was a German trader who came to the Solomons in 1912. He married into tribal royalty on Santa Ana; an old black and white photo on the wall of the family home showed him in a shirt and tie towering 50 cm over his ornately beaded wife Kafagamurirongo on the day of their wedding. As two world wars came and went, the family anglicized their names. Son Geoffrey Kuper, by then living on Santa Isabel Island, was a leading light among the legendary coast-watchers who clandestinely assisted allied troops from 1942 onwards. Geoffrey's widow Clara, daughter (Greta), and son (Henry) now lived on Santa Ana. We spent several lazy afternoons while Greta and her partly deaf mother reminisced to us.

"See this?" Greta would say, handing over a photo from the disorganized pile of curled black and whites she was sifting through, as we sat on wicker chairs in her airy front room. "These are grade-taking ceremonies in the village from 1943, I think. Of course, I wasn't born then, but even Mum wasn't allowed to watch. No women were allowed… And this one?" she said with a smile of reminiscence, and then answered herself.

"It's Mum with the Queen. 1974, I think."

"February," Clara chimed in, nodding in reminiscence. "Star Harbour."

Not quite all of the old ways have been forgotten. On the weather coast of the island there exists a well-maintained "kastom" (traditional) house that is used for ceremonies and where the remains of chiefs and elders are buried. The chiefs' remains are placed in miniature war-canoes two meters long and suspended from the rafters; the skulls and bones of elders are encased in baskets and simply piled up on a large altar. The current chief was happy to show me around. Taboos meant that Jenny could not enter.

"Of course, they won't allow my bones to be kept here," he said a little sadly. "The missionaries say it's a heathen custom."

Off the eastern tip of Guadalcanal Island, a huddled group of small islands and waterways forms Marau Sound. Here we anchored close to a very plush but under-utilized resort, all lawns and rustic chalets, called Tavanipupu. The local chief, Justin, explained to us that the hotel was one of the few such places that had not been sacked and/or burned during The Tension. The ethnic conflict—between native Guales of the island of Guadalcanal, and settlers drawn by economic opportunity from nearby Malaita—had peaked around 1999, but still lay not far beneath surface. Justin and the villagers in his care were Malaitans.

"We spent a whole year cooped up here," Justin said. "Every day, we'd see the people from the weather-coast in their motorboats. They had guns, heavy guns, and they weren't shy to use them."

Now there was a new local dimension to The Tension.

"Pamela," he said referring to the white owner of Tavanipupu, grimacing and pronouncing her name pam-AY-ler. "She is very hard."

Pamela for her part complained that Justin and his friends simply would not do a proper day's work, no matter how much they were paid. She was sounding jaded with island life. In what we took to be a cautiously phrased threat, Justin suggested that if we chose to go ashore at night it would be best to leave a paid guard on board.

"Of course, it's not my village that is the problem," he added. "It is those Roman Catholic boys from over there. They are bad boys."

Across the sound we could see Guadalcanal itself, with all its resonance. This was the setting for USA's first major land engagement of the war, following Pearl Harbor. Guadalcanal was the island on which the Japanese advance towards Australia and New Zealand was halted. Over sixty warships lie on the floor of what is now called Iron Bottom Sound, but Henderson Field (now Honiara International Airport) was the key to the battle. With control of it, the USA could hope to step its way north and west almost to the shores of Japan. Without it they would be hopelessly distant in Vanuatu, and Australia would be exposed to Japanese bombing.

We ghosted our way into Honiara, on the island's north shore, just as a Virgin Blue jet coming in from Brisbane settled into its downward glide path to Henderson. To port was where the first American landing craft had gone ashore. They had next to no air cover and only short-lived support from their mother ships, for word had been received of a Japanese battle fleet steaming down The Slot, from Rabaul, and the US naval commander would not risk his ships to cover the marines.

Honiara today is no place to linger with a yacht. You drop the anchor in uncomfortably deep water and then back up even more uncomfortably to a ragged breakwater and run lines ashore. The place is completely open to winds from the north and west. The locals do not have a reputation among the sailing community for honesty. Our French neighbors on *Ma Ohi* were foolish enough to leave their portholes unsecured when they went shopping ashore one morning and came back to find that everything within reach (an iPod, CDs, a camera) had been literally fished through the small openings.

The Point Cruz Yacht Club is a large A-frame with a bar that serves cold beer and greasy French fries, and it also has an interesting if sad crowd of denizens. Every morning a group of five or six old white guys, most of them generous around the girth and florid, one of them in a wheelchair, would install themselves at the same table. They would stay all day and long into the night. It was difficult not to overhear them. The topics were always the same: the place had gone to hell; the locals were thieves; the Solomons had no future; the beer was piss. They'd occasionally nod or wink at you as one White Man to Another:

"How's it goin' mate? Watch yerself, orlright?"

In the grounds, a small plaque on a plinth commemorates Canadian-born Signalman Douglas Munro, the only Coast Guard recipient of the Congressional Medal of Honour. On September 27, 1942, he was in command of a ten-boat detachment charged with making an emergency evacuation of marines from this point; covering the entire flotilla, he died on the spot.

This is not one of the Pacific's more romantic locales. There are unattractive concrete and tin shanties thrown up after World War II, criminality is rampant and Chinese traders huddle in their own quarter, fearful of some new wave of anti-Chinese violence (there have been several). Particularly ugly is the debris left everywhere from betel-nut chewing: great puddles of red saliva that at first have you thinking you have just missed a bloodbath. When I bought a green tee-shirt with the legend "I (heart) Honiara," a wit at the yacht club remarked:

"Good joke!"

Up on a once-fought-over ridge behind town is a large and well-kept American war memorial. Nobody is buried here: the Americans took all their dead with them. There is a fine view over Iron Bottom Sound and to Savo Island, and a large American flag flutters and flaps quietly in the breeze. It is a peaceful location quite at odds with the history of the place. Back in town there is a dusty one-room war museum with poor-quality photographs and a few yellowing newspaper cuttings. On the wall at the airport is a propeller from a Japanese Zero.

The most popular area for sailing in the Solomons is in and around the Marovo Lagoon and the adjacent island of New Georgia. We spent nearly three weeks moving from island to island, all in gin-clear and well-protected waters. Marovo is home to most of the Solomons' wood carvers and with judicious bargaining some exceptionally beautiful pieces can be obtained. The most well-known carver enjoys the name John Wayne, but he has dozens of rivals. They are nearly all Seventh Day Adventists, having been converted at a stroke by a fiercely evangelical Australian trader in 1948. SDA'ers may not eat products of the sea that do not have scales, so this is a particularly good location to find lobster. Those who are not necessarily 100% devout are known as Backsliders, we learned; they have no qualms about fishing for lobsters for others to eat.

In a number of the small villages were color posters in English. They announced the upcoming visit of a delegation from Japan, in search of the remains of dead soldiers. We talked about the Japanese to a woodcarver:

"I don't know," he shrugged. "They seem alright. Nobody today remembers the war, you know? We don't live that long here."

In the local paper (available only in Honiara), the Japanese Embassy was often in the news. There was an announcement that Japan would be providing constituency funds to every member of the legislature. It was an idea that would make most aid and development experts shudder, such is the scope for corruption when cash is handed over directly in this fashion. One cynical (or realistic?) expat we met in the yacht club bar explained it succinctly:

"Well it's obvious, isn't it? The Solomons have a vote on the International Whaling Commission, like most of these small Pacific countries. And we all know where Japan stands on that."

One night as we went to bed in Marovo, I left our anchor light burning as usual, illuminating the cockpit. Three hours later, again as is usual, I got up to have a look around. So as to be able to see into the gloom, I turned off the light. I forgot to put it on again. Another hour or so on—it was around two o'clock by now—I must have been having a nightmare:

"Wake up, wake up!" called Jenny sleepily from the opposite bunk. "You're having a bad dream."

I started, and settled on my back, my eyes open. Then, very slowly and with creeping horror, I became aware of a figure. There was someone standing, absolutely stock still, between our two bunks. He was so close I could easily have reached out and touched his thigh. He carried a machete. For a second or two I thought I must still be dreaming.

I thought for a moment more. With my heart pumping and oblivious of the fact I was stark naked, I shot to my feet, shouting incoherently, and frantically pushed the figure out into the cockpit and over the rail. He (for I could now tell it was a young man) leaped adroitly into his small dugout and paddled away as fast as he could into the darkness. I shouted at the top of my voice, adrenaline pumping:

"Go away! Go away! Never come back or I'll kill you!"

It took an age for my heart to slow down. Both of us were shaken. Later, comparing notes, we realized that approximately half the yachts that visit the Solomons every year experience something like this. At least in our case we had neither suffered any physical harm, nor had we lost anything. But it was weeks before I could sleep properly and not react to every little rocking of the boat, or a tap as a piece of driftwood nudged up against us. For a long time, we kept at hand a large winch handle and a spray can of Mortein cockroach killer - a cheap local version of Mace.

Our last call, prior to leaving the Solomons, was Gizo: the second city of the island group. Just outside town, we passed a small island on the reef. Old charts call it Plum Pudding Island but the newer ones give it its popular name: Kennedy Island. One dark night in August 1943, John F. Kennedy was skippering his Motor Torpedo Boat, the *PT-109*, in nearby Blackett Strait. He was rammed by the Japanese destroyer *Amagiri* running at full speed and with no lights—the so-called Tokyo Express that resupplied Japanese outposts every night, from Rabaul. The *PT-109* went down quickly. Captain and crew swam to Plum Pudding Island. Under the young Kennedy's leadership, they all survived to tell the tale. The captain was awarded the Navy and Marine Corps Medal, and the rest, as they say, is history.

The *PT-109* lives on in the form of a bar run by a friendly member of the Solomon aristocracy, Lawrie Wickham. Three times a week deafening disco music booms out from the straw-roofed hut over the Gizo anchorage. Every day enterprising locals call by in their canoes:

"Hey man, look what I got here!" and they bring out a dirty and much-handled scrap of paper.

"See dat? It's a thank-you from John Kennedy to my granddad. I make a special price for you, my fren."

I scrutinized one. It was dated 1944, which could be right. But interestingly it bore the White House letterhead and was signed: John F. Kennedy (President).

When Christmas came and went it was time to think about leaving. After a few days tacking to the outer extremities of the archipelago, we edged into a narrow and imperfectly charted strait, Hamilton Passage. On one side is the interestingly named Rob Roy Island and on the other, the also interesting Wagina Island, pronunciation uncertain. The tide turned in our favor. Soon we were rushing north into open water at seven knots, reaching for the Equator.

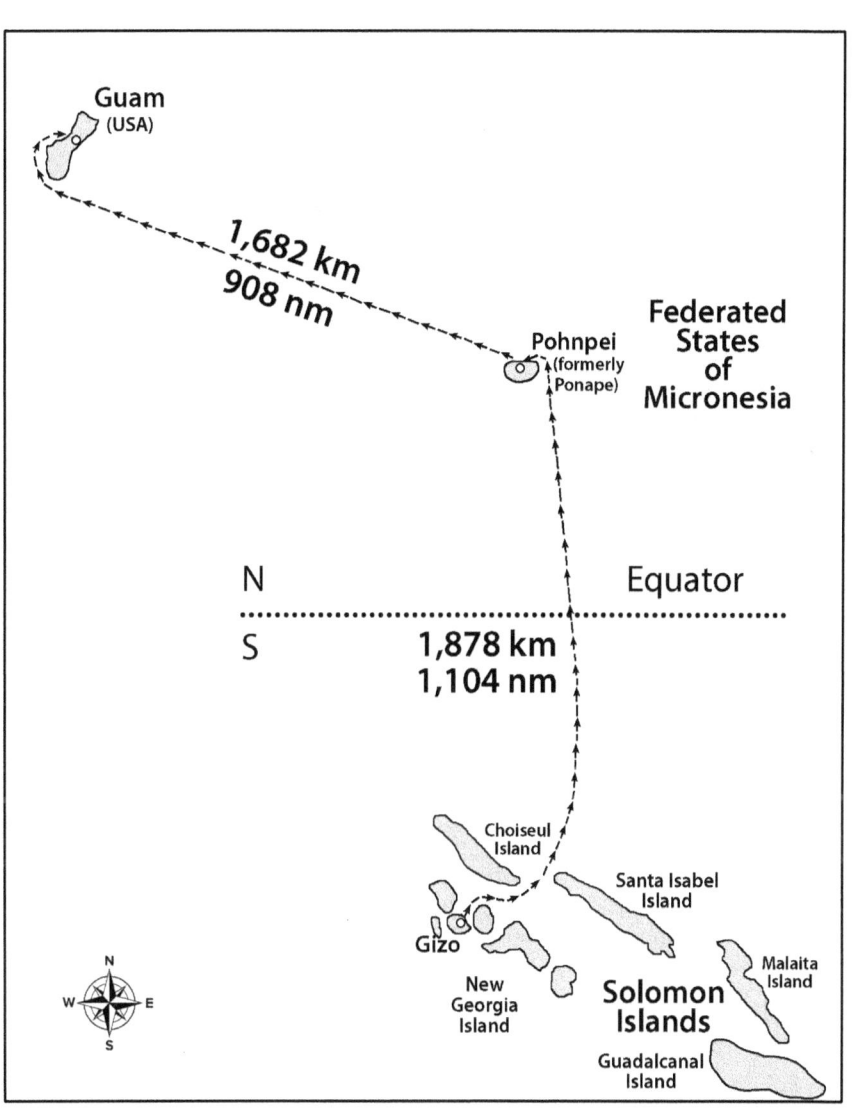

Gizo to Guam

Chapter Three:
Into the Rising Sun
(Pohnpei, Guam, and
the Approach to Japan)

*F*rom the Solomons to the island of Pohnpei in Micronesia it was, we calculated, 844 nautical miles. In trade wind conditions, we would hope to cover that distance in eight to ten days.

The passage was slow. We drifted rather than sailed across the Equator, celebrating—as we do on all special occasions—with a proper written menu for dinner, an exchange of small gifts, and an extra chocolate bar on watch. Fourteen days out, on January 19th, the high green hills of Pohnpei came into view, and the wind and current at last began to cooperate. By flying every inch of canvas that we had, we made 119 miles on our last day and reached the entrance pass on the north coast, below a huge square-topped mountain, just as dusk was coming on. Kindly and at no charge, the Port Captain sent out a launch to guide us to a safe anchorage before darkness engulfed us. Next morning, we motored the final couple of miles into the port and, among dozens of Chinese and Taiwanese fishing boats, checked into the Federated States of Micronesia (FSM).

As we lay alongside the high harbor wall, pondering on the chart the complicated route to the inner anchorage, along came a bearded, white, and half-naked Good Samaritan in his rubber dinghy:

"Hi! I'm Ted. From *Aloha*. First time here? When you're ready, just follow me. And welcome!"

Pohnpei (also spelled Ponape) is one of four big islands—the others being Kosrae, Chuuk (formerly known as Truk) and Yap—that, along with their associated atolls, make up the FSM. The nation's modern history is complicated. Spain was the first outside power to claim the islands in 1886, calling them the Carolines, but they soon sold the group on to Germany, in 1899. After World War I, control in turn passed to Japan, which had been on the side of the Allied Powers during the conflict. Many Japanese quickly settled. With war imminent again in the 1930's, Japan established a seaplane base and heavily fortified the

Wartime guns on Sokehs Ridge, Pohnpei

area around Pohnpei's only town, Kolonia. The town was bombed, but there was no attempt at an American landing here.

From 1945 to 1979, the USA, under a Resolution of the United Nations, administered the Carolines, the neighboring Marshall Islands, and the Northern Marianas as a single Trust Territory. American rule can best be described as benign neglect: the USA never seems to have put much effort into colonial governance, certainly not like the British or the French (sometimes) did. Everything went into gentle decline and this became known informally as the Rust Territory. In 1979, a vote was held that resulted in Chuuk, Yap, Pohnpei, and Kosrae holding together to form the FSM as an independent country in 1986.[7]

Visible reminders of the short era of Japanese control are ubiquitous. One afternoon we walked up to the top of Sokehs Ridge, that dominates the yacht anchorage, and explored the rusting old anti-aircraft installations. And the locals maintain a taste for Japanese cuisine, especially sashimi. But the

---

7   The Marshalls, Palau, and the Northern Marianas, meanwhile, each became their own countries. Guam was different; it had been transferred by Spain to the USA in 1898 and was administered by the US Navy; in 1950 it was established as an Unincorporated Territory of the USA.

USA continues to make investments in all of the former Trust Territory islands under a succession of agreements known as Compacts, and the people look very much to America today. The standard of living is much higher than you would otherwise expect in island groups with so few obvious means of income generation. FSM'ers have full and free access to the USA (and vice versa), and many take advantage of this to enlist in the military and send home their wages. All about town you see bumper stickers such as "My son's a Marine" or "Go Army."

Another source of income is offshore fishing licenses. Every two or three nights we would be awakened at around midnight by the roar of a large jet landing at the nearby airport, and again departing an hour or so later. I knew it wasn't the scheduled Continental Airlines milk-run service along the island chain; that departed in the middle of the day.

"Oh yes," said *Aloha* Ted. "It's a cargo plane. They load up here with frozen tuna and fly direct to Tokyo, in time to make it for the morning auction."

Later we read that a single frozen tuna from Pohnpei had gone for a record USD100,000 at the Tokyo market.

One result of free American access to the FSM is the existence of a large expatriate community, many of whose members are involved in teaching (there is a quasi-university on a purpose-built campus outside Kolonia), with a few living on yachts.

There is also a fleet of derelict sailboats that, local lore has it, a Japanese businessman bought from disillusioned cruisers just because they "make the bay look nice." Ted was one of the liveaboards. His story was a little sad but not untypical of tales you hear in remote and apparently idyllic harbors around the world.

"My wife Lynn and I, we'd always had the dream, to sail way for ever... We saved and saved, bought our boat. We didn't really know how to sail, but a friend came with us from San Francisco to Hawaii. It seemed straightforward enough, so we carried on alone. Well, you know how things go... Stuff started to go wrong. I'm practical and I could fix most things. But Lynn got spooked. We were a day or so out of here, had a big blow. One thing after another broke, one of those sequences. When it was over, I couldn't get the engine going."

In a month in Pohnpei, we never met Lynn; she obtained a job on land as a teacher. It had been a year now that they had been here. Ted tinkered on *Aloha*, but, it seemed to us, in a dispirited way.

"She doesn't want to go on. And I can't blame her. But we can't go back either. We've nothing to go back to, you see."

More recent arrivals were Phil and his girlfriend Mel, from California and Alaska respectively, on *Mira*. Phil, with his shoulder-length hair and love of surfing, was half hipster, half hippy throwback, his conversation littered with "man," "crap," and "dude." Mel was a modern girl: younger, fashion conscious, and a bit worried about how seawater and the sun were treating her. Phil was eternally optimistic, and every lunchtime when we met over sashimi he'd be excited about the latest job prospect; he was a bush pilot and had made some inquiries with the inter-island airline. Mel, we could tell, was more sanguine and possibly not so excited at the prospect of spending a year or more in Pohnpei.

One day when Phil's negotiations hadn't been going so well, he asked us what our plans were:

"Us? Oh well, probably Japan…"

"Japan? Wow, that sounds kinda cool…maybe we could tag along…"

We have never been enthusiastic about sailing in company; one boat is always faster than another, and we don't like to be subject to anyone else's plans. But Phil seemed pretty easy-going; I thought he'd probably change his mind a few times more, but we agreed tentatively to leave at about the same time for Guam and onwards.

Cruiser hangouts in foreign ports shift year by year, often according to the price of beer. A favorite in Pohnpei was Rusty's, which was located in a post-apocalyptic ruined apartment building overlooking the harbor, with an appropriately rusty anchor over the doorway. Here the island's biggest band—"Wetter than Seattle," a meteorologically correct reference to the local climate—performed every couple of weeks. The teachers swapped stories, as they do everywhere, about their charges.

"Oh, they're nice enough… No discipline problems. But they're lazy, no question. Anyone with ambition, they join the US Army or the Marines; spend a few years travelling around the world, making money; come back and retire to the ancestral plot at thirty. Trouble is, joining the military these days has got its disadvantages. Wars, I mean."

The "real" locals meanwhile drank a form of kava called Sakau and the preferred cultural activity was cockfighting, at which vast bets were laid every Sunday afternoon, after Church. Aside from the Japanese dishes, the Pohnpei cuisine wasn't too much to write home about, but there was one surely unique specialty: Ramen seasoned with purple grape-flavored Kool-Aid powder:

"Jim Jones' favorite noodle dish," joked one of the regulars at Rusty's.

One day we chartered a speedboat and its owner and zigzagged through several miles of reefs and shallows to Nan Madol. This is a long-abandoned city, built on artificial islands within Pohnpei's lagoon; it was constructed around 1200 CE, deserted 400 years later. What makes it unique is that the streets are all shallow canals, best navigated today by kayak. The walls of the buildings are constructed of basalt columns laid on their sides, in such a way that they resemble logs; the columns were extracted from a volcanic plug on the far side of the island. It is an odd place—no crops ever grew here and there is no nearby source of fresh water—and very little is known about the Saudeleurs, the then-ruling dynasty of Pohnpei.

Our boat driver was Billy. Muscular, with a buzz cut, he had military insignia tattooed on his thick forearms, one with the word "Desert," the other "Storm;" he had bruised my hand when we first greeted him. Billy had his own theories:

"You guys heard of Moo?"

We both must have looked puzzled. He spelled it out:

"Em-you. You know, the lost continent of Mu. It's kinda like Atlantis...'cept this one's real, and it was here."

Later we looked it all up. Over the years, various pseudo-historians or "antiquarians," with a disproportionate number of intriguing names—Augustus le Plongeon, Ignatius Donnelly, Etienne Brasseur de Bourbourg—have placed the mythical Atlantis in a host of locations. One of the most prolific theorists of the early twentieth century was James Churchward, who insisted that Atlantis, Lemuria (the origin of lemurs) and Mu—the term he preferred— were all one and the same and were the common origin of the great civilizations of Egypt, Greece, and others such as Easter Island.[8]

Nan Madol, which he said was 12,000 years old, was one of this lost world's seven great cities. Mu had a total population of precisely 64 million, he noted.

All this, Churchward said, he had learned "more than fifty years ago," as a soldier in the British Raj. A high-ranking temple priest had shown him a set of revelatory ancient clay tablets, in a long-lost "Naga-Maya language" which only two other people in India could read. Apparently, a sufficient number of people bought into Churchward's eccentric ideas for him to have three full-length books published on the subject. He is tactfully described in Wikipedia as "a British occult writer, inventor, engineer, and fisherman." The entry concludes laconically and intriguingly: "UK-based electronic music record-label Planet Mu has released three compilation albums with titles copied from Churchward's own books: The Cosmic Forces of Mu (2001), Children of Mu (2004), and Sacred Symbols of Mu (2006)."

Jenny glowered at me in warning as Billy gave us a version of all this. But years as a diplomat have accustomed me to take in all sorts of wild ideas without batting an eyelid; we both nodded judiciously and kept our thoughts to ourselves. We hoisted the kayaks Billy had lent us into the water and spent a couple of hours wending our way around the vegetation-choked canals, climbing ashore occasionally to inspect Nan Madol's massive structures. Few tourists ever come here, we'd been told. It was oddly quiet, sinister even. Only occasionally we could hear in the distance the tinny tones of Radio Pohnpei;

---

8   Churchward, James. (2007). *The Lost Continent of Mu*. Kempton, Illinois: Adventures Unlimited Press.

Billy seemed to be listening to a fire-and-brimstone Christian preacher, fond of the Book of Revelation.

Early March and it was time to be off again. Phil's flying plans had definitively fallen through, and Mel was anxious to be on the move. So, when we moved to the port complex to check out, *Mira* joined us.

The 900-mile sail to the west-northwest and the USA's island fortress of Guam was one of our favorites so far, once we had cleared the squally and wet weather south of 10 degrees north. With a warm wind over the quarter, never more than twenty knots and rarely less than ten, and moonlight nearly all the way, this was trade wind sailing how it was meant to be.

Sitting alone in the cockpit at night, the only sounds would be the rhythmic whoosh of *Bosun Bird's* hull moving through the water, the occasional creak as the wind vane made a small adjustment and the tiller moved a fraction to one side or the other. We have a rule of no reading after dark—in order to see the lights on any approaching vessel, your eyes need to be adjusted to the gloom—so all there was to do, was to sit and contemplate the stars and the fading phosphorescence in our wake. Once we were away from land, I'd start to feel a sense of timelessness. This was how the world had always been, the near boundless ocean and the stars. Often it was with real reluctance that, my three-hour watch over, I'd call down to Jenny to wake her, have her put on her tether and come out to relieve me. I'd tell her what course we were steering, whether the wind was rising, falling or steady, whether I had seen any lights. I might point out a star we were steering for. Then I'd go below and pass her up a cup of hot chocolate before going to bed myself.

We had two of our best day's runs yet, 136 and 140 miles in 24 hours. Several days out we heard on the short-wave radio of the earthquake and tsunami at Fukushima, Japan, which resulted in tsunami warnings throughout Micronesia. As in the case of a tsunami wave that hit Tonga and Samoa eighteen months earlier, we must simply have sailed over it. A 30-centimeter difference of height in one wave, when the average height is two or three meters anyway, is not noticeable.

Just short of Guam, we held a little ceremony, each dropping a coin over the side. This was the deepest place in any of the world's oceans: the Mariana Trench, which bottoms out at about 11 km (2 km deeper than Everest is high). We wondered how long the coins would take to reach the bottom, and whether some deep-sea explorer long in the future would one day find them.[9]

---

9   Googling this, you will find pages and pages of speculation, with estimates ranging from three to ten hours.

Guided by a friendly but efficient naval radio operator on the VHF radio, we took a mooring in the spacious, choppy bay off the Marianas Yacht Club, on the island's lee side. Phil and Mel—who had beaten us here by a day—shouted over to us from their mooring that there had been a 90-cm tidal rise and fall in nearby Apra Harbor (the main port), an hour or two after the moment of the Fukushima disaster, repeated several times. But the only damage on Guam was several submarines breaking their moorings; and Phil gestured behind his back. We could make out what must be Polaris Point, marked by a (presumably disabled…) nuclear missile. Here was the entrance to an inner bay that was used by the US Navy, closed by a boom that would be pulled aside as and when warships needed to enter. The approach, we soon observed, was permanently patrolled.

The yacht club is an airy, open-sided building in a grove of pine trees. Although we were welcome to use it at all times, including its delicious cold showers, it was active only twice a week: a bar evening on Fridays, and dinghy racing on Sundays. The caretaker was a veteran cruiser named Bob, with the pale, blotchy face of someone who has spent too many years out in the sun:

"Yup, been here twenty years now. Couldn't find a reason to move on: great climate, good sailing, free mooring, and American beer at American prices."

"But those cyclones?" we asked.

We could tell immediately that Bob was relishing the prospect of telling his next story.

"Typhoon Alley," he said in a practiced way. "That's what they call it. There's what they call the typhoon shelter in those mangroves over there, but I wouldn't risk it myself. No one's looked at those moorings since they were laid. And the Navy? No, they won't let you in. I rode out the last one right here." He gestured out into the bay where his grubby-looking sailboat lay pointing into the brisk trade winds.

"It was a Super Typhoon. At Andersen Field they recorded gusts of 160 knots. I kid you not. I was on board. I'd put down an extra mooring, secured her with chains. Had green water breaking over the decks for hours. But she was OK."

In the rafters of the club were painted signs left by passing cruisers. We found boards painted by old friends: *Yawarra*, who had been here no less than three times since the seventies; *Ludus Amoris*, last met in the Strait of Magellan; and *Sunstone*, ahead of us in Japan's Inland Sea. Before leaving we added our own roughly painted sign to the gallery.

The Club had the usual supply of old sailing magazines which we read religiously from cover to cover, so as not to deplete our meagre stock of paperback reading on board. In a months-old[10] edition of *Latitude 38*, a popular free magazine published in San Francisco, we were shocked by a short item in the letters section.

An acquaintance of ours, nicknamed Freeloader Bob in the cruising community, had written in and mentioned that he had met our Japanese friend Chinami in the Marquesas Islands. The editor responded to say Chinami had since gone missing "near Cape Horn." Later we learned that, after leaving New Zealand, he had throughout his long crossing of the lower South Pacific maintained regular contact by satellite phone with his wife in Japan. His last call was from 300 miles west of Chile, after which there was silence. An air patrol by the Chilean navy found no sign of *Kifa*. I passed the magazine over to Jenny, indicating the item:

"You should read this."

I found myself remembering a young French sailor named Antoine, whom we'd first met in Mar del Plata, Argentina, where cruising boats gathered every southern spring before jumping off on the 1,200-mile dive south to the Strait of Magellan or Cape Horn. Deep into the Chilean channels, Antoine had eventually decided Patagonia was too cold for him, the life of a single-handed sailor too lonely. Before turning back for Rio, he'd sent us all a cheery email, wishing us all well and saying he'd be thinking of us as he lounged on Copacabana beach with some Brazilian girl in a skimpy thong. He'd then sailed east, back into the Atlantic, and straight into a gale. His battered 21-foot Mini Transat sailboat was found months later, wedged into a ravine on an isolated island in the Falkland group, 400 miles out. Antoine's body was never found.

We were saddened, shocked by Chinami's death, just as we had been at Antoine's. But what was there to say? We knew the risks, as doubtless they did. Perhaps it was some consolation to Antoine's mother—and to Chinami's friends and family—that they had died doing what they loved. I wasn't actually too sure about that. Jenny passed me back the magazine without any comment.

Urban Guam was a massive culture shock. Tumon, sometimes described as the poor man's Waikiki, was lined with Hermes and Gucci shops along with US chain-restaurants: TGI Friday's, Texas Steak House, and so on. At the multiplex movie theatres we did not recognize the name of even one of the dozen or more movies showing, an indication of how out-of-touch you can become at sea. With Phil and Mel, we rented an ancient rust-blistered Toyota to get around in. Out in the burbs at the Micronesia Mall we toured together the aisles of a massive Payless supermarket, gaping at products we had long since forgotten. The only reminder of Guam's remoteness was the advice given to us to shop for produce on Tuesday evenings or Wednesday mornings, just after the ship from San Francisco had unloaded. At a vast Home Depot—reputedly the biggest in

---

10   January 2011.

all the USA—it was a true pleasure to pay only USD4 for a can of WD-40 that in the islands would have cost us USD20 or more; and at K-Mart we bought clothes in anticipation of the colder climate in Japan.

Unlike the rest of the Marianas, Guam is a US Territory, ceded by Spain to America in 1898. Virtually undefended, it was seized by Japan the day after Pearl Harbor. The occupation was brutal and is remembered with bitterness by the native Chamorro population. Following massive aerial bombardment, US Marines launched an amphibious assault on July 17, 1944, with air cover provided by, among others, Lieutenant George Herbert Bush, who flew a torpedo plane. The Marines landed either side of Apra harbor, at Asan and Agat.

In a pattern that was to become familiar—as, island by island, US forces progressed painfully north towards the Japanese mainland—the invasion of Guam was fiercely resisted by troops well-concealed in excavated cave systems prepared for the launching of so-called "banzai" (suicide) attacks as a last resort. In various locations, including behind the yacht anchorage at Piti, defensive guns could be found almost overgrown in the dense jungle.

There were discreet monuments to the war in many places. Asan beach, where 2,500 Marines died, was now a grassy park where children flew kites and people picnicked on the weekends. The Japanese flag flew alongside the Stars and Stripes and most of the tourists were Japanese. Strangely, and in contrast to Normandy, there were no US war cemeteries. As on Guadalcanal all of the bodies had been repatriated. It was odd too that there was no officially sanctioned war museum on Guam. The very few Spanish colonial buildings that survived the bombing were falling down, and the only collection of war relics, which included the tail section of a Japanese Betty bomber, was a private one.

In the city museum there were some photographs of the immediate postwar years. One in particular caught my attention. It stays with me now. A burly, grizzled, and grim-faced white American NCO in a khaki shirt is holding a young Japanese man by his upper arm and guiding him past a group of similarly solemn onlookers, up a short flight of wooden steps. The Japanese man is thin but fit-looking; eyes front, he looks calm; his hands are lashed behind his back; he is walking stiffly upright. The typed caption under the photograph explains that it is September 1945. The man is about to be hanged for war crimes committed during the occupation of Guam.

It is understandable that for most Europeans, and Canadians even, the War in the Pacific seemed to be something of a sideshow. For Americans it is less understandable. For the enemy in the Pacific was just as redoubtable as in Europe; the logistical challenges were greater; and here it was a question not just of one very high-risk landing operation, but of a whole string of such invasions. Each was fiercely opposed and each only took the USA a little closer to the real objective: the four home islands of Japan. We were humbled by visiting these battlefields.

Back in the anchorage we talked about what we'd seen with Lloyd, the New Zealand skipper of the only other visiting yacht, *Ti Haranui*:

"Yeah, I guess I used to be anti-American, in the way that everyone else is, you know, since George Bush junior and all that… But, coming up through the islands, all the way from home. It makes you think. We'd be speaking Japanese now, if it weren't for the damn Yanks."

Of course, there is older history as well. A "must" on our list of sights to see was Umatac Bay, on the southwestern corner of the island. On March 6, 1521, Ferdinand Magellan here made his first landing since leaving the stormy waters of the Strait that now bears his name, 7,000 miles behind him. The experience was not a happy one. He first named Guam the Island of Sails, on account of the sailing canoes seen off its shores. But then, after his three ships had anchored at Umatac, hundreds of native Chamorros paddled out. They did not share the Spaniards' concept of ownership and removed everything on deck that was could be lifted. Magellan had to fire off a few cannonballs from the *Trinidad* before a trading arrangement was reached.

When after a scant three days the Spanish flotilla sailed off, they found that one of their ships' boats had been stolen. In disgust, Magellan renamed Guam and its immediate neighbors the Ladrones ("Thieves"), an appellation that stuck until relatively recently.

Having sailed from the Strait of Magellan ourselves it seemed incredible that the great navigator had crossed such a vast expanse of ocean without sighting a single speck of land. Ferdinand Magellan was not a lucky man (and his luck would definitively run out in a grim manner soon after he left Guam).[11]

Umatac today is a quiet village, with a small bar called Magellan's Landing. Its sign is sponsored by Budweiser and it urges patrons to drink responsibly. A white concrete column marks the presumed landing site. The bay is surprisingly small and would only take one or at most two modern yachts. Magellan must have anchored his unwieldy flagship well offshore and landed here in his small boats. Overlooking Umatac is a small fort of a slightly later period. Also from the subsequent Spanish colonial period are the remnants of an old coast road, including beautifully constructed stone bridges.

Much of the north of Guam is occupied by Andersen Air Force Base, but there is good hiking on the southern coast and in the interior. We made several walks to island peaks, waterfalls, and to the beaches. In this remote and densely wooded hinterland a Japanese sergeant, Shoichi Yokoi, hid out for 28 years after the end of the war. He was finally captured close to a tacky resort restaurant called Jeff's Pirate Cove, whose music he could apparently hear from his jungle cave. Shoichi's picture and story now adorn Jeff's plasticized and gaudily colored hamburger menu.

---

11   Magellan was killed in a skirmish on the island of Mactan (Philippines) on April 27, 1521.

What a life story, I thought. Did Shoichi ever have doubts during those 28 years? And what about afterwards? Did he have regrets? Did he feel he had been let down? How must his homeland have looked to him, when he went back in 1973? On his return to Japan, he sent a message to the Emperor:

"Your Majesties, I have returned home… I deeply regret that I could not serve you well. The world has certainly changed, but my determination to serve you will never change."

Shoichi received USD300 in back pay and became a television advocate of austere living.

In between shopping and tourism bouts we were, as usual, scrutinizing the weather outlook. Phil and Mel shared their own sources with us, but they were more than happy to follow our judgement. I was intimidated by this unsought-for responsibility and became aware that, like it or not, we were now considered as "older" and more responsible cruisers. I couldn't quite pin down when we had made the transition from happy-go-lucky but had seen it coming for a while. We were almost unique these days in having books on board (as opposed to e-books) and the titles and authors of the cruising books that had meant so much when we got started in the eighties, said nothing at all to Phil and Mel.

It was late March. It was early for any typhoon activity in the North Pacific, but some persistent lows were hanging around in the islands of Yap and Palau to the southwest. The risk was growing that one of these would "go cyclonic" and then start moving west towards the Philippines. Then, typically, it would either continue due west or recurve to the northeast, towards Guam or the gap between Guam and Japan. The weather charts indicated that two or three days out we would have to cross a "shear line," a kind of front, with increased winds and rain. But we decided it was better to get moving than linger in Guam to see what that irritating low intended doing.

First, there was a more mundane problem to deal with, one that would soon become part of our lives: Japanese bureaucracy.

Arriving in a new country, on a yacht from overseas, you can't just show up wherever you like. You must come in at a designated Port of Entry. Japan is no exception. What was perplexing was the discovery that there are dozens of small Japanese ports that have Customs officers, but only a very few that have Immigration as well. Why would you have one without the other, we wondered (we never got a satisfactory answer to this one). Having selected your Port of Entry, you then had to notify officials by fax of your exact date and time of arrival.

"Who has a fax these days?" Jenny asked in frustration as she pondered this requirement on the screen of our laptop.

"More to the point, who has a fax on a yacht? And who can forecast a yacht's time of arrival a week in advance?"

We invented a date and time virtually at random, paid to use a fax at the Guam Seamen's Mission and, after a final phone call to the very helpful meteorological officer at the US naval air station, checked out in company with Phil and Mel. The course: 320 degrees, destination Kyushu, Japan. We had guessed that the passage, which theoretically would have us close reaching in northeasterlies all the way, might be a difficult one. Certainly, it was uncomfortable.

After our first night, we could make out a low grey outline to starboard: the island of Tinian. Captured by US forces shortly after the fall of Guam, it had the great prize of an 8,000-foot runway. The Americans for the first time now had an airfield that gave its B-29 Superfortress bombers the ability to reach Japan and return. Seven squadrons of the 58th Bombardment Wing were later based here. But it was two B-29s in particular that put Tinian in the history books: the *Enola Gay* and the *Bockscar*.

The *Enola Gay*, named after the mother of its commander, Colonel Paul Tibbetts, loaded up on Tinian late on August 5, 1945. After a six-hour flight, the aircraft was over Hiroshima at 8:15 a.m. the next morning. After the successful detonation of Little Boy, a uranium-235 fission weapon, President Truman warned:

"If (the Japanese) do not now accept our terms, they may expect a rain of ruin from the air, the like of which has never been seen on this earth. Behind this air attack will follow sea and land forces in such numbers and power as they have not yet seen and with the fighting skill of which they are already well aware."

Three days later *Bockscar* followed the *Enola Gay* from Tinian, with a slightly different kind of weapon, code-named Fat Man. The initial target was the industrial city of Kitakyushu on the straits of Simonoseki between Kyushu and Honshu. Cloud cover diverted *Bockscar* to its secondary target, Nagasaki.

Bosun Bird sailed on. Three days out we began to traverse the shear zone that our laptop files indicated would bring winds of 26 knots; in fact, they were around 30 to 35 for the best part of three days, with unremitting 100% cloud cover and squalls. The only comfort was that the seawater that was constantly drenching us was still warm. Adding to our stress was uncertainty over a threatening depression near Palau, which the Guam forecaster, in his daily analysis, began calling "the elephant in the room."

Barely were we through the shear zone, with the skies clearing, when the elephant began to move to the northeast, along the very shear line that we had just left behind. At one point, as we made all possible speed to the northwest, Guam upgraded the chances of its developing, within 24 hours, into the first typhoon of the season as "Good" (the scale being "Poor," "Fair,"

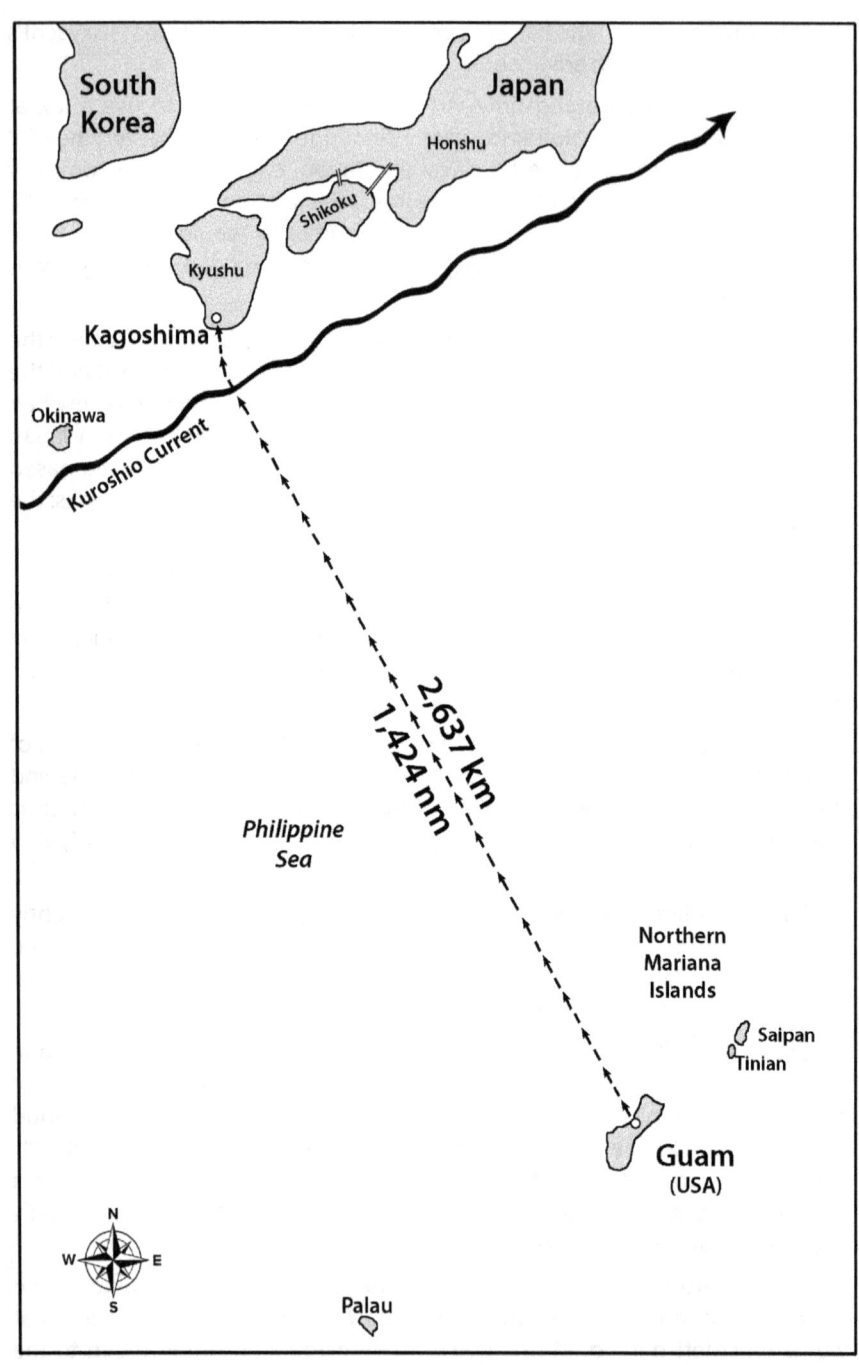

Guam to Kagoshima

and "Good"). But our luck held. The system continued on its track, which led to an intensification of the wind in the area we were now in, once again to 35 knots, but no more.

Thirty-five knots in a 27-foot boat is quite a lot of wind, but the angle was such that we were able to hold our course with four reefs in the mainsail and our storm jib hoisted. *Mira*, a little way ahead of us, suffered a knockdown and some damage in the same gale. We were corresponding with Mel and Phil by email transmitted through our satellite phone. I sensed with some consternation that Phil, for the first time since we had known him, was seriously worried.

In these circumstances the deck and coach roof are constantly swept by breaking seas, and it is impossible to stay dry; the area below the companionway, where you put on and take off your foul weather gear, is permanently wet. Jenny would announce:

"I'm sleeping on the floor tonight. I'll keep my wet-weather gear on. Call me if you need me."

She argued that by staying fully dressed she would be able to react more quickly in case of emergency. In reality, every time this happened, she would plead for a few minutes:

"I just need to go to the head…"

Going to the toilet (for a woman at least) with all your wet weather gear on is a lot more complicated and time-consuming than without.

Heavy weather in the shipping lanes;
the bridge of this tanker is barely visible from our cockpit

By now we were beginning to encounter more shipping than we had ever seen, bound to and from Japan. Our newly installed Automated Identification System (AIS)—a sort of low-budget radar that uses a small black box and the regular VHF antenna—allowed us to plot almost every ship within twenty miles or so, and gave us a read-out on their name, speed, and course. As and when the AIS further indicated with a beep that we were close to being on a collision course, we would call up the vessels by name on the VHF radio and assure ourselves that they could see us. Such conversations became routine, with the watch officers almost invariably replying courteously, even though they might have to go out onto the wet and windy bridge wing with their binoculars to make us out against the foam-flecked background of the ocean.

After the wind had subsided, a tired Red-footed Booby spent a whole night perched awkwardly on *Bosun Bird's* bow pulpit. More unusually, as we closed Japan, three swallows took up residence under the cockpit dodger: two males obviously competing for a female's attention. The competition resolved, the winning pair blithely flew below and set up home on the port bookshelf, just behind a book on meteorology. They stayed overnight; one died of causes unknown, the other flew off in the morning. We felt there was substance here for a haiku, but we couldn't remember the rules; we'd have to Google them once we got to Japan.

Our strategy for approaching Kyushu, the westernmost of the four big home islands, was to head west until we picked up the fast-flowing Kurushio current (the Pacific's Gulf Stream) then ride it north to the island. A good plan, but to our consternation we found ourselves in a powerful south-flowing arm of the current, just as a northwesterly gale was building. Once again, we reefed down heavily; the motion became violent, and for the first time ever, Jenny retired to her bunk with seasickness. At one point we found we had steered due west (270 degrees) for five hours, at great effort, only to be set due south (180 degrees) by over ten miles. The crew began muttering despondently from below:

"Maybe we should just think about going to Okinawa…it's dead downwind."

But wind and current eased and, after a detour of nearly 100 miles, we were able to re-set our course just as the first islands of Japan came into view.

In light winds and/or dead calm we worked our way north. A highlight was passing close to the great volcanic outlier of Io Shima Island, girdled by high cliffs and belching grey smoke from its fumarole. Closer to Kyushu, we started to encounter not only more heavy shipping but many smaller fishing boats with their bewildering arrays of unfamiliar lights, notably orange strobes indicating "keep clear." As dusk fell on our last evening at sea, we eased our way onto a northerly course and crept into the long, wide bay at whose head lies the large city of Kagoshima. The horizon at sea level was perceptibly darker and was starless: we were looking at land. By four in the morning, fishing boats

First sight of Japan

returning to port were steaming past us, leaving us rocking in their wake and sniffing diesel.

In the pauses there was another, suddenly familiar smell: spruce, or was it pine? For a second or two it seemed we were back in British Columbia, waters we'd last sailed twenty-five years earlier. The sun rose slowly, and a light fog dispersed. Colorful hydrofoils, one advertising Fuji Film, buzzed past at forty knots, more sedate passenger ferries overtook us in both directions. A prop-driven Air Force surveillance plane with a large red disk on its fuselage buzzed us. Dead ahead another active volcano (Sakurajima) let out great burps of smoke in welcome.

Every time we make a landfall at a new, unfamiliar destination there's a sense of excitement, of nervousness even. How will we know where to tie up? Will the local officials be welcoming? Will we be able to get ashore today, maybe for a meal out, or at least a hot shower? This time there was something extra. We'd never been to Japan before and hardly any cruisers came this way, so we had little to go on. In fact, we'd chosen Kagoshima as our landfall for no better reason than the only book we'd ever found on sailing these waters, Hal

Roth's *Two on a Big Ocean*,[12] had Hal and his partner Margaret arriving here too. The book had come out no less than 40 years earlier.

"Don't worry," said Jenny, and she recalled the set of instructional language CDs we'd been listening to on the night-watches coming from Guam. "We'll be able to deal with the obvious situations."

Using the notes that accompanied the disks, I gave her a quick test. She got "hello" and "goodbye" the wrong way round but managed an acceptable "good morning."

"Well," she responded defensively, "they said that if in doubt you can always just say 'Sou desu ne?'[13] We'll try that. It should cover most situations." Pause for hesitation. " Or was it 'Sou desu ka?'[14] I'm not sure anymore."

Up went our home-stitched Japanese flag on the starboard side spreader, the courtesy flag that it is customary to fly when entering a new country. And, below it, our much used yellow "Q" flag, which signifies "I request quarantine clearance," (or "pratique"); this is more obligatory than customary. We switched on the engine, I ran my finger over our paper chart, along the coastline, and we set the GPS to its final waypoint.

---

12   Roth, Hal. (1972). *Two on a Big Ocean*. New York, NY: Macmillan.
13   "Is that so?"
14   "That is so" (if pronounced flatly...).

Chapter Four:
Kagoshima and Kamikazes
(Southern Kyushu)

Massive Sakurajima almost blocks off the head of Kagoshima Bay (Wan - 湾 - in Japanese). Beyond the narrows, between its slopes and the city of Kagoshima on the western shore, the water becomes shallow. In 1941, Admiral Isoroku Yamamoto, Commander in Chief of the Imperial Japanese Navy, noticed a superficial resemblance between the strait and the lagoon behind it, and the main anchorage of the American Pacific Fleet at Pearl Harbor, Oahu. Realizing that the key to a successful attack on Pearl would be ensuring that his air-carried torpedoes did not bury themselves in the unusually shallow muddy bottom before hitting their targets, he had his torpedo bombers practice for weeks at Kagoshima until they chanced on the perfect modification that allowed for shallow running.

Jenny wasn't impressed that I'd been boning up on my history. She was looking anxiously ahead through the binoculars.

"Do shut up! We need somewhere to tie up."

We scanned the heavily built-up shoreline south of the narrows. There were miles and miles of dockyards at the foot of high, green hills and no obviously friendly place for a small yacht to moor. The giveaway would be a cluster of masts. I took the binoculars from Jenny, but there were none to be seen. We slowed down.

"Why don't we try *Mira* on the radio?" I said. "They've been here a couple of days already. They must have sorted things out."

Jenny went below, grumbling that we never keep our radio on in port, so why would Phil? But he came up almost immediately once she made a hailing call on Channel 16. There were advantages to buddy-boating after all, I had to admit. Phil read out to us his precise GPS position, Jenny wrote it down and quickly located the spot on both our chart plotter and the paper chart I was following in the cockpit. Soon, we were heading into a narrow concrete cut, deep in the harbor, with sailboats moored to the vertical walls bows-in. The

Sakurajima volcano and the Kagoshima harbor breakwater

harbor walls were so high, a precaution against typhoons, that their masts could not be seen from outside.

Phil hailed us and guided us into a slot formed by large foam buoys while simultaneously asking about our passage and telling us about *Mira's*. Distracted as I was by his chitchat and the perplexing mooring arrangements, it was ten minutes before I noticed a line of ten or a dozen smartly dressed men on top of the harbor wall. Some were in uniform with peaked caps, some in bright blue blazers, all wore white gloves.

"Looks like the Toyota sales team's here!" I said to Jenny, in poor taste.

Then, more seriously, I wondered if we were interrupting some sort of civic parade. Finally, I recalled that by an amazing coincidence we had arrived in Kagoshima exactly when we had randomly indicated we would in that fax, sent so long ago from Guam. This must be the official reception committee.

They all came aboard in pairs, as if boarding the Ark: two from Immigration; two from Customs; two from Agriculture; two from Health…and two from the Police. All were exquisitely polite but serious. Their English was rudimentary but comprehensible. All had multiple forms for us to fill in. One of these, the appropriately named General Declaration (with which we would later become excessively familiar), was put before us three or four times. Several people wanted to photograph our passports, then us, and then the boat. Light-heartedly I asked:

"Can I photograph you as well?"

There was immediate consternation, that stereotypical indrawn breath, and quizzical glances were exchanged. The answer was obviously no. Japanese officials had to be taken seriously.

Coming ashore at Kagoshima; next to us is Mira

We became worried when one pair, whom we had deduced to be from Immigration, politely gestured us towards their car, waiting on the quayside; the officers' English did not run to explaining what this was about. We looked to Phil, who just shrugged with a smile. We were whisked into Kagoshima, clearly a very large, modern city. The half-hour ride was exotic and foreign, not so much because of the modern buildings but because we could not understand a single word on the street or shop signs. Our guides in white gloves pointed out landmarks, looking at us questioningly when not sure of the English word:

"Here is train. Here is convenience store. McDonalds. Sento. You know Sento?"

We shook our heads negatively. More consternation.

"Is bus."

Another silence on our part. There were no buses anywhere in sight.

"Sento? Hot water!"

Ah! Bath! A public bath! The Japanese obviously had problems with the "th" sound.[15]

---

15   A Sento is a communal hot water bath that uses ordinary water that has been heated up; an Onsen is similar but uses naturally hot volcanic spring water.

More paperwork at the office, more General Declarations to be filled in. One question, written in both kanji[16] characters and English, asked for my mother's unmarried name. The official's finger lingered on my written response; he looked up at me and, speaking in Japanese, asked what seemed to be a question. Jenny caught my eye and shrugged almost imperceptibly.

"Sou desu ka," I said after a pause, with more firmness than I felt.

He frowned, looked stern then nodded. I smiled triumphantly at Jenny. There were low bows; a "Welcome to Japan!" and we had officially arrived.

We had a surprise when we got back. Sitting in the cockpit was a six pack (cold) of Asahi beer, a small package of assorted sushi, a watermelon, and a bag full of chocolate chip rolls. There was still a price-tag on the watermelon: we weren't yet sure of the exact value of the yen, but it seemed to be the equivalent of at least USD20. Phil smiled:

"It's just passers-by… The word was out that there were new arrivals… It was the same for us."

Mi-Chan, a pretty young woman in her early thirties, appointed herself as our host in Kagoshima. Her English was about as limited as our Japanese; we were never really able to work out if Hiro, or maybe Nakamura, was her boyfriend; whether she was paid for the small jobs she did around the boatyard; how well-off she was; or even where exactly she lived. Every day she would come down to our boat or to *Mira* with small gifts, which we were embarrassed to be unable to reciprocate, and a plan for the day's activities. Mi-Chan liked to be on and around sailboats, although she didn't have one of her own. One morning, pointing out the expensive yachts stored in rows on land around our mooring, I asked:

"Mi-Chan, who likes to sail in Japan?"

Puzzled for a moment, she consulted her hand-held electronic dictionary, typed in a couple of words, then took me by the sleeve and we walked down a row of boats. She pointed up at one after the other:

"Doctor, doctor, professor, dentist, doctor…all old men!" she said with a big grin.

---

16   Kanji is a Japanese writing system that uses characters (ideograms) mainly derived from Chinese writing. Or it can mean an individual character in this system. A second, complementary but phonetic system, called Katakana, is used for transcription of words from foreign languages or loan-words; another phonetic system, Hiragana (also phonetic), is used primarily for native or naturalized Japanese words and grammatical elements. Romaji is a Roman alphabet version of Japanese.

It didn't take us long to learn that she was right. You had to be wealthy to sail in Japan or, more to the point, you had to have been wealthy twenty years earlier, when the Japanese economy was booming. Since the crash, scarcely a sailboat had been sold, and the yachting community had inexorably aged. Many of the boats had English names: *Shangri-la, Blue Fantasy,* and *Windward Coconut.* But that didn't necessarily mean their owners spoke more than a word or two of English. Oddly, almost none had anchors on their bow rollers; odd, that is, until we realized that Japanese sailors don't anchor, they just tie up on harbor walls or in marinas.

Some of those who still sailed were still wealthy. One day at the marina there was great excitement as Hagiwa San, the marina owner and crane operator, conferred with our friend Nakamura. After Hagiwa strode away to his BMW, Nakamura explained:

"You remember that big yacht that left last week for Tokyo? They have radioed to say they have broken their mainsail halyard and need a new one. I must take them one."

"But how are you going to do that? They are at sea…"

He smiled.

"Didn't I tell you? My job is as a helicopter pilot. I will take them a new line in my helicopter!"

As word of our arrival spread, so more gifts began to arrive on a daily basis: melons, vacuum-packs of dried squid, mochi rice cakes, and various confections made of adzuki (red bean paste which we found to be an acquired taste). One day Oota San—his visiting card read *"Wind Word;* I am a boss; Captain Oota"— gave us a folder of full-sized Google Earth photos of harbors on our projected route onwards along with, mystifyingly, a small solar-powered lantern. Mi-Chan smiled when she heard:

"Oota San very kind man. He love Internet shopping."

Mr. Bamboo (his real name resembled the Japanese word for bamboo, but he liked to be known by foreigners this way) politely ascertained our age; we learned the Japanese have no scruples about asking. Then a day or two later he presented us with a specially compiled set of his favorite CDs from the sixties and seventies: the Monkees, Tommy James and the Shondells, and the Archies.

Mi-Chan took us everywhere we could possibly have wanted to go and she would never accept payment for a meal, a bus ticket, or a train ticket. It was especially useful to have her guide us on and off the trains. Our suburban stop at Sakanoue, above the docks, was not a tourist destination by any stretch of the imagination. Every single word in the station was in kanji characters, such that we could not even tell if the trains were coming from or going to Kagoshima proper, let alone figure out how to pay. It was all very familiar and yet very alien at the same time. The suburban trains were modern, but the passengers were startlingly uniform, all unmistakably native Japanese. Everyone obeyed the instruction not to take cell phone calls nor to make them; there wasn't a scrap of litter in sight, nor any graffiti. You could buy newspapers at the station, except perplexingly, when it was a holiday: a newspaper holiday, that is, not a national holiday. I found myself scrutinizing the "Most Wanted" posters on the platform, wandering what sort of crimes get you onto the Japanese list. Advertisements for the new Kyushu Shinkansen (bullet train), which showed a Darth Vader-like locomotive approaching head-on through a mist of cherry-blossoms, were oddly beautiful.

Need an ATM? Go to any post office, of course; and there seemed to be lots more of those than in any other country we had been to. Or a sandwich, a razor, or a magazine? Drop in on one of the ubiquitous Family Mart or Lawson convenience stores—each one with an identical layout and identical stock, down to the last cream doughnut.

Finding somewhere to read our email was more of a challenge. Mi-Chan, Nakamura, and Mi-Chan's friend Hiro were all perplexed. They all had their hand-held devices, of course, and spent half their waking hours online, but what was a Gaijin (foreigner)[17]—who was simply not allowed to buy a SIM card even if he had an appropriate device—to do?

In downtown Kagoshima we found a place that advertised itself as a Cybercafé. It was a dark and smoky place occupying an entire floor of an apartment building, with carpet on the walls. Its main function was as a library for manga comics, most of them pornographic (I checked). But you could also rent semi-private booths with comfortable faux leather reclining chairs. People used these to play video games for hours on end but if you pressed, you could get normal Internet access. There was free juice and coffee, and you could even get curry or French fries from a machine. Some people seemed to live in these gloomy places, many stayed the night.

One day Mi-Chan and Mr. Bamboo took us, along with Phil and Mel, half an hour down the train line to Ibusuki, at the entrance to Kagoshima Bay. This, we knew, was a famous natural spa, or Onsen. We also knew that there were special rules, which they carefully explained to us on the train:

"First, different entrance for man, for woman…"

We nodded.

"Inside take off all clothes. All," Mi-Chan emphasized seriously. "Put in box and…" (she consulted her dictionary) "lock."

"Small towel," she went on, pulling out a washcloth to show us. "Only small. Not…not…" Again, the dictionary, with a giggle. "Ah! Not hide parts! Maybe put on head."

---

17 Sometimes considered a derogatory term, usually applied to Caucasians.

"Now most important," Mr. Bamboo chimed in. "Wash first. Not pool. Use bowl. If not, big problem! Mundai!"

We'd read all this and were more or less prepared. But for most persons brought up in the UK or North America, getting completely naked in public is not a common experience and it can be nerve-wracking. Gaijin do attract some attention, we found. But there was no inordinate staring at the wrong places, and we soon got used to it.

Ibusuki was unusual in that as well as having a modern hot water spa inside the five-star hotel, it had hot sands. You were given a light blue cotton kimono to make the short walk from the indoor spa to the beach (our hosts showed us how demurely but casually to hold the flap of the gown so that the fresh breeze did not expose everything), and then asked to lie down in your gown in a designated location on the black sand beach. Old ladies then covered you up with hot, steaming sand, leaving only your head exposed. They would plant a miniature parasol carefully, so your head was in the shade. And then you lay there as long as you could take it. It was all quite bizarre, even more so when, as you got up, you looked around and saw twenty or thirty heads in the sand, each with its small and brightly colored sunshade. When we'd all finished and met up outside, Mel whispered conspiratorially to me:

Jenny and Mel, en route to the Onsen, Ibusuki

"I had a problem!"

"What?"

"I've got a small tattoo...here," Mel whispered, and she pointed at her hip. "One of the old ladies made a bit of a fuss, wagging her finger at me..."

Mi-Chan, overhearing, chimed in to explain quietly:

"Yes, in Japan, tattoo very bad...mean Yakuza."

"Yakuza?" I asked in a normal voice.

"Sssshh! Yakuza is mafia!" she whispered.

Later, the ever-resourceful Mi-Chan presented Mel with a roll of pink Elastoplast so that, in future, she could mask the offending butterfly and hopefully avoid arrest as a gang leader.

We learned the basic etiquette in temples (Buddhist) and shrines (Shinto), and how to spot the difference between the two; the familiar vermilion Tori gate was the giveaway pointer to a shrine. Gamely we tried every kind of noodle, fish, and crustacean on offer, along with the local alcohol: "Shochu," usually distilled from sweet potatoes and often drunk hot. We learned very early on that if you show any interest in their culture and can demonstrate having done even a little homework, the Japanese love you for it. And by no means do they always take themselves as seriously as we'd been led to believe. Mel and Jenny had a hilarious and occasionally ribald evening trying on the beautiful kimonos (with associated medieval underwear) of Mi-Chan's mother and grandmother.

One day, we politely excused ourselves and set off on our own to a small country town called Chiran, an hour away by train and bus. We hadn't been in Japan long enough to know whether our interest in Chiran might be offensive. For this was the principal base from which, in 1945, wave after wave of kamikaze pilots were dispatched in a last-ditch attempt to turn back the American fleet that was then preparing to take Okinawa, the last and most important big island before Kyushu. I'd just finished reading a moving novel by Horoyuki Agawa, entitled *Burial in the Clouds*,[18] and found myself fascinated by the phenomenon.

There is a museum now at Chiran; the airfield has long ago been built over. It is a simple and somber place. There are few explanatory plaques. Just walls covered with equally-sized sepia photographs of young pilots, with their name, their age, and the date of their mission. Following a key, you can contemplate the final messages they left, usually for their mothers. Some are almost unbearably sad. And some of the photographs are as well. One has a group of five pilots standing in a small group together smiling; they are in their fur-lined leather jackets, goggles around their necks, leather helmets on. One young man has a small puppy in his hands and the others are competing to pet it. It must have been taken within an hour or so of their take-off. I was reminded of photographs from the Battle of Britain: pilots of much the same age waiting to be scrambled, wearing similar sheepskin jackets, holding in their arms dogs with names like Blackie or Winston.

---

18 Agawa, Hiroyuki. (2006). *Burial in the Clouds*. North Clarendon, VT: Tuttle Publishing.

In a corner, a grainy black and white video runs over and over; there is no soundtrack. The scene is an open airfield, on a breezy morning in April 1945. Young fliers stand in front of a table where a white cloth is snapping in the wind. One by one, they step forward, stand to attention and knock back a single tot of Sake. The next sequence has their planes taking off, one by one, wagging their wings. On the left of the screen is a line of schoolgirls; they wave the pilots goodbye, with bunches of flowers in their hands, then shade their eyes as they watch the aircraft disappear.

I'd served as a diplomat in Pakistan, where suicide bombing is a daily fact of life. And yet I had never really been able to comprehend it. There, I'd never been able to put myself remotely near the frame of mind of young men with everything to live for, who had chosen to kill innocent persons in their "cause," whatever it was. The objective of the kamikaze pilots was perhaps more comprehensible—defense of the homeland, of the Emperor—and their targets were by no means innocent non-combatants. But I still couldn't see myself doing it. What was going through the boys' minds as they took off, I wondered, or as they lined up their target? What did they think of at that final moment?

The museum was busy but quiet. Every other visitor, I guessed, was over sixty; some were silently crying. What were they crying for? Was it admiration for the young men in the sepia photographs? Pity? Or frustration at the waste? As we sat quietly on the train going back to *Bosun Bird*, I thought I'd have liked to have had my Dad with me, to have heard his thoughts. He didn't often talk about the war. But he did tell me that when he went into action, he wasn't motivated by hatred for the enemy or love of his country. He kept going because to have done otherwise would have been to let down his friends; and he'd have looked like a coward. Perhaps it was the same for the kamikaze pilots. And, for that matter, the suicide bombers in Pakistan. It was more important to belong than to live.

Since Hal and Margaret Roth had come to Kagoshima on *Whisper* in 1972, very few other foreign yachts had passed through. Everyone had warned us before coming to Japan that complicated permits would be needed for each stage of the voyage. But when we checked with each of the agencies that had visited us on arrival, they were reassuring and told us simply go ahead and enjoy ourselves.

We consulted the Kagoshima sailors about good places to stop before setting off to work our way around the bottom of Kyushu and up its west coast. Especially helpful was Maika San, who was about to set off for Fukuoka in his small green Cornish Crabber yacht, *Summertime*. He supplemented Captain Oota's Google Earth photos with a detailed typewritten schedule he had prepared for us, with every day's daily run and each night's stop listed:

"Very good Maika San. Very detailed. Thank you!"

"Yes, in Japan all sailors make schedules."

"Why? Does someone require it?"

He looked perplexed.

"No. I don' think so. You don' make schedule?"

"Well yes, we usually have a rough idea of where we're going, and we try to estimate when we might arrive… But you have timings to the minute. What if there is no wind or the weather is bad?"

He looked at us as if we were stupid.

"Of course, I put engine on. Must keep to schedule."

A day before we planned to leave, Mi-Chan bustled us off anxiously, to meet Hagiwa, the marina owner. Mi-Chan's English was limited, Hagiwa's non-existent. But he had taken our early fretting about bureaucracy to heart and had made extensive enquiries. He pulled out a map of Kagoshima and said he had made an appointment for us at the Ministry of Transport. No such officials had visited us on arrival, but Hagiwa looked very worried, Mi-Chan too. We really needed to see these people now, it seemed.

At Transport there was much courteous listening, whispered conversations at the back of the room, phone calls to other offices. Gradually it emerged that we too would need to produce a schedule, just like Maika's, with every port we intended to stop at, and exact times of arrival and departure. The only places we were not required to list were Open Ports.

"And what is an Open Port?"

"Ah, so. Kagoshima is Open Port, Fukuoka is Open Port… Some others, maybe Yokohama, yes maybe Nagasaki…"

Open Ports were an historical relic from Japanese history. For most of the Edo period (1603 to 1868) Japan was effectively shut off from the outside world. Nagasaki was the only location where foreign trade was permitted, and on a very controlled basis; it was known as an Open Port. Following the arrival of US Commodore Matthew Perry off the coast of Japan in 1853, with his threatening gunboats (the Black Ships), a small number of additional ports were decreed as Open. The vast majority were termed Closed. As they still are. In order to visit Closed Ports, we would need a permit for each and every one.

"Why is this so?" we several times asked.

"It is the rule."

"Is it a security issue?"

"No. It is the rule."

"Why is it the rule?"

We could tell at this point that our insistence was regarded as rude. But even officials with whom we later became friendly, and there were many, could never explain why it was still the rule. It was just that it had always been so. With Captain Oota San's schedule in hand, we drew up our own plan and handed it to the officials at the Ministry of Transport for consideration.

Phil and Mel had meanwhile been having their own discussions. Mel had not enjoyed their passage from Guam; a fall in rough weather onto the hot galley stove had left an impressive square burn mark on her leg. The prospect of the long crossing to Alaska, which would probably be just as rough, was not appealing. Within the space of 36 hours, Mel got on a plane back home, Phil put *Mira* up for sale and we said our goodbyes, promising to meet up again in Alaska one day.

Our plan was officially approved. Or we supposed it was. For our vellum permit, though covered in impressive-looking stamps, was entirely in kanji script. Only by comparing the dates (which were in Roman numerals) were we able to deduce that we had been granted what we had asked for. Even so, we had to make a complicated conversion from the Japanese calendar (based on the reign of the current Emperor).

Mi-Chan took us on an extended round of goodbyes; we'd agreed to meet up with her a few days later, and she'd sail with us for a short stretch. Laden down with gifts, we motored out of the harbor and set a course south, to the entrance of Kagoshima Wan.

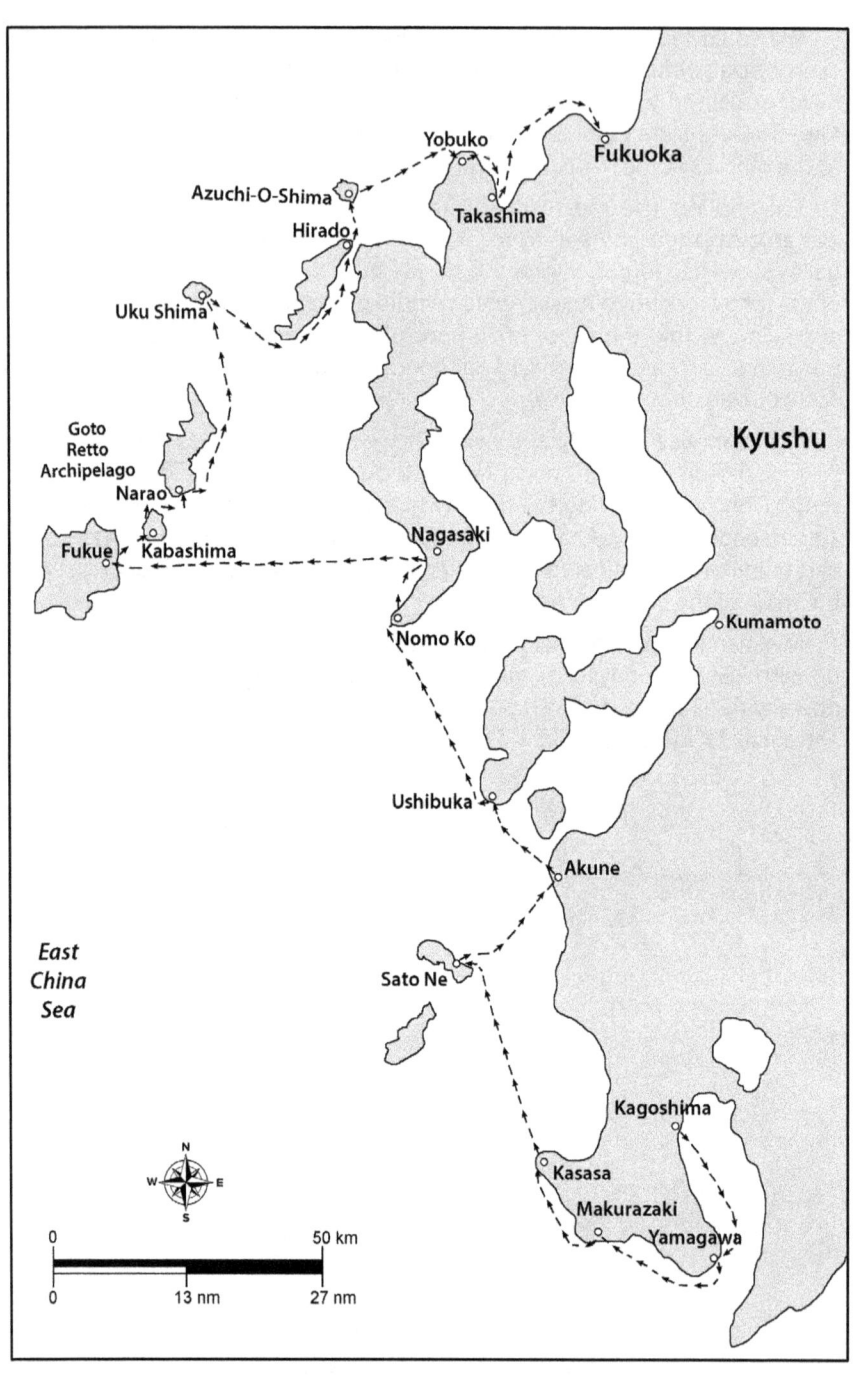

Kagoshima to Fukuoka

Chapter Five:
Embarrassing Encounters in the Nude
(Sailing the East China Sea)

*A*s we pored over our charts of Japan, with tiny nooks and indentations along every mile of coastline, it looked like a cruiser's paradise. But Maika, poring with us over his Google Earth photos, had warned us:

"Many bay, yes. But see, bays full of fishing harbors. Never anchor. Always wall or, best, pontoon."

We saw a few little coves on the shoreline as we sailed out of Kagoshima Bay; they were indeed all encumbered with fish-farms or had tiny artificial harbors where fishing boats were packed tight behind concrete walls. Yamagawa, our first stop, was a bigger bay but its center was occupied by two enormous floating docks, and every part of the shoreline was built up. One corner had a small walled harbor. Very cautiously we poked *Bosun Bird's* nose in: no room. We motored over to a large, green-painted pontoon, its side protected by automobile tires. Nobody ran down to object, so we tied up.

Late in the afternoon it began to rain. One or two men wandered down with a questioning look, frowned when they saw we were evidently Gaijin, then walked away again. We sensed that the default instinct was "no, you can't stay here," but no one wanted an argument, least of all in another language. At exactly five o'clock there was an electronic crackle in the damp and misty air. Over the town's loudspeakers came a few bars of *Love is Blue*; then silence again. We didn't know it then, but in rural Japan the times for children to go to school and come home again, and sometimes their lunch hour, are signaled in this way. Every village has its own tune: just a few bars, usually something a little sentimental.

"I quite like the idea," said Jenny. "It gives you a sense of community. I wonder who gets to decide on the tune?"

Next day was a brisk sail west, along the bottom of Kyushu. To our right there was what we had imagined to be a classic Japanese seascape: a small but perfectly conical volcano, one or two steep-prowed white fishing boats puttering about tending traps, the blue-grey hillsides bathed in a gentle haze

Tied up at Yamagawa

that never seemed to disappear, whatever the season. But when we came to Makurazaki, we were reminded that this can be a wild and storm-bound coast. A zigzagging waterway led us in through a claustrophobic maze of towering concrete walls, the outer ones of which were a full ten meters clear of sea level at high tide. Again, the hesitant search for a pontoon in a crowded harbor, again the visit by some official who this time tried to tell us "No" with the classic crossed-arms signal. But he gave up quickly when we pleaded "ashta" (tomorrow) and pointed to 7:00 a.m. on our watches.

Now it was Golden Week, one of the busiest holiday periods in Japan when four national holidays cluster together to give most people their longest break of the year. It didn't seem the ideal time for holidays—the weather was usually rainy at this time, we later learned—but the Japanese get famously few breaks, and they are not to be wasted. Makurazaki was festooned with flags of all sorts, especially huge colorful tubes of light nylon that represent carp ("Koinobiri") and that are flown as kites for Boys' Day (to bring them health and prosperity) on May 5th. All along the wharves a bustling market had been set up with all the usual plastic junk to buy but a few unusual games to play as well. In one, you paid a few yen to be given a twig to which was attached a short piece of cotton thread and a bent pin as a hook. In open tanks or bowls, you then fished to catch one of the dozen or so ten-centimeter eels that might be swimming around. We watched for a long time; the eels occasionally bit but in that case the twig always broke. As at fairground attractions all over the world the odds were very much stacked in favor of the proprietor. But the Japanese instinct to fish is so strong that there was always a line-up of willing punters.

海

In the evening Mi-Chan, who apparently lived nearby, came down to see us.

"Mi-Chan, is there a girls' day as well?" asked Jenny.

Having learned the classic western gesture for puzzlement, forefinger on lips, slight frown, Mi-Chan thought hard and theatrically, then got out her electronic dictionary.

"Hmmm…maybe," she said, after typing in various entries.

"Perhaps…Hina Matsuri. Doll festival? March?"

The doll festival had indeed been appropriated by girls, we learned, but it was not a national holiday; there's little doubt who gets to rule in a household where there's a boy and a girl.

"Now we go Sento," Mi-Chan went on. "Real traditional, old Onsen in house, we call Sento."

In an unpromising location just off a car park, she led us to a porch with a curtained door either side; one curtain had a red kanji character (女), the other a blue one (男).

"Boy blue, girl red. Remember?"

"Or maybe other way?" she added, pretending to be puzzled.

I held back a moment, just to be sure, and let Jenny and Mi-Chan go in first.

This was a real Japanese Sento; Ibusuki had been the modern, deluxe version. As you entered, you handed your 200 yen (about three dollars) to an old lady—it was always an old lady, usually bespectacled—who sat ensconced in a kind of elevated pulpit, from where she could sternly survey the men's side and the women's side over either shoulder. Past her pulpit, the two sides were divided by a high wall that stopped a meter or so short of the ceiling. In the wood-paneled changing room, with the mistress of the Sento looking round to coolly survey things over the top of her glasses, you stripped off, left your clothes in a small locker with a key on a wrist band, then stepped through a sliding glass door (the old lady could still see you…) into the bathroom proper. This was lined with white tiles but high on the far wall, visible from both sides, was a marine scene in blue-painted tiles. Around the walls at waist height were shower heads, with low plastic stools. You shower sitting down in Japan, not standing up. In the center was the main pool, a meter and a half deep and piping hot: here, as usual, a little too hot for North American or European tastes. At the far end of the room was another, smaller pool, this one filled with murky cold water that, Mi-Chan later told us, was infused with some kind of health-giving seaweed.

If I have gone on about Sentos (and will continue to go on…) it is because we became quite enamored of them. The whole experience was a lot more relaxing than having a shower, sitting naked with other people was somehow liberating. And you never knew who you might meet. Once or twice, I did end up in the tank next to heavily tattooed men. Whenever I told my Japanese friends, a frisson of excitement went through them:

"Yakuza!" they would hiss dramatically.

But all my mobster neighbor would have to say was:

"Plis here is shampoo!" as he beamed at his own English prowess.

Of course, every Gaijin has his or her Onsen or Sento story. Ours didn't come at Makurazaki but at our next stop, a tiny snug harbor called Kasasa with a luxury hotel, the Ebisu, at its head. By now we considered ourselves veterans but just in case, Mi-Chan—who had sailed with us that day and was horribly seasick all the way—came with us once more. Admission was a lot pricier than Makurazaki, but through a huge plate-glass window you had a wonderful view of the East China Sea as you lay gently cooking in the hot water.

So beautiful that next day, after Mi-Chan had gone home, we went again. There was no one else around; Golden Week was over. I was lying half asleep in the steaming water on the men's side when I heard the sliding door open. There was a pause, then:

"Oohh!"

I glanced over. At the door, faintly visible through the steam, stood a naked figure. The small washcloth was to little avail; it was unmistakably a woman of a certain age and she was holding one hand to her mouth in horror, revealing even more. Oh dear, I thought, the poor woman has come in the wrong side. I shrugged and dozed off again. Ten minutes later the door opened again. This time it was a man, fully clothed in the peaked cap, blue blazer, and white gloves uniform of the hotel staff. Very hesitantly he came over and, with his hands in the praying position, whispered:

"So sorry. Ladies' side. Please to go."

Massive embarrassment all around. It didn't take Jenny and me long to figure out what had happened (she had undergone a parallel experience on her side). So fine was the view, but from only one of the baths, that the management considered it fair each day to switch the men's side with the women's side. Here there were no red and blue curtains to distinguish, just the black kanji characters for "Men" and "Women" which, of course, we had failed to learn yet.

One side of the pontoon below the Ebisu had a modern Yamaha yacht tied up and a plaque in front of the boat, which was evidently not going anywhere soon. And on land there was another, older 28-foot yacht named *Kairen Tarachine*, this one mounted in a wooden cradle with a walkway around it. Both were well-travelled: one around the world, the newer one (inspired by the first) across the Pacific and back. In Europe, the USA, or Canada they would scarcely have merited a second glance, even if you had known their history. Our own vessel was smaller and older than both of these and had been further. It said something about Japanese yachting that the two boats at the Ebisu had been singled out for museum-treatment, their single-handed skippers for hero treatment. Inside the hotel there was a museum about one of the two sailors. I didn't want to belittle anyone so when I spoke with the curator, I phrased my comments carefully. He took some time before replying:

"Yes, you see for a Japanese man (or woman) it is still not so usual to… to break away, to rebel. You know the saying 'The nail that sticks up gets hammered down'?"

I nodded.

"Well our society is still like that. We admire those who do stick up, but we think they are a little crazy."

With hindsight, this kind of interest accounted in some degree for the extreme and unexpected warmth of the welcome we were given everywhere we went on our small, sailboat in Japan. We wondered too if the very small size of Japan's offshore sailing community—and the consequent lack of relevant information on the topic in Japanese-language books and magazines—had accounted in part for our friend Chinami's puzzling behavior. Yes, he was that nail that stuck up; he had bucked the trend. But he wasn't just a nail, he was a casualty of the Galápagos syndrome.

According to the Galápagos syndrome, Japan is so large, so advanced, and so self-sufficient in most respects, yet physically and linguistically isolated, that trends in the "outside" world sometimes pass the country by, almost unnoticed. The country develops ways of doing things that are perfectly adapted and suitable locally, but which don't work when the wider world intrudes. The most well-known example of this is Japanese cell phone technology, which has evolved along a path quite different to everywhere else—and which is consequently no longer transferable.[19] In the case of Chinami, so unusual was his initiative that there had been nobody to tell him that on a long voyage you just keep sailing at night, and that you need to keep watch at all times for ships that might be on a collision course.

Leaving the rugged Kyushu coast astern, we sailed out westwards to a small archipelago centered on Koshiki Shima, with sleepy fishing villages, and found

---

19   Takeshi Natsuno, professor at Tokyo's Keio University: "Japan's cell phones are like the endemic species that Darwin encountered on the Galápagos Islands—fantastically evolved and divergent from their mainland cousins." Quoted in the San Diego Tribune, https://www.sandiegouniontribune.com/sdut-japans-cell-phone-prowess-fails-create-global-clou-2009jul21-story.html

a handy pontoon in front of an empty resort hotel. By now we were wrestling with what was to become a cruising problem for us: garbage. On the one hand the Japanese seem to generate huge amounts of surplus packaging, especially in their supermarkets, but on the other they approach disposal and recycling with great energy, nay fanaticism.

It was very rare indeed to find any kind of garbage can in public. Every neighborhood, sometimes every apartment block had its disposal area. But these were almost always inside locked cages to which only the local people had access, and there were designated days for the collection of different kinds of garbage. Often there were detailed explanatory signs with small pictures of everything from fish heads to tape-recorders

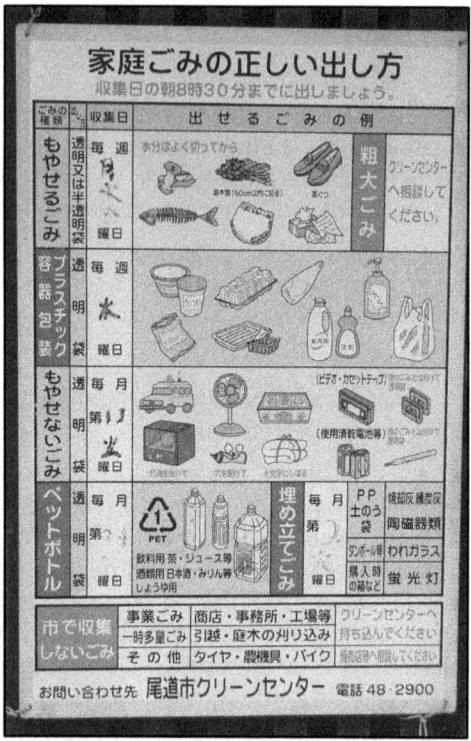

Recycling guidance at Sato One

and refrigerators; of course, they were in kanji. Each kind of "gomi" (塵) has a different name or term to describe it. The phrase used for items like large, broken refrigerators or couches was "sodai gomi" (粗大). This, we learned, is also a term used by annoyed Japanese housewives to describe their inactive and passive retired husbands as they lie around the house, while they are busy vacuuming or dusting. Such wives (and we would later meet a number) nodded appreciatively and seriously when we suggested that the nearest equivalent in English might be Couch Potato.

At Sato One we made three nocturnal forays and were successful in locating a cage whose padlock had been lost; but we spent the rest of the night in dread that we had been seen by the Gomi Police.

In a park above the quiet harbor one afternoon, four men were sitting companionably round a barbecue, smoking fish and getting quite drunk:

"My frens, my frens…you come… Plis! Plis!"

They all worked together and had come for a week of sustained drinking and camaraderie to the island where they had grown up. The conversation faltered, as it often does when everyone has had too much. And there were dead ends when our respective linguistic abilities failed us.

"What is your job?" I asked one of the group.

"Stim!" (or that is what it sounded like). This accompanied by puffing sounds and energetic back-and-forth hand motions. Train driver? Laundry technician? Dry cleaner?

"Sensei!" said the leader eventually, in desperation, gesturing to his cell phone as he pulled it out.

"We call Sensei. He help with English!"

I was sure the local English teacher would be less than keen about being summoned out here on a Sunday afternoon, but Jenny and I were amazed when fifteen minutes later up drew a car and, to drunken but enthusiastic shouts of welcome, Sensei (a little embarrassed for us) shambled over.

For an hour or so we talked. These four men had all grown up on the island together, been at school in the same class, gone to the big city together, and now they all worked in the civil engineering department of the local government in the city. What this had to do with "stim," was never clarified. In their fifties now (this teacher must have been a successor to their own Sensei, we deduced) they were still the best of friends.

"Two, three times a week," Sensei explained, "they meet, maybe for noodles, maybe in a bar after work; eat, drink, maybe karaoke; every year, there are class reunions, office parties, and each year they come to Sato One."

"I think they are good men," he said in a quiet aside to us. "Honest men."

And their wives, where were they? There was a partial answer when, with the light fading, another car drew up, and a middle-aged lady in a trouser suit stepped out decisively. Time was evidently up. After greeting us politely but a little suspiciously—Had we perhaps been encouraging the drinking?—she briskly began tidying up around the quartet, clearing away the remains of the barbecue and corking sundry three-quarter-empty bottles. She bowed politely to Sensei, whom she evidently knew, and bundled the four men into the car, like so many tired small children. With a happy wave, off they went.

Earlier, Mi-Chan had taken me on one side and asked me:

"Nick San, how you persuade Jenny San to sail?"

I must have looked bemused.

"Japanese woman, Japanese man, even if husband and wife, have different lives, I think. Not do things together, so much…"

We had had a brief glimpse of what Mi-Chan had meant; we were to have many more.

We worked our way back from the islands to the coast of the big island of Kyushu, first to the port of Akune, then Ushibuko. The fishing harbors, some squeezed into tight inlets with steep green hills behind them, were packed with modern white fiberglass fishing boats, usually in the 25- to 30-foot range. But they were always quiet: of a hundred boats, only eight or ten seemed to go out any given morning or evening. At the covered fish markets there might be a few old ladies packing squid into ice or shelling shrimps. But it was obvious they'd once seen far busier days. When an old, short-sighted man in a pharmacy in Akune bravely tried out his English on us, we took advantage of the opportunity to quiz him about life in these small towns:

"Yes, many boats," he said. "But now the fishing mans all old. No young mans. All young mans go to Nagasaki or Fukuoka, do not want to fish any more. And diesel, it is expensive."

We'd noticed colorful large-scale murals on the iron roller-shutters of the shops in the main street. One had the Beatles crossing Abbey Road, another had American comic book heroes, another Godzilla:

Storefront painting, Akune

"Yes, good idea of the city. Everyone very happy. They help with paint. Now some tourists come to see the paintings, spend money. But the city forget one thing…"

We waited. He chuckled.

"To see painting, shutter must be down. Shop cannot open. So no make money."

Nomo Ko was approached through a fifty-meter-wide channel in which the green sea heaved and sucked at the steep cliffs either side. Concrete walls lined the narrow inlet beyond the pass, and houses with the traditional, grey-tiled roofs were squeezed into every available space. It was teeming with warm rain. There was not a soul to be seen as we moored at a free pontoon and set off to find someone to ask for permission to tie up. Finally, behind a couple of closed doors in a building on the wharf we found a uniformed office worker shuffling papers dejectedly under a weak fluorescent light. He looked up at us in shock, as if we had come from outer space. But we took his shrug of incomprehension as a yes.

When the rain eased we wandered through the damp and shining streets. A couple of old ladies coming back from their shopping, stooping forwards over their walkers-cum-shopping trolleys, smiled politely at us. Two Grade Three girls in matching pink baseball caps, satchels on their backs, and holding hands, stared and giggled. We found the village store whose ancient owner—

everyone seemed to be very old or very young in these places—waved us in. At least half the items on the shelves were still quite unknown to us. Was this seaweed or some kind of vegetable? What about these meter-long root vegetables? What did you do with them? That melon, surely the price could not be 30 dollars? But by now we had a few favorites; one was a kind of half-moon shaped bun studded with dark spots: Chocolate Chip Melon Pan.

That night a thick, wet fog came down. It cleared sufficiently around nine in the morning for us to be able to make it safely out of the harbor entrance, but soon we were enveloped again. It was too late to go back. Every so often we'd hear a fishing boat sound its horn or the noise of an engine rising then fading. An hour or so out there was a partial lifting. I called Jenny up to the cockpit:

"What do you make of that? An island? A big ship?"

Away to starboard (a mile, maybe two?) was an eerie, ghostly sight. It looked like a huge World War I Dreadnought: grey black, a long forward section with those characteristic forward-sloping bows, slab-sided superstructure with radio towers on top. For a moment or two it seemed to be moving; you could just make out breakers under the bows. But then I realized it was an optical illusion.

"Gunkanjima," Jenny finally said after a close study of the chart. "Battleship Island," after an even closer study of the dictionary.

Later, we Googled Gunkanjima (軍艦島). From 1887 to 1974, this was the site of a set of coal-mining shafts that gave access to extensive undersea seams. On the island itself, which covers a bare six hectares, accommodation was built for 5,500 persons, which made this once one of the most densely inhabited places on earth. Now it is completely deserted, but increasingly studied as an example of the degradation of large concrete structures over time. It is also occasionally used as the set for post-apocalyptic movies, including the James Bond film *Skyfall*. Gunkanjima eerily faded away into the mist again.

By mid-morning the fog had cleared, and the wind was picking up. Over an increasingly rough, grey-black sea with scattered whitecaps, we zigzagged past one green island then another. We were going too fast but had not far to go; it wasn't worth reefing. An outgoing ferry passed us close by, too close for comfort; inbound a hydrofoil buzzed past like an enormous water beetle. We turned to port under a high and elegant grey suspension bridge, heeling hard. On both sides were giant floating docks; letters ten meters high told us this was the site of the Mitsubishi Shipyards. To the right, houses tumbled down the steep hillside, a few of them wooden and looking to be a hundred years old or more. Up ahead, as the inlet narrowed, was a complex of high rises and a peculiar silver dome: Nagasaki.

Chapter Six:
Dying Islands and Closet Christians
(Nagasaki and Goto Retto)

One thing we learned from the Nagasaki Atomic Bomb Museum was that the bomb destroyed the largest Christian Church in Asia. We also learned that although in 1945 Nagasaki, as today, was an important shipbuilding center, the Mitsubishi Shipyards were not the target. Rather it was the business and semi-residential area of what is still the city center. Part of the rationale for the choice of Nagasaki (as for Hiroshima) was that it had not been heavily damaged by prior conventional bombing: accordingly, it would afford the scientists an excellent laboratory to see exactly how devastating an atomic bomb could be.

A display of documentation from British and American archives convincingly made the case that in the mid-stages of the war—before Germany had been defeated—the decision had been made by Roosevelt, Stalin, and Churchill that the first atomic weapon would be used against Japan, not Germany. The viewer was tactfully left to draw their own conclusions from this.

The museum was moving; we had expected it to be. There was pathetic debris from the bomb blast: broken spectacles; a schoolgirl's lunch box; a half-burned pair of shoes. If the aim of these displays was to show the enormous tragedy of the bombing, in which 80,000 civilians died, then it succeeded. Where it was less successful was placing August 9, 1945, in its broad historical context. There was an account of the wave of Japanese expansion into Asia in the 1930s, but it was sketchy. There was a reference to the infamous Rape of Nanjing, in which an estimated 250,000 to 300,000 Chinese civilians, many of them women and children, died at the hands of Japanese troops. But it admitted only that "there is controversy over this matter."

Among that documentation on display from the western allies was no mention of what had been at the top of my father's mind as he awaited his embarkation orders: estimates of the losses likely to be incurred in a land assault on Kyushu and Honshu. The most conservative saw the allies suffering between 1.7 and 4 million casualties, of whom 400,000 to 800,000 would be dead, while

Japanese casualties would have been between 5 and 10 million. And among the Japanese exhibits there was no reference to the Emperor's lack of response to the first bomb.

The ethics were not easy to decide upon. We thought it good, when we toured the tranquil and shady gardens near the Hypocenter, that schoolchildren were being lectured to in groups. But I wondered what their teachers were saying.

Schoolchildren at the Nagasaki Atomic Bomb Museum

An old man came up to us as we sat on a bench:

"What do you think of all this?" he asked quietly.

"It's very sad…" I said slowly and vaguely, not sure. As per my diplomatic training, I was waiting for a prompt.

He waited too. When I didn't go on, he nodded gravely and strolled on.

We had moored *Bosun Bird* at a perfectly placed little marina in the historic center of Nagasaki, Dejima Wharf, where in 1543, the first European contact with Japan was made (an off-course Chinese junk with a few Portuguese adventurers aboard). It was adjacent to the enormous silver dome we had seen: this was a ferry terminal and staccato departure announcements could be heard all day.

In 1560, St Francis Xavier stepped ashore here. Christianity briefly flourished until in 1597 the authorities decided to clamp down in dramatic style, crucifying twenty-six Japanese and European Christians; the Christian Church went underground. But Dejima was allowed to remain as the single point of Japanese contact with the outside world. For the next 250 years the Dutch were allowed a toehold of a trading enclave here, through which odd fragments of western science and erudition leaked in, and wild rumors of exotic Japan leaked out.

Dejima has been recreated, tastefully and life-size. But, as a reconstruction of seventeenth century Dutch warehouses, it is probably of more interest to Japanese than to westerners. Tanaka San, the friendly marina manager who had arranged for an army of officials to visit us on our first day here (for this was an Open Port: it was as if we were entering Japan again for the first time) sensed our interest in more obscure history:

"Over bridge," he gesticulated. "Many dead persons. Gaijin. Interesting."

After a dozen wrong turns among the hectares of graves in the cemetery on the mountain, we found what we were looking for. There was a small square building with an onion dome; all around, under the trees, were dozens of Russian Orthodox crosses in stone, most with legible inscriptions in Cyrillic. Many of the graves bore the date 1905. Here were some of the dead from the Battle of Tsushima at which, in the waters between Korea and Kyushu, Japan decisively defeated the Russian Grand Fleet. In the nearby American section of the cemetery, one inscription caught my attention:

Horace Peter
Admiral's Secretary
U.S. Flagship Hartford
November 21, 1867

Meanwhile, in the Dutch section is the oldest European grave in Japan, that of Hendrik Duurkop of the Dutch East India Company, who died in 1778 on his way to take up his post at Dejima; at its head is an hourglass (its time near expired…) with wings. More mysterious is the marker commemorating Gustav Wilckens, who died in 1869, aged 37. Carved on the side of the stone, in kanji, are the words:

Tamagiku of Tsunokuniya.

Tsunokuniya, we learned, was in those days known as a high-class brothel; the gravestone was likely paid for by Wilckens' geisha, Tamagiku.

And here is a European child's grave:

Father, Mother, God Loving Me
Guide Me While I Sleep
Guide My Little Feet Up to Thee.

You could write a history of the foreign presence in Nagasaki, based entirely upon the cemetery.

We wandered back through modern Japan. There was a street full of enormous glitzy Pachinko[20] parlors where players were enticed in by posters of sexy manga girls winking exaggeratedly. From inside came the racket of hundreds of pinging machines and, when the doors opened to let someone in or out, clouds of pungent blue cigarette smoke puffed out. A nearby sign, wordless, showed a row of upstanding citizens (one with their pet dog) evidently saying "No!" to scowling Yakuza in black suits: Pachinko is often associated with organized crime. There were several blocks of apartment buildings with illuminated panels in their doorways, each advertising small drinking clubs. Some had complicated all-you-can drink packages to offer, a few had karaoke, and others had pictures of dusky girls with their names:

Anti-Yakuza poster, Nagasaki

"Are they prostitutes?" we later asked Tanaka San.

"No, no!" he exclaimed in horror. "Just barmaids…but very pretty. For conversation only."

It sounded very Japanese, but we were never entirely convinced. Who would really pay ten dollars over the odds on their beer just to be winked or smiled at by a pretty girl?

"Oh yes. Oh yes. Sure. Japanese man like this." Tanaka insisted. "Especially if has not pretty wife."

In the supermarket near the marina—intriguingly called YouMe—I hunted around for Chocolate Chip Melon Pans and then caught up with Jenny at the meat counter. Video screens were playing an endless loop of a silly but very catchy song called Suki Suki, featuring schoolgirls in short kilts bouncing around happily. It was our first, but no means last introduction to the phenomenon known as J-Pop. Later we found that there are dozens of You Tube[21] versions of this song, which was at YouMe somehow promoting the sale of meat.

---

20   Pachinko is a form of pinball. The object is to win as many balls as possible; these can in turn be exchanged for prizes.

21   "Cute japanese song-suki suki daisuki*1Hour*Loop," YouTube, 2022, https://www.youtube.com/watch?v=vWbB5iRY88Y

The most famous manifestation of J-Pop was an all-girl group called AKB48: the AKB stands for a district in Tokyo (Akihabara), and forty-eight was the number of girls who constantly rotated through the group's permanent shows. Every parent-age Japanese friend to whom we mentioned AKB48 would laugh in delighted recognition. But a few did then confess to us that they worried if AKB48 was actually pornography being marketed as bubble-gum pop. Wikipedia seriously describes AKB48 as a social phenomenon.[22]

Every Japanese sailor we had met insisted that we should never sail at night. There were far too many fishing boats out there and:

"Fish man not like yacht man. Sometimes he want you to hit net. Then you must pay big money."

But it was sixty miles west from Nagasaki to the Goto Retto archipelago. We wouldn't make it in a day, so we set off one evening and successfully dodged those fish men; I listened to AKB48 on my iPod to while away the night watch. We came in to the medium-sized port of Fukue, at the south end of the island group, shortly after dawn.

Goto Retto ("Five Islands") is a chain of islands running in a northeast to southwest direction, rugged and deeply indented. In an enlightened bid to persuade more yachts to stop by, the municipality had reserved a space on Fukue's main ferry pontoon. Here we had one of only our very few unpleasant human encounters in Japan.

"Excuse me," I said in slow, clear English, gesturing so that I would be more clearly understood.

A working boat had moored unnecessarily close to us and had carelessly bumped our stern section as it tied up. Now it was about to do so again. I clambered out onto the pontoon:

"Please. This is not good! Do not touch!"

It was odd. The young man whom I was talking to, from one meter away, simply made no eye contact whatsoever and looked stolidly into the distance. He didn't walk away or respond angrily; it was as if I was not there. I tried one more time.

"Please. My Yotto. Too close."

He seemed to be deaf and blind. Rather angrily Jenny and I ostentatiously retied our lines so as to edge a little further away. Next day, after we returned from some chores in town, we found one of our mooring lines untied and trailing in the water; it must have been done deliberately. There was little wind, and it was not dangerous, but if bad weather had developed, *Bosun Bird* could

---

22 "AKB48," Wikipedia, https://en.wikipedia.org/wiki/AKB48

have been damaged. Later, other Japanese sailors to whom we spoke said that they too had had similar experiences. Fishermen and people who work on ferries do not like yachts and consider that they have no place in fishing harbors:

"They really think they own the sea and the ports, that they are theirs," said one friend. "It doesn't matter if the place was reserved for you, that you were paying, they don't agree with pleasure boats on principle."

The silent treatment, sailing friends thought, was likely more to do with our being Gaijin than anything else:

"They think you will not understand, which will make them look foolish if they try to speak to you or respond to you. So, they pretend you are not there."

We experienced another clash of cultures in Fukue. It wasn't unpleasant but it was frustrating. By now it was late May and there had already been one or two typhoon warnings that had come to nothing. But Tropical Storm Songda, now close to Taiwan, looked likely to be coming our way. We walked over to the nearby Coastguard office, to seek advice as to where we might move to that would be a little more sheltered. The smartly uniformed officials were very helpful. We jointly pored over our charts and our Google Earth pictures, and by consensus it emerged that there were two or three more sheltered locations on the north side of the island we were now on.

"But so sorry," one of the officials eventually said with a nervous smile.

I had noticed that he had occasionally been consulting a thick file on his desk. Now he put it on the table, turning it so we could see. It was our own latest list of approved Closed Ports, which we had updated with the authorities in Nagasaki.

"Only Fukue allowed for you," he said calmly, running his finger down our itinerary.

"But maybe a typhoon is coming…"

"Yes, maybe big typhoon," he agreed. "But *Bosun Bird* need permission for other closed ports. So must go to Nagasaki now and make new list." And he positively beamed at us.

By now, everyone in the office was listening. They all looked at us attentively. We knew there was no point in arguing, even less in (again) querying the rationale for the Open/Closed Port system. If we had said nothing and simply moved to a safer bay, probably they would have said nothing either. We nodded and left.

Fortunately, Songda stayed clear and we made lots of friends in the meantime. The evening of our encounter with the Coastguard, a tall, shy man showed up by *Bosun Bird*, tapped politely on the hull, and presented us with a bottle of wine, some marmalade, a jar of olives, and a jar of sauerkraut:

"Matsumoto," he said, bowing and introducing himself.

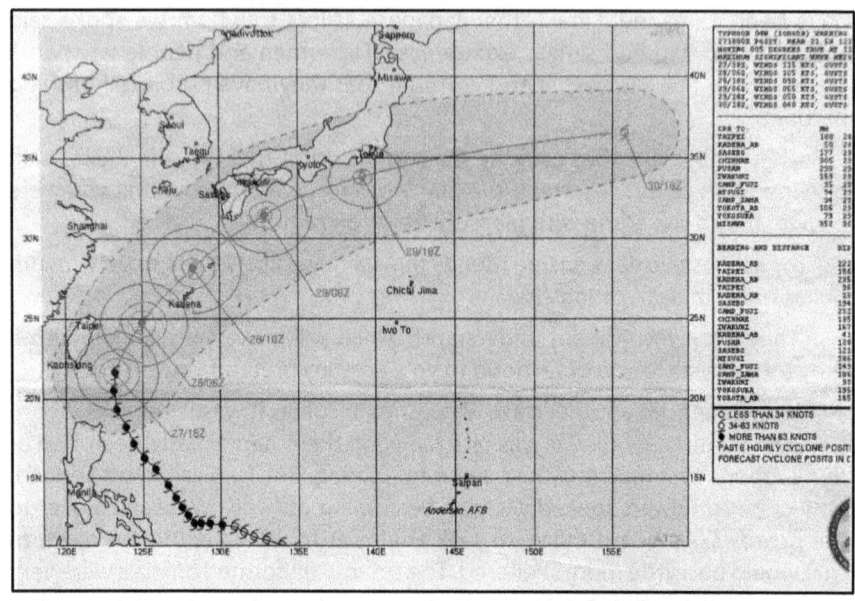

Joint Typhoon Warning Center: the approach of Typhoon Songda

Matsumoto was the local vet and one of two yacht owners in Goto Retto. Next day he was back. He took us to view his boat, *Micawber*, and then without further ado, having correctly assessed that we had no shower on board, stated:

"Onsen. Now?"

Following Matsumoto's lead, we strode boldly into Fukue's only five-star hotel, making no eye contact with the staff, and took the elevator up to the penthouse, where we spent an hour naked, contemplating the skyline from enormous black slate tubs. There was more to come. A little bewildered—Matsumoto's English was scant—we were ushered into a small tatami-floored dining room which he had evidently reserved for us. There followed a sumptuous multi-course meal served in traditional style by a kimono-clad waitress as we sat cross-legged. We marveled over the various kinds of sashimi and other kinds of seafood that were placed before us. A very useful Japanese word that is worth learning early on is "Oishi!" (delicious). But Matsumoto kept looking at his watch. Eventually there was quiet tap on the sliding door, and he sprang up, visibly relieved:

"Ah, my captain!" he exclaimed, and more introductions were made.

Yoshinoro and Taeko, with their son Sin (just back from after-school soccer practice and proud of his red and blue-striped Barcelona FC shirt) owned the other yacht on the island.

Within the next couple of days we had met everyone in Fukue who had ever been sailing or knew about yachts, everyone who had been abroad, everyone who spoke either English or French. There were some cosmopolitan encounters: one evening we had dinner with the island baker, who had trained in Paris and spoke fluent French; his friends in turn included a Fukue lady and her Swiss husband, who was an ex-diplomat with whom we shared various mutual acquaintances.

One day we remarked how although Fukue evidently marketed itself as a holiday town and the holiday season was upon us, it was strangely quiet, with everything shut up after seven. Very few of the boats in the harbor went out either. Yoshinoro, who spoke excellent English, nodded.

"Yes, you are right. The town is dying. I was a small boy here. I grew up in Fukue; I went to Nagasaki to train as an ophthalmologist, but I have been back some time now. I like the quiet life. But you know what? When Matsumoto and I were boys, there were seven classes in our grade at school. You know how many there are now? Two."

While Japan's cities seem as crowded as ever, he explained, it is deceptive. The birth rate is falling fast; as the economy stagnates, people get married later and later; there is virtually no immigration. The young people go to the cities to find work and they don't come back. Matsumoto added something in Japanese, and Yoshinoro translated:

"In the islands, like Goto Retto, there are now likely fewer people than at any time in the last five hundred years. That's partly why we like it. But for many Japanese people, they want the cities; it is not like Europe or America."

At one point, we got out a map and showed our route from New Zealand to Japan. I pointed out Vanuatu, the Solomons, Guadalcanal, Guam, making passing reference to the war. Yoshinoro, Taeko, and Matsumoto were about our age and would have grown up in the fifties and sixties. I'd assumed that Guadalcanal would ring a bell. But it didn't. We felt we knew them well enough by now to ask a couple of risky questions:

"So, what do you learn about the Pacific War at school?"

Yoshinoro looked up with a smile, not in the least embarrassed.

"When we went to school: nothing. By the time we reached the 1930s it was always the end of the class or the end of the year…and that period was never in the exams either. We didn't learn about it at all. History for us starts again in 1945, with the Bomb."

Fukue Island with its low green hills, farmland and intricate bays and inlets, was Irish-looking in the warm spring drizzle. We'd been given a brochure that was entirely in Japanese except for the enigmatic title *"Road To Church in Goto"* and we used this as an excuse to find some of the old and now largely abandoned Christian churches that are scattered around the smaller villages. One at Dozaki dates from 1868 and is preserved as a museum. Built in red brick, in a vaguely Italian style, it stands at the end of a quiet road that leads nowhere, overlooking a calm inlet. Inside are various artifacts from the long period, starting in 1614, when remote Goto Retto was a refuge for Christians who were being persecuted on pain of death on Kyushu and the big islands. Even here, Christian worship was clandestine. Kannon, the Buddhist Goddess of Mercy, was venerated in lieu of the Virgin Mary and Dozaki church had several examples of sly Kannon statues.

For over 200 years the Kakure Kirishitan (Hidden Christians) maintained their faith in complete isolation from the outside world. Understandably, in some areas there was a gradual drifting away from conventional tenets, as books and Bibles were too dangerous to own. Ancestor worship crept into some rites and odd mélanges of Latin and Portuguese took on the rhythms of Buddhist chants. When persecution ended in the mid-nineteenth century, most of the Kakure reverted to conventional Catholicism; some did not. The holdouts still practice in Goto Retto and are known as the Hanare Kirishitan (Separated Christians).

海

With Typhoon Songda safely past, we motored out from Fukue early one morning onto a calm grey sea and began working our way up the hazy east coast of the archipelago. Yoshinori and Matsumoto had recommended Kabashima, only five or six miles away, as a good first stop.

With the aid of the GPS coordinates our friends had given us we were soon puttering into a quiet bay of emerald-green water, with steep forested hillsides all around and a welcoming empty pontoon near its head. Incongruously there was also a set of three large white-painted concrete buildings at the end of the bay. It looked like a school complex, and as nine o'clock came around a small fleet of cars arrived: it must be the teachers. Oddly, there did not seem to be any pupils; maybe it was a local school holiday, but the teachers still had to come in. But an hour or so later a young man ambled down, leading by the hand a six-year-old boy. We invited them aboard for tea.

"I am Hideki, elementary school teacher; this is Kenji; Kenji please say hello."

We were right: the buildings were Kabashima's elementary and junior high schools, with a shared gymnasium. But there was only one pupil in each school, in facilities that could have handled four hundred between them. The schools still had ten teaching staff and three support staff, including a dinner lady, assigned to them. As we talked, Kenji was looking at us intently; it was evident he had Down Syndrome or some similar condition.

"Yes," said Hideki. "He is a nice little boy, but he has some problems. His mother lives at Fukue, with a new man; she is, how do you say? Simple and cannot look after Kenji. So, he lives here on Kabashima with his grandmother."

Hideki pointed to the very top of the mountain where you could just make out the curling and gold-painted eaves of a small wooden temple. 77-year-old grandma was a soothsayer—we had to look up the word in the dictionary, when Hideki had trouble explaining it—who made a small living by telling the fortunes of the occasional pilgrim who climbed to the top of the mountain. The old fortune teller and the lonely boy, living in a temple on a hill on a small island: I thought there might be an enigmatic Japanese novel or art-movie there.

Later we were invited to visit both schools. We helped Hideki and Kenji make some colored paper masks in Kenji's large home room. There was a solitary child-size desk in the middle of the room, a carefully charted weekly timetable in Hideki's writing on the blackboard, crayon pictures by Kenji on every wall. When it was time for break, Kenji tugged us by the hand and showed us around the rest of the school: a well-appointed music room, a science lab, six or seven shuttered empty classrooms, the teachers' room.

"Of course, it is very expensive," Hideki admitted. "But the law says every child has the right to go to school, so we keep the school open. Kenji will be here for four, maybe five more years, then he will go the Junior High… It is lonely for him, but he has special needs, so I think it is also good: we can give Kenji much attention."

Over at the Junior High, 12-year-old Hiroki shyly tried out his English on us and gave us a similar tour of his school. A bell rang. Apologizing, he hurried off to change; it was time for Phys Ed. Hiroki was an accomplished athlete and for an hour we sat on the sidelines as the track-suited teacher put him through his paces around the school's oval 400-meter track. Of course, there was no one to compete against on Kabashima but in the track season, his coach told us, he and Hiroki would go over to Fukue, even Nagasaki, to compete in inter-school meets. When Hiroki was old enough, he would go on to Fukue for High School, taking the ferry every day.

"And then this school will close…but not for so long," said the PE teacher. "Because then we must re-open for Kenji. On Kabashima," he added, "there are two villages, with maybe 150 or 200 people in each. But Kenji and Hiroki are the only people under twenty."

Working north up a rugged coastline of white limestone crags we came to Narao and its twin harbors: one deeply indented in a natural narrow creek, the other a perfect hollow square of concrete walls. We tied up in the newer basin. Over our stern we could look out on a kilometer-long wharf lined with three-story fish-processing buildings; piled up neatly were huge piles of black and deep-red nets. At the small ferry terminal were large but fading color photographs of what Narao was like in its heyday, twenty years earlier: huge modern tuna boats were tied up ten deep on the now-deserted wall, the quay was crammed with trucks loading fish, everywhere there were men and women working on their nets while tourists looked on and took pictures.

"Is it the wrong season?" we asked the sole occupant of the ferry terminal, a ticket seller in uniform, who sat behind a glass screen.

"No," she said, shrugging apologetically. "Fish all gone; fishermen all gone; no more boats."

Narao had once been a holiday town as well. High up on the hill dividing the two harbors was a seventies-vintage brick-built hotel, with an oversized lobby in which three or four overstuffed couches, spotted with cigarette burns, looked lost. We were in the holiday season, but the place was sepulchrally quiet:

"It is Fukushima maybe," said the man who sold us our 200-yen tickets to the Onsen. "This year nobody want to come on holiday."

At the north end of the archipelago, on the island of Uku Shima, the local fishermen's union had taken what must to them have seemed a desperate step to stem their small community's decay. They had converted one arm of their harbor into a snug and well-appointed yacht marina, with low floating pontoons behind intimidatingly high outer walls. There were maybe 40 slips. We were the only boat here.

We knew the routine now. We went to the ferry terminal in the main harbor to find out the lay of the land. A man enthusiastically thrust a wad of brochures on us, gave us two cream buns for nothing, and walked us down to the port's only supermarket. It seemed like they didn't get too many Gaijin here. As we picked at items in the three narrow aisles, a young woman eyed us speculatively, then shook off her inhibitions and walked over to greet us in prepared but excellent English:

"Hello! I am Katsuko Kawamata! Welcome to Uku Shima. I want to help you!"

Katsuko was mystified about why we had come to Uku Shima; she asked us several times, but she gave us helpful advice about how to get around and walked with us back to the ferry terminal. Here we jointly worked out how to take a ferry to the neighboring island of Ojika. When we eventually made it to Ojika we spent a morning exploring a huge and overgrown fort deep among the hills and then found a noodle restaurant in the tiny harbor:

"Hallo Nick San! Jenny San!" called out a friendly woman at the next table, as we sat down.

Goto's a small place. Katsuko must have phoned all her friends in the archipelago with the exciting news of the newcomers. Tiny Myori and her incongruously tall teenage daughter in turn adopted us for the day. Myori's husband (now separated) had been an American sailor at the vast US navy base at Sasebo, close to Nagasaki, and daughter Liza spoke English with a perceptible American accent. Myori ran a little English-speaking kindergarten called Miyori International Club, out of her own home, but times were hard. Although older Japanese children all routinely attended after-school crammers to get themselves through highly competitive school exams, immersion English at this age was now considered a luxury.

"And of course," (this was by now no surprise to us), "there are very few young children anyway."

Katsuko sent us next to yet another nearby island: Nozaki. Our company on the small passengers-only ferry was unusual: five or six young and very switched-on Tokyo-ites in aviator sunglasses, heels and spiky hairdos, who had come to do a fashion shoot on the famously white beach of this island. We arrived at the tiny two-boat harbor. As they minced off with some difficulty down a goat track, we made our way through the eerily empty village of Nozaki, across some overgrown terraces, to another remarkable red-brick church in the same Italian style as Fukue's.

This island, 6 km by 2 km, with three villages, was once home to 600 people. Now there are none, save a caretaker in summer at the old school, which functions sometimes as a hostel. And there are day trippers such as us. Deer have multiplied, and being quite tame and unafraid, wander through abandoned farmhouses, around the harbor and on the terraces below the church.

Seeing us coming, the caretaker scrambled up to the church ahead of us, opened its wide double doors and flung open its shutters. We wandered in. Sharp beams of brightly colored sunlight shot inwards through the restored stained-glass windows, illuminating a simple vaulted interior, painted white with gilt trim. The unpainted pine pews looked old, well worn. The church was built in 1908 with funds raised by the seventeen Christian families that then lived on Nozaki; the last service was held here in 1985. What would have been unremarkable in Tuscany was here quite astounding: unexpected, un-Japanese.

The Christian church on Nozaki Island

We made a forced march for two hours, along the spine of the hilly island: there was only one ferry back and we had been warned it would not wait for us. High on a crag, with a spectacular view back to Uku Shima, we found the old Jinja (shrine). Flanking the moss-covered paving stones before it were the two customary Koma Inu (guardian dogs), one with its mouth closed, the other open. Both were off-kilter and as moss-covered as the flagstones. They were slightly menacing in this silent place. By tradition, the open-mouthed dog (on the right) is supposed to be saying "A!" the closed-mouth dog "Um!" These are respectively the first and the last letters in the Sanskrit alphabet and have the same symbolism as Alpha and Omega in western culture: the beginning and the end; life and death. Together they spell "Aum," a syllable sacred not only in Shinto but Buddhism, Hinduism, and Jainism.

Far down below on the shoreline, barely visible through trees, was a stone Tori, a traditional Shinto gate, built to show the gods the way up to the shrine.

I gingerly pulled aside the wooden sliding door on the small front-building (or oratory) of the shrine. Inside was a wooden chest with a slotted lid (the offertory box) while behind it, recent pilgrims had left bottles of Sake, a pair of oranges, and a tin of peaches. Half-concealed behind white cotton curtains, another wooden stairway led from the back of the oratory and up to the main shrine. The floors had been swept; a twig broom stood neatly against the wall. Everything smelled of pine, with a faint whiff of old incense.

The only sounds were the gentle creaking in the wind of the high, ancient pines outside the shrine and the tinkling of a nearby stream. The last man to leave Nozaki Island had been the shrine priest, in 2001, years after the Christian priest. It was an atmospheric, haunting place, strangely and oppressively quiet; you felt there was someone watching from the forest.

The currents are strong in the East China Sea, so we had to carefully time our passage back over to the big island of Kyushu. In pre-dawn darkness, we felt our way carefully out of the high-walled marina, its red and green entrance lights winking, and into the open water. There was a flood tide heading northeast and, aided by a light wind that had trouble in dispersing the morning mist, we were able to sail most of the twenty-five miles across. At noon, with the current picking up now, we made for the wide, funnel-like approach to Hirado, between Hirado Shima (island) on our left and Kyushu on our right.

At the head of the channel was a Golden Gate-look-alike red suspension bridge, one of the hundreds of massive infrastructure projects in which Japan invested in the eighties. From the amount of traffic on it (none) you had to wonder whether they would have been better off carrying on with the little ferry it replaced. Just past the bridge—we were being swept along at such a speed that we nearly missed the turn—was a snug, green-watered nook on the left, down whose steep hillsides the centuries-old town of Hirado tumbled. We made for the abandoned ferry pontoon.

Chapter Seven:
The Bosun and the Pilot's Brother
(Hirado to Fukuoka)

The Matsuura clan ruled Hirado for eight hundred years. The magnificent pagoda-like white castle that overlooks the harbor dates originally from 1599. But only fourteen years after he had completed it, Matsuura Shigenobu deliberately burned down his own stronghold in one of those very Japanese episodes of obeisance and honor. There had been a change of Shogun[23] in distant Edo (modern Tokyo)[24] and the Daimyo (feudal lord) of Hirado wished to show his humility in visible form. Like all castles of the day, it was built largely of wood and was destroyed many more times. We would ask Japanese friends:

"Why didn't they build in stone? Wouldn't that have been much better in war time?"

There would be a pause. Then a serious:

"Ah yes, perhaps. That is why all are now concrete..."

And indeed they are: a fit of post-war nationalism in the sixties coincided with the new love affair with concrete so that dozens of decrepit or derelict castles like Hirado's were torn down and replaced with concrete replicas. From a distance they look good, and with elevators and specially designed visitor galleries they are convenient to visit. But they lack atmosphere. Japanese visitors appear not to mind in the least: another triumph of pragmatism over sentiment.

Down in the town is the old Matsuura house, still built in pungent wood. In a long glass case along a wall is a rolled-out parchment five meters long that

---

23 The Shogun: hereditary, military rulers of all Japan, who co-existed with the Mikado (the Emperor) but held the real power in the land, until the end of feudalism in 1867. The term can indicate singular or plural.

24 Edo was re-named in 1868, following the end of the last Shogunate.

shows the route the Daimyos would take from this remote corner of Japan to Edo, to pay tribute to the Shogun.

We studied the map carefully, for we'd be following much of the same route. The lord and his retinue would hug the northern shore of Kyushu in their unseaworthy vessels, before threading the Kanmon Kaikyo strait between Kyushu and Honshu and entering the secure and calm waters of the Inland Sea. Then they'd hop from island to island, riding the tides more than the wind, as far as Osaka at the sea's east end. There they would climb into their palanquins and the long journey to Edo would continue overland. It was an expedition that could take months each way but that was half the idea; the Edo-era Shogun debilitated their subject lords quite deliberately by requiring frequent tribute in person, and the splitting of the Daimyos' families. The parchment shows dense forests, towering snow-capped peaks, raging torrents to be forded and mythical beasts lurking in the bamboo as the chain of stickmen laboriously wends its way to fabulous Edo, where the Shogun waits in serene splendor.

There are other strains of Japanese history here too. On a secluded patch of lawn on the hillside opposite the castle is the gravesite of William Adams (1564-1620). Known in Japanese as Anjin San, he was perhaps the first Englishman to reach Japan. But he had already crammed in several lifetimes of adventures before he reached these shores in 1600: service under Francis Drake in the defeat of the Spanish Armada, an expedition across the top of northern Russia in search of the Northeast Passage, and an epic voyage from England via the Straits of Magellan to Ecuador, Hawaii, and Usuki (on the eastern shores of Kyushu), where he was nearly crucified by a mob led by Portuguese Jesuits.

Starting in 1604, Anjin San helped the then-Shogun to build the first western style sailing ships near Edo, became an intimate of the Shogun, and earned the sobriquet of the First Western Samurai. In 1613, he moved to Hirado and helped establish a trading post for the (British) East India Company, in tandem with the already existing Dutch East India Company station. He died in Hirado after many more adventures. Anjin San is also commemorated in his hometown of Gillingham (Kent) but is probably best-known as the inspiration for the character of John Blackthorne in James Clavell's *Shogun*,[25] and to a lesser extent, for his portrayal as a sexually frustrated Elizabethan in Japan in the near-pornographic *Lord of the Golden Fan*.[26]

Back at the ferry pontoon, another yacht was in: *Skal*. The name sounded (and was) Scandinavian but the crew were not. In the way that these things seem to happen in Japan (fueled by a little alcohol), by eleven that night its crew were lifelong friends. Ishii, trim, with short silver hair, a perpetual nervous smile, in his sixties, had responded to our first invitation by coming round with an armful of charts and two carrier bags that turned out to contain bottles of

---

25   Clavell, James. (2020). Ashland, Oregon: Blackstone Publishing.
26   Nicole, Christopher. (1987). *Lord of the Golden Fan*. New York, NY: Bantam Books.

vintage whisky and Sake, vacuum-packed squid, a tin of sausages, assorted pickles, a jar of marmalade, and bundles of tourist literature.

"Ishii," he said clearly, pointing directly at his chest, adding with a beam: "Captain of *Skal*. And Akihara San. Artist. My fren..."

Within minutes the cabin was festooned with charts that would be half-unrolled as Ishii frenetically stabbed at one of his favorite anchorages after another, then would roll themselves back up, so that soon we had no idea what part of Japan we were looking at. After half an hour and at least one bottle of Sake we reached a chart that seemed to be from somewhere near Osaka. Ishii gestured excitedly at a set of Japanese characters on an east-west coastline, and said:

"Suma! Very good marina! Home of *Skal*!"

Within a minute he had speed-dialed his friend Miyazaki San, the marina manager, who must have been startled to receive this business call at home at eleven o'clock on a Saturday night. But he apparently agreed on the spot to give us one free week's moorage on arrival (no mean sum financially).

"One week ..." Ishii shrugged philosophically. "But in Japan all can be discussed... Later I talk to Miyazaki again."

Next evening we were over on *Skal*. Like all the Japanese sailors we met, Ishii never cooked on board unless there was absolutely no alternative; and then it would be instant ramen at most. As Ishii said, with no sense of irony:

"Japanese man, don't cook. Except sushi chef."

Frugality would be the order of the day in many

At the old ferry dock, Hirado

regards. Cruisers were alarmingly prepared deliberately to arrive at marinas after hours and then leave at dawn so as to avoid paying, or to falsify their boat-registration decals with a felt-tip pen so as to gain a year or two's free sailing. But in port the first quest was always to find the best (which was usually the most expensive) eatery.

The Japanese cruiser's boat, it seemed, was partly for drinking aboard and entertaining your old (male) friends and was a sanctum into which wives or lady friends would very rarely be invited. Just as well. Hanging on Ishii's bulkhead was a calendar entitled Hawaii's Best, consisting of buxom dusky-skinned Vahines named Leilani or Sandra whose only items of clothing were flower leis.

Much later in our friendship I would ask how it was that the Japanese stereotype of a sexy woman was one with large breasts; even the big-eyed schoolgirl heroines of pornographic mangas had size 40Fs that burst excitingly out of their sailor smocks. And yet the classic Japanese beauty is demure, flat-chested, whatever natural attributes she may have almost smothered beneath tight underwear... But I digress; we weren't quite there yet.

"Palo San," said Ishii, gesturing to another silver-haired man who had joined us for the evening. "Okayama University," he added after some brow-wrinkling thought and whispered consultation with Palo and Akihara. "University Sailing Club. Old friends..."

I don't remember too much about the evening. In our logbook there is taped a color photograph (Ishii had a printer on board) of myself with a tea-towel wrapped around my head performing a traditional Japanese eel-fishermen's song that involved intricate gestures imitating the way in which eels are drawn from the water into the net. At another point in the evening, as heavy rain began to splash onto the coach roof, Palo San pulled from nowhere a roll of rice paper and a beautiful small box in which he laboriously prepared black ink from powder. From another pocket came a brush. As we unsteadily held the paper in place on the cabin table, he turned thoughtful for a few moments and theatrically tested a few words before his now-expectant audience. In surprisingly steady strokes of the brush, biting his lower lip in concentration, he penned three vertical columns of calligraphy, whispering as he went. It was a poem to our presence, here in the rain in Hirado.

"Pitter patter," Palo tentatively explained, pointing to the first characters. "Pitter patter..."

After that, the explanation became more complicated. Every character seemed to be a pun, a double meaning, and our three friends could not agree on how to explain it to us in their fractured English. Eventually we rolled the parchment up. I hope that when we one day find someone who reads Japanese, it will be truly poetic (but probably it won't; with the amount of alcohol he consumed that evening, Palo cannot have been at his best).

Jenny sat through this quite stoically and smilingly. Every time I was offered another shot of Sake or whisky, she was politely proffered a soft drink or juice. And she was not actively included in the conversation. We'd been in Japan long enough to not be offended by this. Much later Ishii would take me on one side and ask, as Mi-Chan had:

"How did you persuade Jenny San to sail?"

It wasn't that easy to explain. We'd met, as people do in the west, because of shared interests, so that doing things together as a married couple was just a natural extension of that; and including others in our activities, regardless of their gender or status, was also natural. But for Ishii's generation in Japan marriages had often been arranged ones. As men progressed through their famously long-houred and arduous working lives, their friendships were those they had made at university, likely through same-sex clubs, or at work. These often spilled over from working hours into late-night drinking sessions, from which wives and girlfriends were excluded.

By the time we got up next morning, a little the worse for wear, *Skal* and her crew had long gone. They had their schedule to keep, and the heavy rain meant that they were now a day behind their carefully planned timings. We did some more historical homework and took a bus around the coastline to Kawachi.

Boarding a public bus as a foreigner in Japan is not as intimidating as you might imagine. The white-gloved drivers, while rarely having any command of English, are unfailingly polite and will respond clearly to place names uttered in a questioning tone. You take a ticket from a machine when boarding, which has the number of the stop where you got on. An illuminated board at the front of the bus shows your fare climbing as each successive stop is reached. If you don't have exact change, there are change machines. It cannot be economical, but pretty much anywhere not reachable by train has a bus line. As each stop approaches, a pre-recorded, perky (or were we just imagining it?) woman's voice announces the name of the place, twice just in case. After only a few days in Japan, if nothing else you know the Japanese for:

"Next stop Bungo; the next stop will be Bungo."

Jenny was carefully reading, in preparation for this particular expedition, a very tatty copy of James Michener's *Rascals in Paradise*,[27] acquired in a book swap at some forgotten stop in the Pacific and partly consumed by bookworms.

"In 1622," she recited to me, "a young Chinese merchant named Nicholas Iquan settled near Hirado."

---

27 Michener, James & Day, A. Grove. (1987). *Rascals in Paradise*. New York, NY: Fawcett Books.

Coxinga's birth rock

He met a girl named Tagawa: hooker or high-class scion, it depends on your political agenda. In 1624, so legend has it, she was taken by sudden labor pains and gave birth behind a large prominent rock on the beach at Kawachi.

Her Chinese/Japanese half-caste son would become known as Coxinga. He was the most successful, the richest, and the cruelest pirate in history. In one legendary episode he assembled a fleet of 3,000 junks, with an accompanying army of 200,000 men, with the aim of taking on the entire Manchu empire. But in true pirate style, he celebrated his thirty-fifth birthday, on the eve of battle, with a stupendous drunken binge that allowed the Manchus to counterattack and rout him. In 1661, he declared war against another enemy: the Dutch occupiers of the island of Formosa (now known as Taiwan), then the richest island in the Pacific. There was a long siege in which Coxinga was triumphant. He installed himself as King and ruled in splendid fashion before overreaching himself and attempting to expel Spain from the Philippines. He died a horrifying death of rabies (or possibly malaria) in Formosa at the age of 37, in 1662, known by now in the west as the Attila of the Orient.

The birth rock is still there, its base thirty centimeters under the water at high tide. Kawachi is a quaint, compact fishing village. The ubiquitous 22-foot white Yamaha fishing launches were tied up neatly with their sterns to an ancient harbor wall; fishing nets were laid out to dry on parapets; and the waterfront was a combination of small engine repair shops, fishmongers, and mini-markets. As always it was a quieter place than we had imagined when planning our little trips. It was perpetually Sunday afternoon in rural Japan.

A bilingual plaque at one end of the village indicated to us that Kawachi had seen more riotous times. The English-language text informed us that this had once been the "gay" quarter. This was presumably a misleading translation for what in English would be known as the red-light district. A literal translation of the Japanese term, we later learned, was poetic if enigmatic: The District Where the Water Trade is Plied.

Up on the hill behind it was a gaudy red and green temple-like building with a bus drawn up beside it, and the bus's contents—forty or so tourists of Asian descent—wandering around with brochures in their hands. It was Coxinga's mausoleum. We gleaned from a uniformed tour guide with halting English that back home in Taiwan, whence came this group of tourists, the pirate was a demi-god with political overtones. He was the Chinese/Japanese warrior who had taken on the invincible Manchus, freed Taiwan from European oppression and established it as a great kingdom in its day. As such some see him as a prior incarnation of Chiang Kai Shek. He is also revered in the Shinto pantheon, presumably as a seagoing enemy of mainland China.

My Japanese (or Chinese?) was not up to asking whether Coxinga was really buried here; given the nature and place of his death it seemed unlikely. And no doubt it was beside the point if he was a God.

All of our Japanese sailing friends who had been this way had been following their schedules. On such itineraries, days of less than thirty miles were unthinkable, as were diversions to places that might be slightly off the direct navigation routes. Our own plans called for shorter distances, allowed for side-tracking and favored places that, strictly from the chart, looked to be safe. So we found ourselves sometimes in locations that had probably never seen a yacht before.

Azuchi-o-Shima, only seven miles north of Hirado, was one of these. A small but high island off the northwest corner of Kyushu, it had a very snug L-shaped inlet on the southern shore, lined with smooth concrete walls with no overhangs: a cruisers' dream. At this particular time of the month the tidal range was not large, and Jenny was able easily to climb ashore and secure us to a pair of rusty old bollards.

We wandered into the village, the quietest and in some ways the quaintest we had yet seen. There were narrow streets lined by wood-framed houses with overhanging balconies and eaves so big that they almost roofed the alley in; carefully channeled streams that ran the length of the streets; old English-style post-boxes painted orange; and blue and red barbers' poles. We went into the first poky little store we came to. The shopkeeper, in the aisle, stood stock-still staring at us for a full twenty seconds before rallying herself to respond politely to our Konichiwa (Hello). Some children returning home hand-in-hand from school stopped dead and, open-mouthed, stared at us as we walked past; we were used to this by now. In the post office we were clearly the event of the day, if not the week. The girl at the sole small counter anxiously gestured to us to

Exploring the village, Azuchi-o-Shima

wait, then came back with two Japan post office fans and customized packets of Kleenex which she presented to us with a small bow.

Way above the town, reached after a hot fifty-minute climb up a path that cut off the road's hairpins, was a large sixties-vintage hotel. Was the Sento open, we enquired of the myopic old man on the desk?

"Hai," was the surprised and hesitant answer. But he gesticulated for us to wait and disappeared.

It was clear the place was deserted of guests. Some anxious whispering could be heard from a corridor in the back. Ten minutes later the man reappeared and, after he indicated to us to take off our shoes, we followed him though darkened corridors. We arrived at the usual double-set of curtains, and he gestured us both into the ladies' half. Sensibly given the lack of guests, only one bath had been heated up.

"Please take off clothes," he said. And waited expectantly.

We looked at each other and hesitated. At last, he seemed to get the message. With a little shrug, as if to say, "crazy Gaijin," he turned and left us to it.

Azuchi-o-Shima was as far north as we'd be going for quite a long time. Now, for the first time in many months the course was due east and the distance to Alaska—which we used to amuse ourselves by checking once in a while on the GPS—began for the first time to diminish rather than grow. We had two very unsatisfactory nights in the vicinity of the squid-fishing port of Yobuko. Unsatisfactory not because the place was uninteresting. In fact, it was an unaccustomed hive of activity even on the shore, where motorized squid-driers whizzed around like miniature carousels, the pale, flattened squids flying out at a 45-degree angle. But throughout the night squid boats came and went, revving at full speed through the harbor entrance where we were tied up, causing us to rock dangerously against the wall. And at low tide—which occurred in the middle of the night in pouring rain—the wall itself threatened to suck us under its overhang, which we had failed to notice in daylight.

"I really don't care how quaint it is here," Jenny muttered irritably as she took her turn fending us off in the dark from the wall, with a boat hook. "As soon as it gets light, let's just get out."

For a year now we'd had that paper napkin tucked into the back of the logbook, with a rudimentary sketch-map of an oval island with an artificial harbor built into its southern shore. The only western characters read: "Nozaki San; Takashima" and "Bosun." We fished the paper out now and scrutinized Chinami's map, comparing it with our nautical chart.

The chart showed a round island, Takashima - maybe a mile in diameter - in a bay a few miles off the city of Karatsu, with a pair of artificial harbors occupying the shoreline facing Kyushu. We weren't greatly tempted to go to Karatsu itself. The normally charitable *Lonely Planet* guide describes it thus:

"…the beach is grotty, the castle a reconstruction and the town is at the end of the line…"

Cautiously, with the depth sounder showing only 1.20 meters (the exact depth of our keel) we edged into the little walled harbor Chinami had indicated, backed by a village of twenty or thirty houses with grey tile roofs. We tied up first at a small pontoon, but an old man edged up to us and explained in sign language that it would be needed for the passenger ferry that plied between here and Karatsu. When we handed him Chinami's note, his face lit up and he hobbled away, gesturing for us to wait. A few minutes later, Nozaki himself—the Bosun, short, stocky with a buzz cut and beaming smile—was rushing towards us from his waterfront home. He pumped our hands enthusiastically, bowed repeatedly, muttered a few words of broken English, then pointed over to where his yacht lay, next to a fishing boat:

"See fishing boat? My fren! You tie up…," and he demonstrated with his hands that we should go alongside.

Half an hour later we were taking turns to use the ingenious mini-hot tub that Nozaki had installed in a wooden shed behind his home: a kind of large tin can with a hinged lid and a seat inside, in which you sat up to your neck in scalding water. Boiled, red but clean, we then sat while Nozaki's grey-haired mother fussed over us, bringing us cups of tea. Nozaki proudly showed us some of the mementoes of his Navy career, that cluttered the tiny front room:

his red Bosun's stripes, black and white pictures of ships he'd served on, a ship's wheel and bell, old ships' oil lanterns. We leafed through a photo album as our host leaned over our shoulders and explained every faded picture:

"My fren' the chef...an' here we arrive in Hawaii. Flowers, girls! Now big expedition to Japanese base in Antarctica, one year! Very very cold!" and he shivered theatrically.

Jenny with Nozaki's mother

Nozaki was not an educated man but, having served in close proximity to the US Navy for years—out of Sasebo, near Nagasaki—he was fluent in certain technical terminology. It was odd to hear him talking about Aegis-class Destroyers, Sonar, and AWACS while struggling to explain other simpler matters.

When Jenny and his mother stepped out briefly to the kitchen, he beckoned me into the corridor and, with exaggerated stealth, retrieved from under the stairs a package wrapped in newspaper. Reverently he unwrapped it. It was a curving, sharp samurai sword, but of no particular antiquity as far as I could see.

"Ssh! No tell!" he whispered.

I had no idea why I was being enjoined to silence: was possession of the sword illegal? What was its history? I was frustrated by my own lack of Japanese, again.

Nozaki's father, in his late eighties as far as we could deduce, was very sick in hospital in Karatsu, and Nozaki and his mother travelled to the city almost every day to visit him. Nozaki pointed out a color picture on the wall of a Betty bomber[28] in wartime camouflage: Nozaki senior had spent the war working at the Mitsubishi aircraft factory.

---

28 Betty bomber: twin-engine, Mitsubishi-made aircraft operated by the Japanese navy between 1940 and 1945; "Betty" was the name given to it by the Allies.

I knew that soon we'd have to talk about Chinami. Nozaki's eyes brightened as soon as I mentioned him. But I had to pass on the news: Freeloader Bob's letter in *Latitude 38* and the editor's response. Nozaki seemed initially perplexed; it was taking him some time to digest the news:

"So…Chinami San? He is gone? And boat is, how you say, sunk?"

But eventually he smiled sadly, his eyes bright, pulled over a bottle of Sake and we jointly toasted Chinami.

That night Nozaki and his mother fussed over us even more, plying us with mountainous quantities of a pancake-like specialty cooked on a hot plate (Okinomiyaki) and then dressing Jenny up in one of the old lady's beautiful, hundred-year-old silk kimonos. We all posed in turn and laughed over how Jenny's long arms protruded from the hanging sleeves. Before we went home that evening, Nozaki thrust upon us a package of eight or ten nautical charts, waving away our protestations at his generosity. He walked us down to *Bosun Bird*, sitting on glassy water under the stars. Jenny and I were silent. I don't know if it was because we were remembering Chinami, or because we were humbled by the generosity of Nozaki San and his gentle mother, who had taken these two strangers so warmly into their home. A bit of both.

Nozaki's island of Takashima, small and under-populated though it was, had two shrines and the town fathers had worked hard to build up a certain unique mystique around them, with a view to attracting tourists and cash. At one, a tradition had evolved by which you could take a lottery ticket or a bundle of cash, purchase a specially designed velvet bag, insert the items within, then go and have the ticket or the money blessed by the High Priest. This was meant to bring luck for the ticket and good fortune to the blessed money, which pilgrims would then go on to invest. This procedure was helpfully explained with small pictures on leaflets handed to all visitors as they stepped ashore at the ferry pontoon. In return, you were expected to deposit a "very large" sum of cash with the shrine. So what was the point then? You had to pay a fortune to make a fortune?

Ah—it was explained to us—not exactly. In the shop you could buy fake bank notes of very high denominations and leave packages of those with the shrine instead. The God would not know the difference. Sure enough, there in the kiosk outside the shrine, as well as those velvet bags and the ubiquitous lucky cats, you could buy a couple of million counterfeit but, to us, quite convincing yen for the equivalent of a dollar.

"So if I've got this right…," Jenny said. "On the one hand you attribute to the Gods the power to make your cash or your lottery ticket lucky; on the other you make the calculation that they can be fooled with indifferently forged banknotes…"

The creative owner of this particular shrine shop hadn't stopped there. When Jenny stooped to stroke one of the several cats that were roaming around the aisles, the lady beckoned us over to a TV set, put in a videocassette, gestured to us to watch, and turned it on. It was one of those jokey news items that you find at the end of the daily bulletin. Here was our shrine, here was our shop, the leering TV host in a bow tie and oversized spectacles…and here were the cats, filmed walking around on their hind legs and occasionally putting their forepaws up in what could pass as a praying motion. The manic commentator in his spotted tie peered into the camera and cackled in exaggerated, possibly ironic, amazement.

"See! Holy cats!" beamed our lady.

It was evident the cats were good for business. As we edged out politely, a boatload of tourists was heading determinedly our way, all clutching brochures featuring the famous felines. Our friend was disappointed we weren't buying but as we left pressed on us a pair of small towels for the local Sento, with appropriate cat paw-prints.

海

We departed Takashima at 6:00 a.m. on a still morning, with thin mist hanging over the water, the stars fading. We were touched when Nozaki and his mother—notwithstanding our insistence to the contrary and the early hour—came down to help us with our lines and wave goodbye. Not for the first time in our short stay in Japan we felt uncomfortable; these people had taken us right into their lives for a couple of days, expected nothing in return, and we would never see them again. All we'd brought Nozaki was the bad news about Chinami.

The mist lifted and we had a bright and sunny sail eastwards along the north shore of Kysushu, with green hills to starboard, the Sea of Japan to our port, Korea well away over the horizon.

Thirty or forty miles off the port beam was the stretch of ocean off Tsushima Island where in 1905 Japan's naval fleet, commanded by the legendary Admiral Togo, ambushed Russia's and annihilated it. At a stroke, and only three or four decades after its first substantive contact with the great western powers in two hundred years, Japan was in the Big Leagues. Now she was a major military nation, one that could dream of empires, just like England, France, and Prussia. As such Tsushima was one of the most significant battles in modern history; naval buffs will also point out that it was the only decisive battle ever fought by battleships against battleships.

A little nervously we passed through a narrow tidal passage that the Pilot described as "needing local knowledge" and entered Fukuoka Wan. At the head of the bay were the twin cities of Fukuoka and the older Hakata, with a combined population of 1.5 million. Dodging freighters and car carriers we edged our way towards Odo Marina, a large yacht harbor carved, like so many of Japan's marine installations, out of reclaimed land.

"I wonder what that is," said Jenny scanning the shoreline through binoculars as we approached. "See that Ferris wheel, just to the right of it. Looks like a huge white Gothic cathedral; there must be a lot more Christians in Japan than we thought."

We settled quickly into Fukuoka. Helping us along were Jan and Lena aboard the Dutch yacht *Hoorn*. They'd been based here for years, maintaining a useful website for any and all cruisers planning to come to Japan. Jan worked occasionally on a local fishing boat, and they had virtually been adopted by the friendly fishermen in whose harbor they kept *Hoorn*. They both spoke Japanese and repaid the hospitality of their friends by delivering extra English classes for their elementary-school-age children, in the fishermen's union building. Jan would often drop round on his bike to say hello, have a cup of coffee, invite us to the morning fish market. You could tell that he genuinely enjoyed helping the few foreign yachts that came this way.

One way or another *Hoorn* and her crew had been away from Holland for thirty years. We discovered we had mutual friends whom we had known when we were both cruising the South Pacific in the late eighties. Jan visibly missed the easy camaraderie and the constantly changing island scenes of those days. Japan was way off the usual cruising routes. With Lena it was different. She had found her own life here in Japan and had little ambition to go back to sea, let alone to re-settle in Europe. She was openly indifferent to the lengths Jan went to help us out and she passed up all our invitations to visit *Bosun Bird*. Although Jan repeatedly insisted we come and visit them on *Hoorn*, we never felt that welcome or comfortable there.

Jenny and I had often talked about simply going to sea for good, becoming perpetual sea gypsies. We had no children, we had sufficient funds if we were careful. It's what *Hoorn* had done. But Lena had tired of the constant vagabondage, of meeting people knowing you might see them for a few weeks, only to never see or hear from them again. She wanted roots, Jan didn't (yet). One problem was they had nothing to go back to in Holland. It had been many years since they had lived there; they had no house; so, they'd ended up here. Oddly, although they knew the coastline of Kyushu that we had sailed along and had now been here for years, they had never taken *Hoorn* into the Inland Sea or anywhere else in Japan.

We talked a lot about Japan and the Japanese. I was feeling that with next to no knowledge of the language we were barely touching the surface of the country. Jan and Lena both appreciated our evident and ongoing interest:

"So many visiting yachts don't really show an interest. The Japanese are very proud of who they are: flatter them and they'll repay you."

We mentioned how embarrassing Japanese hospitality sometimes was; there was no way we could reciprocate it.

"Yes," mused Jan. "You can't really… But you know what? The longer you stay, the more the expectation of repayment does arise. First you have to understand that if you go away anywhere, even for a weekend, maybe sightseeing or to some temple, the routine is that you must bring back presents for pretty much everyone. And more than once we've had a friend unexpectedly show up with all his family and half of his friends from work and expect to be taken out to sea for a sail. It's often inconvenient, and they don't understand that you may have to pay attention to tides or the weather. But that's how society here is held together: mutual obligations."

Back at Odo marina, we were soon firm friends with Nori, who owned the boat moored next to us, named *Lei*. He was shy about his English but in the typical way of Japanese yachtsmen he broke the ice with a simple question:

"You like Japanese beer?"

Nori, a semi-retired architect, was in his seventies. He would come down to *Lei* most days on a little Honda electric bike, take off his helmet and greet us politely. He didn't sail that much these days: many of his friends were now too old or too sick to go out. One day he arrived clutching, along with the usual two or three cold cans of Asahi, some rice paper and bamboo shoots.

"Today is Tanabata Festival," he explained.

And he set up everything in the cockpit. Tanabata is the Festival of the Star Weaver. Orihime, the Princess Weaver of the Stars—so Nori explained after a few false starts, consulting the notes he had made—fell in love with Hikoboshi, a humble shepherd. In punishment she was sent to live on the other side of the galaxy. But one night every year their stars come close enough almost to touch: that would be tonight. Nori paused after his explanation.

"Now I come from the hospital," he said. "My good friend, my crew, is very sick. I cannot take him beer, nurse says no. But we make traditional Tanabata wish anyway."

We waited expectantly.

"My friend's wish: blue skies and more cold beer!"

Holding the rice paper carefully, Nori asked us separately to whisper our wishes to him and he transcribed them in Japanese characters. We copied them carefully onto paper sheets to keep as souvenirs, while we placed the original with the bamboo shoots to blow in the wind in *Bosun Bird's* rigging. Nori cracked up when he saw my copy:

"This not Japanese character…no, no, certainly not! You have copied…how you say…crossing out!"

When Nori asked us where we'd like to go on a day out, I recalled our visit a few weeks earlier to the kamikaze base at Chiran, near Kagoshima. *Lonely Planet* told us that there was a similar "peace museum" at Tachiarai, an hour's drive from Fukuoka. So, we asked if we could try to find it.

The museum was a modern one, evidently just revamped, located in a non-descript sprawl of suburbs on a flat plain with green hills in the distance. Here had been an Imperial Japanese Army Air Force Base and later, after 1940, the Tachiarai Army Flight School. Runways had crisscrossed the plain in those days and as the Allies inched their way up the island chains towards the home islands, the base had become increasingly busy.

That ended on March 27, 1945, when Tachiarai was the target of one of the largest B-29 raids to have taken place thus far. Suspended from the hangar-like ceiling of the museum was a life-size skeleton of a B-29, dwarfing the carefully restored Zero fighter that sat grounded below it. In a side room was a simple memorial of photographs and names, to the two Flying Fortress crews that had gone down over Tachiarai that day. In its way this was as moving as the sepia photos of the kamikaze pilots I had scrutinized at Chiran. I wondered if any war museums in Europe had similar memorials to their attackers.

Nori wandered around thoughtfully, ever further behind us. Uneasily I wondered if we had been tactless to ask him to bring us here. But he had seemed prepared to talk about the war. On the way back he opened up.

"One of my first memories is the B-29s," he began. "We used to hear them. We'd come out and look up. There they were."

He was four years old at the time. Almost every day they flew over Nori's hometown of Kumamoto, in the center of Kyushu, often bound for the steelworks and associated industry at Kitakyushu, or Nagasaki and the nearby naval base at Sasebo.

"And I think I can remember my brother."

He paused, gathering his thoughts.

"In 1944, he was sixteen. He ran away to join the Navy Air Force. It's what all the young men wanted to do in those days. My parents wouldn't talk about it for years; it was like he never lived. Much later my other brother made many investigations. He found out what had happened."

We listened quietly. The boy was exactly sixteen years and eleven months old when he set off on his final mission, in April 1945.

"They were five of them. All his age, all friends. They were given enough fuel, poor quality alcohol or ethanol, to reach Okinawa. No more. You have seen the pictures. They wrote their last letters, drank their Sake, like the Samurai tradition. Pretty girls waved them off."

Nori tailed off, his face working expressively. It was a minute or two before he was able to continue.

"Only three of them made it to the target. The others must have crashed on the way. It was quite common. They had hardly any training; the fuel was no good. My brother, the other one, he went through all the records, even the logs of the American ships. They record the attacks that day. They were all shot down."

Nori was proud of his brother's bravery, but intensely bitter about the generals and the politicians who had led Japan to such a pass, to a point at which they were recruiting teenagers to commit pointless suicide. It wasn't like "those samurai films you have seen," he said. Seppuku was always meant to be for the nobility, "not for ordinary people like us," certainly not for sixteen-year-olds.

海

Summer was now upon us. It was thirty degrees (Centigrade) every day and increasingly humid. There was a small beach close to the marina, with a public park behind us. It seemed odd to us that no one ever swam.

"Is it polluted?" we'd ask.

"Oh no; very clean; now no pollution in Fukuoka."

"So, the beach is dangerous in some other way, then?"

"No, no...but swimming forbidden."

"But why?"

"Swimming season start July 1st; end August 31st; only permitted to swim two months."

Another mystery solved was that of the enormous Gothic cathedral we'd seen when sailing into Fukuoka. No, there wasn't much of a Christian population here, at least not so that you'd notice. The cathedral was a very popular full-scale wedding chapel: a commercial operation, whereby you paid professional wedding-arranging companies to rent the faux-church and arrange for a Christian-style service. The term "style" was the point. The chaplain who performed these ceremonies was typically a foreigner who was in Japan to teach English, and who was prepared to put on ecclesiastical garb and learn a few lines from the classic Christian marriage service so as to make some extra cash.

Such ceremonies have no legal validity. They are often held as part of a sequence that may also include a Shinto ceremony and a visit to a drab civil registry office. While Mendelssohn's Wedding March is a popular choice, so is Celine Dion's theme song from Titanic. Bridesmaids, bouquets, and western-style wedding gowns are all on the menu of optional extras. Western Wedding Arranger, we learned, is a career path all of its own, very popular with young female university graduates with a reasonable command of English.

With summer came an ever-increasing sequence of typhoons. The chances of undergoing a direct hit were relatively small, but the statistics said we would at least be touched by one or two if we spent an entire summer in Japan as we intended. So we always plotted their progress with some concern.

Tropical Storm Meari gave us pause for thought in late June. But after closing in on Shanghai it mercifully decided to keep going north and died in the Yellow Sea. In mid-July Typhoon Ma-On was more menacing. Odo Marina's more conscientious yacht owners came down to double up on their lines, take off their roller furling sails (which risked coming loose and flogging to shreds in very heavy winds) and we received several concerned offers to stay over in people's houses. No one seemed quite to understand that the boat was our home and that if severe conditions threatened, we wanted to be on hand.

And summer is the season of festivals (Matsuri) all over Japan. Fukuoka has one of the more famous, called Yamakasa. This 750-year-old celebration sees each of the traditional, old neighborhoods of the Hakata district constructing towering floats that typically depict—in vivid colors and with extravagantly costumed figures—scenes from Japanese history. Often the historical tableaux mimic the weekly costume dramas that for years have been the showcase of NKK television. The more ambitious floats have cannons that periodically emit sparks and smoke. Many have nodding heads or waving arms. Some incorporate more modern folk or manga heroes such as Doraemon, the smiling blue mechanical cat with magic powers that is the fondest childhood memory of sentimental middle-aged Japanese men.

Each float is carried by a band of muscular young men decked out in loose cotton jackets and a jockstrap that exposes their buttocks in their entirety. The floats are heavy, and it takes much grunting, heaving, and coordinated cries of encouragement before they can be lifted and carried in a rush for a couple of hundred meters at a time. Replacement carriers dart in every few minutes to spell their friends off. The culmination of two weeks of practice and parties is a dawn race around the city center on July 15th which attracts Le Tout Fukuoka. The crowds encourage the men with cries of "Oisa, oisa, oisa!" (unique to this event) and cooling buckets of water; women don't have much of a role in things, except in organizing the après-parade festivities.

In a celebration as old and well-known as Fukuoka's there are of course plenty of tourist onlookers. But the enthusiasm and interest of the younger generation is genuine; there is no financial gain here. No one is in it for religion either, although Shinto is at the root of this and most other Japanese festivals. It's all about belonging to your community with pride, playing your part in traditions that have been going on for far longer than anyone can remember. Some of the young men had smartphones tucked into their jockstraps; many had a smoke while they rested. None of them looked the least embarrassed or self-conscious; no young American or Canadian would have been seen dead doing this, I thought with regret; far too uncool.

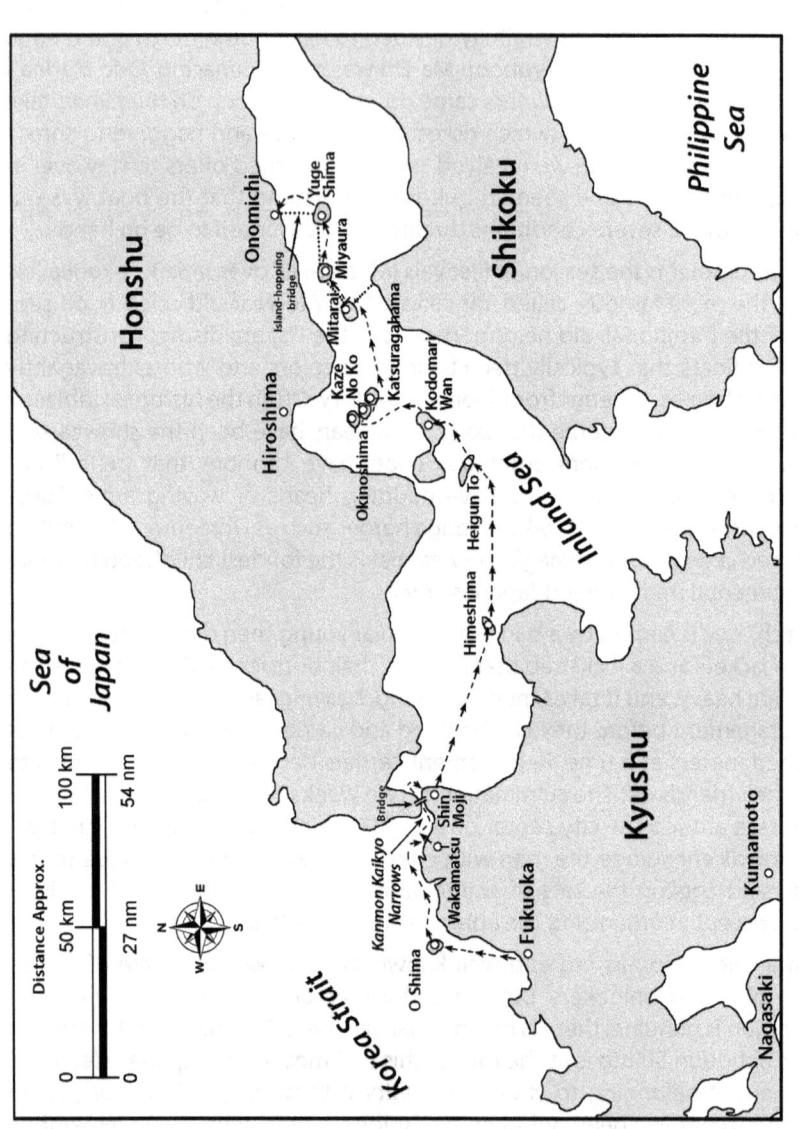

Fukuoka to Onomichi

Chapter Eight:
Through the Barrier Gate
(Into the Inland Sea and Hiroshima)

With Yamakasa over and the rhythm of approaching typhoons growing in intensity, it was time to move on from Fukuoka and gain the security of the Inland Sea: Seto Naikai (瀬戸内海). Nozaki's charts in hand and Google Earth online, we sat on a sunny afternoon in the large upstairs club room of Odo Marina, consulting with Ohara as the overhead fans whirred. Ohara, small and lithe, deeply suntanned, had a grey goatee like the Sensei in The Karate Kid. He also had a sense of humor:

"My name is Ohara," he said when we first met him. "Japanese, descended from Irish pirates."

A day or so out from Fukuoka we would have to thread a narrow tidal channel between the great islands of Kyushu and Honshu and hit it at exactly the right time. Complicating things, Ohara told us, would be the fact that the channel doubles as one of Japan's major ports, and is heavily industrialized on both shores:

"Difficult to find a place to stop and wait for the tide..." he mused, but his finger roamed carefully over the detailed chart and stopped on two or three locations where we might be able to tie up wait for a few hours if we had to.

"And many ships...you will see, the channel is narrow, and they stop for no one. Sometimes a big one, two hundred, three hundred thousand tons, needs to turn and nobody can get past."

We were up at 5:00 a.m. to start a slow sail eastward from Fukuoka in near calm seas. Mid-morning, as we ghosted along under sail at a knot or two, a large luxury yacht doing seven or eight knots under power caught up with us. The captain and his crew were clearly well into their second or third case of Asahi beer, and for a few minutes I thought they were going to ram us up the stern. Then Jenny realized:

"They just want to pass us something," and she waved back.

It was a bottle of the finest whisky. Our benefactors (complete strangers) rushed on, no doubt with a schedule that had them in Osaka late next night.

Such is Japan's ongoing love affair with concrete that it is very difficult to keep up with the latest construction in and around harbors, financed by a government cowed by the powerful fishermen's associations. At our stop that night, the island of O-Shima, Google Earth showed that there was an entirely new harbor not indicated on our chart, with what looked like welcoming pontoons on one wall, but a strange raft-like structure in the middle.

Sure enough we were able to tie up. The raft was in fact a series of semi-submerged cages heavily stocked with fish, where Japanese fishermen came to try their "luck," renting rods and lures for twenty or thirty dollars a day. It was another attempt by the authorities in these dying island communities to entice tourists. Some such attempts were more creative, but also more desperate. As we strolled along the waterfront later that afternoon, a bowed old man in a fishing smock beckoned at us from his doorstep. In many countries you might be suspicious, but in Japan we knew we had nothing to fear. We kicked off our shoes and followed him into his cramped front room, where a lady who must have been his wife smiled at us shyly but without any surprise. Wordlessly, he waved his arm as if to say: "Look around."

Crammed into every possible nook—on the windowsill, above the fireplace, covering half the floor, hanging from the ceiling—were thirty-centimeter-long incandescent light bulbs of the kind that the squid boats carry at night to attract their prey. The filaments had been removed and through the tiny gap in the lamps' bases our friend had ingeniously inserted model boats of all vintages: ships not in bottles, but in light bulbs.

We were impressed, but quite lacked any appropriate vocabulary of appreciation. The useful standby "Oishi" (delicious) was clearly not appropriate in this instance. And our friend had no English either. He looked at us politely questioning. We smiled back. There was a pause. We bowed and left. We were not sure whether we had been invited to buy or just to admire.

Next day was bright and sunny. We tacked east again in freshening headwinds, with the hazy shoreline of the big island gradually closing in on our right. By afternoon we were also fighting a strong ebb current that was draining out from the Inland Sea, through the narrow strait that now lay ahead of us: Kanmon Kaikyo, the Barrier Gate. It was slow work, with the few hundred meters painfully gained on a tack often all but lost when we had to pay off downwind to stay out of the path of some massive tanker or freighter exiting the strait.

On the shoreline now we could make out fifteen or twenty tall wind turbines, their twenty-meter-long blades turning lazily, facing towards where we were headed and confirming that our contrary wind was no local effect. Out of the haze derricks, steel frameworks, and massive bulbous tanks began to emerge. Kitakyushu is sometimes known as the Lucky City; it was the initial target for the bomb that was dropped on Nagasaki, but it was too cloudy here that morning. But from this perspective, and even on a pleasant summer afternoon it looked like a particularly grim example of large-scale industrial blight.

Jenny put the binoculars to her eyes:

"Five knots and rising; ebbing."

She had spotted the first of a series of huge LED-illuminated boards that are located on the banks of both approaches to Kanmon Kaikyo. Changing minute by minute, they indicate the maximum current at the Strait's narrowest point, whether the speed is rising or falling, and its direction. It was clear we wouldn't get too far into the Strait tonight.

With our VHF radio now on—and tuned to the English language Kanmon Kaikyo traffic control—we edged our way into the half-mile wide entrance, the brown and oil-flecked water starting to become agitated with whitecaps. With one finger on the chart, Jenny carefully counted off the big red buoys to starboard—a few of them ominously dented by careless tankers—until, at Number 10, we were able to peel off downwind and into a progressively more sheltered channel. Here we could make a more leisurely search for somewhere to spend the night.

On one side were the sprawling installations of the Nippon Steel Works, low-flying smoke from rusting stacks now overtaking us. On the other, small to medium-sized coasters rode gently at anchor. There was constant chatter on the radio:

"Kanmon Kaikyo Control, Kanmon Kaikyo Control…Maersk Tiger approaching Number 35 westbound; permission to proceed…"

"Maersk Tiger, Maersk Tiger, Kanmon Control…hold to starboard; maximum current now eight knots and ebbing; proceed with caution."

The Japanese radio operator was a very cool-sounding young woman with impeccable British English, in contrast to the rough, broken, and mangled language of most of her interlocutors. Once or twice, she had politely to remind the skippers of Japanese vessels to repeat their requests in English.

Three miles down our side channel, cruising now-flat black waters deep in urban and industrialized Wakamatsu, we could see one of the options that Captain Ohara, back in Fukuoka, had mentioned as good moorage:

"Just look for the Space Shuttle, the *Endeavour*, I think…or is it the *Discovery*?" he'd said enigmatically. "You'll see what I mean when you get there."

It was one of the oddest places we had ever moored. We tied up to a rusting floating pontoon that looked as though it had once served as a landing dock for tourist boats. At the head of the ramp was a clearly closed-up Space Museum—yes, there was the full-sized *Endeavour* replica, angled skywards at

60 degrees—combined with an amusement park, all surrounded by high-rise apartments. Suburban trains could be heard clattering past on elevated tracks, unseen, every few minutes. But it was quiet in between, and there wasn't a soul to be seen. On the other side of the still inlet was a dock for container ships with great spider-like yellow gantries capable of reaching out over the water and plucking shipping containers off the ships' decks. We expected someone to come and bother us, but nobody did. It seemed that while the Japanese were, as the cliché went, great rule-followers, they sometimes had no idea how to cope with people who did not follow the rules or who might not understand them.

The night wasn't as quiet as we had hoped. At some point, a ship slipped silently in, and at about 1:00 a.m. began to unload. Those yellow spiders got to work and over an echoing loudspeaker there began endless variations on what was evidently the Japanese equivalent of:

"Left a bit; right. Down. No! Up again; OK! Ready…"

Careful study of our current tables—the script for which Ohara had kindly transcribed from kanji into English on our behalf—indicated that next day, Tuesday July 26th, it would be slack water under the Kanmon Kaikyo bridge (the narrowest part of the Strait) at 6:31 a.m. After that there would be a gradual turn to flood (i.e., the current would turn in our favor), reaching a peak speed of 6.8 knots at 11:07 a.m. We wanted favorable current, but not too much; if we faced an opposing wind, which was likely, the combination of wind against current could kick up some very unpleasant chop in the more open parts of the strait and at its eastern exit.

So an early start was in order: 5:00 a.m. On mirror-flat black waters that reflected the apocalyptic industrial cityscapes to either side, we retraced our route out of the inlet and back to the west entrance of the lazy "U" that is Kanmon Kaikyo. The illuminated signboard showed that we still had opposing current of 3 knots—it was supposed to be turning by now—but the speed was decreasing rapidly. We stayed just out of the frighteningly narrow designated shipping lane, keeping the engine on at all times in case of the need for a sudden maneuver, but rolling our foresail in and out as puffs of wind came and went. A stubby-prowed ocean-going tug lurched out in front of us unexpectedly. We backed cautiously away as its skipper, who ostentatiously made no eye contact at all with us, put his vessel through an aggressive set of tests: full ahead, full astern, hard to starboard, hard reverse. It was just like warming up your car for the day's activities, we supposed.

More slowly, a 200-meter-long unladen tanker, most of its usually hidden hull now exposed and red, was carefully nudged out of its berth by four small, busy tugs, turned around 180 degrees, and placed back in an adjoining berth. For fifteen minutes it blocked the entire strait. As slack water took hold and

Under sail in Kanmon Kaikyo

the current began almost imperceptibly to turn in our favor, more and more ships began coming up from behind us, plowing past, leaving us rocking in their wake. Sometimes they were only thirty seconds apart and because of the gentle curve of the "U" it always seemed as though they were going to ram us. Fishing boats weaved nonchalantly between the stream of vessels; ships' horns sounded constantly. But the fishermen always seemed to get out of the way just in time and without giving the impression that they had in any way hurried to move.

On a small yacht in a place like this you feel very vulnerable and out of place. I kept having to remind myself not to grip the tiller so hard in my nervousness and—as nearly always in situations like this—grew snappy with Jenny if she couldn't instantly place us on the chart or tell me what buoy to look for next. By now the current was with us. This meant we were moving faster, but passing through tidal rapids in this way imparts a sense of powerlessness. You know that a point will very soon be reached when, should you wish to turn around for whatever reason, you will not have sufficient engine power to make any headway and will just be swept on.

To starboard, and in spite of my intense concentration, I was distracted by a cluster of reddish buildings with a tower and some odd domes.

"It can't be!"

"I think it is."

A two-thirds-size replica of St Mark's Square in Venice, complete with the iconic campanile. We'd been in Japan long enough now to know this had to be another wedding palace.

A grey metal suspension bridge loomed high over us: Honshu to the left, Kyushu to the right. The chart showed that deep below us were vehicle and rail tunnels, one carrying the Fukuoka to Tokyo Shinkansen (bullet train). Now it was 9:00 a.m. The maximum current was not due for another two hours or so, but the next sign board, below the bridge, already showed six knots favorable and rising. As we'd half feared and expected, as the eastern mouth of the strait neared, so the opposing wind picked up. We plunged into a roller-coaster ride that had solid water coming over the bows and cascading rearwards along the side decks. More clenching of the tiller. But soon we were through, the wide horizon of the Inland Sea opening up before us.

Jenny and I have sailed enough—and been married enough?—that in certain situations no words are needed. This was one of them. The wind was on our nose, our intended destination—a place called Ube, on the Honshu shore fifteen miles to the east—would be very hard to reach. But if we turned south instead, we would have a short fast sail with the wind on our beam, to the Plan B location we had plotted way back in Fukuoka with Ohara: Shin Moji and its new marina. Jenny already had the right Google Earth photo ready, in its transparent sleeve, the chart book turned to the right page (not as easy as it sounds: all the script was in kanji and we'd had to have friends transliterate every single location). Now she was entering a new set of waypoints into the GPS:

"Six miles to Shin Moji. A very shallow entrance. Stay well offshore until the last minute."

Sometimes in Japan it was tempting to ignore the GPS because things didn't always look like you thought they should from your (not necessarily up to date) charts. This was one of them. To the left of our course and to seawards there was an unmistakably man-made structure.

"It looks like a low bridge, but where can it be leading to? Is it an optical illusion?" I asked.

Jenny checked the chart. Nothing; it should be deep, open water. Then she picked up the binoculars.

"Whatever it is, there's a large jet aircraft landing on it; or maybe crashing into it."

It took some time before it dawned on us. This must be a newly constructed airport for Kitakyushu, doubtless on an artificial island built well out into the Inland Sea. The low framework structure was a set of pilings that ran out from the end of the runway into the water, bearing the approach lights.

Off Shin Moji Marina, which was a bay carved out of semi-abandoned docklands, there were, disconcertingly, jagged metal poles sticking up out of the water. And there were great soggy rafts of what looked like intermingled driftwood and ships' rigging undulating in the one-meter green seas: seaweed farms, we later learned, and the bane of cruising sailors in Japan. You never know where you will come across them. They can extend for miles, and they are rarely lit at night.

Shin Moji was a marina posing as a smart yacht club, with an expensive-looking restaurant, a high lobby decorated with nautical items like ships' wheels, and its own adjoining wedding chapel in the style of a small white church in the Greek islands. The pontoons were only one quarter occupied, the buildings empty and echoing; we had to hunt around to find someone to accept our payment. Ishii, our friend from Hirado had cheerfully advised:

"You must arrive at Shin Moji after five in the evening; then leave before eight in the morning. Like this, no need to pay!"

But while this strategy would probably have worked for us, it seemed a bit of a cheap trick. We paid up.

The Inland Sea is a 280-mile-long stretch of sheltered water, aligned approximately east-west, and protected from the open ocean by the three great islands of Honshu, Kyushu, and Shikoku. It has two wide exits southwards into the Pacific (at either extremity of Shikoku) and Kanmon Kaikyo, the much narrower strait leading westwards to the Sea of Japan that we had just transited. The central section of the sea narrows down and is crammed with islands in such a way that three sets of multi-span bridges now allow for Shikoku to be reached by car and rail from Honshu.

The Sea is by no means immune from typhoons. Now, in late July, we were approaching the peak season for storms. But the mountains on the southern shores of Kyushu and Shikoku usually take the brunt of the approaching systems and in such an enclosed space seas cannot build to dangerous heights. So, it was with a sense of some relief and pleasant anticipation that we unrolled the set of three charts, spanning the entire Sea, that Nozaki had given us back at Takashima. They were old—he'd "borrowed" them from his last assignment in the Navy, years before—so one of our first tasks was to pencil in that new airport (Kitakyushu), just south of us. Then we added the sets of bridges in the east and, right at the eastern end of the last chart, Kansai International Airport, which is built on a large artificial island in Osaka Bay.

I've always loved maps and charts, and can spend hours tracing my finger over them, stopping at places that look interesting from their shape or even just their name. When I was a child, Celebes—that huge island with three legs and a flying mane, in the eastern Indian Ocean, now known as Sulawesi—fascinated me. And I always thought I'd like to go to Wau, in South Sudan, just for the sound of it; I've made it to Wau, several times (along with Yei and Bor), but Sulawesi still beckons. Now we had hundreds of islands before us—over 3,000, said *Lonely Planet*—and an almost infinite variety of routes we could take.

Jenny had to bring me back to reality:

"Alright, we need a plan, at least to start with. Here's the list of ports we got clearance for in Fukuoka; here are the Google Earth pictures; the Japanese chart book for Seto Naikai; we've got the notes Ishii gave us; *Sunstone's* blog"—here she meant the website constructed by our friends who had passed through the previous year— "and some old notes from the Seven Seas Cruising Association, from the nineties I think; an article from *Yachting World* from 1998; and there's always *Lonely Planet*..."

In Fukuoka, having learned an important lesson as we awaited the typhoon in Goto Retto, we had applied for permission to visit every single possible harbor on our next leg, reasoning that it would be acceptable to skip half of them but we would have a problem if caught stopping in one that was unauthorized. The rules stated, frighteningly:

"When making a call at a closed port without special permission, the captain shall be punished by imprisonment with work for not more than two years or by a fine of not more than 1,000,000 yen. And the relevant ship may be confiscated."

Our impossibly long list had been approved without hesitation. Now, I penciled into the back three pages of the logbook a vertical list of the most appealing potential stops, with arrows between each stop and the distance to be run. In several places there were arrows that went out from one side or the other and took in alternate destinations before returning to the main itinerary. Seven to ten stops, over 120 miles or so, and we'd be at the next Open Port (where we'd have to seek permission all over again) of Hiroshima.

Japan's building mania was nothing new. As Jenny took the list from me and began laboriously entering into our chart plotter GPS coordinates that would allow us to steer a safe route even in fog, I settled in to start reading a classic we'd long been looking forward to starting: Donald Richie's travel masterpiece from the seventies, *The Inland Sea*.[29] I'd barely opened it before I was interrupting her to read to her the thousand-year-old Japanese poem that serves as its preface. I can remember it still, its tone of gentle self-mockery:

> *I hear they are building a bridge*
> *To the island of Tsu.*
> *Alas.*
> *To what now*
> *Shall I compare myself?*

---

29   Richie, Donald. (1971). *The Inland Sea*. Kyoto, Japan: Weatherhill Publishing.

海

The neighborhood of Shin Moji was not enticing, so next morning we were up and off at 5:00 a.m. This part of the Inland Sea is the most open and has the fewest islands: today's, at 35 miles, would be one of our longest day's runs. The course was 110 degrees, the wind was from exactly that angle, and it didn't look as though the time available would permit us the luxury of zigzagging under sail all day. Much of the time we motored. It was a perfect warm day. Freighters chugged past at regular intervals. One or two detoured over just to have a look at us, which is rarely comfortable. Although Kyushu was slowly receding to our right, its hazy blue hills, some of them in classic volcanic shape, stayed with us all day.

It was easy to see why those stereotypical Japanese watercolors favored the ethereal look. There always did seem to be a haze, except very early in the morning; it wasn't pollution; it had always been there. When there were no ships to be seen and we had chosen to sail for an hour or so, to give the engine a rest, the silence seemed total. It was not what you would expect at the heart of the most industrialized and densely populated country on earth.

We tied up an hour before sunset to a wall in Himeshima's compact little harbor, on the hilly island's south side. The village behind the harbor had two or three all-purpose shops and a post office. There were few people about, and after dark the streets were silent, the lack of lights in many of the houses revealing that they were unoccupied. Nori, our Fukuoka neighbor, had left us a small folding bike, which we now extracted from below and assembled. We set off in the morning to explore, one on the bike, one on foot. Of course, we had to agree on a rendezvous point where we would swap roles, but the idea worked well and was one we would often repeat.

Freighter in the Inland Sea

It was four or five kilometers from the harbor to the lighthouse at the east end of the island. Jenny had gone on ahead on the bike, and in gathering heat I found my way through the narrow backstreets of the small town, with its overhanging grey-tiled eaves, to the road that runs along the island's hilly spine. In a few minutes I was already on the north shore. Here were great enclosed ponds where little paddlewheels powered by electric motors circulated the muddy water sluggishly: shrimp farms, Himeshima's attempt to keep a few jobs on the island.

The road wound its way up into the hills. Everything was lush and green. The overgrown verges and the dark woods behind hummed and buzzed surprisingly loudly with the characteristic sound of Japanese cicadas. In an hour and a half, not a single car passed. Our rendezvous was of course the island's Onsen: a natural hot spring harnessed and channeled into a modern brick building just above the sea. When I arrived, there were two minibuses parked outside. The local seniors had been brought here for their free weekly outing by the island's social services. The attendant explained to me:

"Yes, our old people, they like the Onsen very much. For them, for their generation, they never had baths at home. Now they do, but Onsen is where they want to come to talk to old friends."

It was enlightened of the town to offer this service, I thought. But Japan was very fast becoming a population of old people. The young—because of the depressed economy?—were marrying late or not at all and having fewer children. Immigration was non-existent and those old people, on account of their healthy diet and excellent medical services, were hanging on determinedly. For how long would the government be able to afford to take them on their outings to the Onsen, we wondered.

Jenny emerged looking a little flushed, with a gaggle of old ladies behind her, giggling quietly as they eyed me; the attendant gently edged them down the steps into the sun.

"Yes…" said Jenny sighing, anticipating my question. "You guessed it. I went in the wrong side again and scandalized the old fellows…or made their day, maybe."

Next day presented us with a semantic/linguistic challenge of some difficulty. We hadn't been long in Japan before we learned that Shima (or Jima) meant Island. In fact, we had learned to recognize the kanji character on the charts. Now our next island destination was Heigun. There again, sure enough, was the character for Shima (島) included in the island's name: 平郡島; but in this case the character was written in western script as Tō, thus Heigun Tō, not the Heigun Shima we had expected. Later we learned that Tō is an alternative word for island, but with slightly different connotations. But how was a Japanese person seeing the kanji characters that describe this island, to know whether to say Tō or Shima? In a word, they couldn't. You just had to know which was the correct spoken word for the context.

In the same way, it was a conventional precaution that when one Japanese person received a business card from another, he/she would courteously check how to pronounce the characters.

There is of course linguistic history to explain how potentially confusing situations of this kind have arisen. And it is incorrect to suggest that any language is "better" than another; every language is uniquely adapted to its context. The issue here, it seemed to me, was actually not about Japanese per se, but how it is conventionally represented in written form.

I recalled a conversation I had with Mi-Chan in Kagoshima, when she was texting a short message to a girlfriend, and wondered if modern smartphone technology might soon start to play a role in that:

"Show me how you text Konichiwa," I had asked.

She made two keystrokes, made a choice between a couple of kanji options, made another stroke, then selected another one of three for "Send."

"But you typed the Romaji (Roman alphabet) characters…"

Indeed, she had: first "k," then "o." Her phone had then tried to guess what she wanted to say and presented her with a succession of options in kanji, until the right one came up (今日は or, in the hiragana form of writing, こんにちは). In other words, the Roman alphabet had to be used to send messages in kanji, because no more efficient way could be found. More recently, some smartphones allow their owner to sketch the character they desire with a single finger, but the technology is far from foolproof and results in many misreadings.

Periodically over the next few months, I would test on friends the provocative idea that developments in the transmission of information could go so far as to threaten the continued use of ideograms both in Japan and China. Reactions were so shocked that I soon learned to speak with a smile, as if I were deliberately teasing. It was earnestly pointed out to me that 120 million people in Japan communicate with each other using kanji characters; kanji is not in danger. Maybe so. Many went on to insist that kanji is at the very heart of Japanese-ness. This I wasn't at all sure about. In reality this system of writing had come into the Japanese islands from China maybe fifteen hundred years ago. And the great classic of Japanese literature, *The Tale of Genji*, is not written in kanji at all, but in a phonetic script more relatable to Hiragana and Katakana. But any suggestion that any aspect of Japanese culture is somehow a subset of Chinese is taboo.

Heigun Tō, the linguistic oddity in question, was another 35 miles on, another quite hilly island, this time with a tiny harbor on the north shore, near its east end. The harbor didn't show at all on any of our charts. We had just one reference to it from an American yacht named *Lorelei* that had stopped in here

The village, Heigun Tō

years ago, and we'd taken the precaution of printing a Google Earth image. We tied up on the most obvious free wall, only to have a youngish-looking man in a wet suit hurry down and very politely point out we were at the ferry dock.

"There is place for yacht, I think," and he gestured to a tall, slightly sloping and barnacle-encrusted wall. "One yacht come before, I think, long time, American maybe."

We were at a time of large tides now, maybe three meters, so it took an hour to get ourselves installed. If the tide is low when you come in (as it now was) just getting a person ashore can be a major challenge in such harbors, involving climbing part way up the rigging then stepping sideways while the yacht, unattached, tries to go the other way. Jun—that was our new friend's name—helped us, and after a short break came back with his wife, daughter, and a basket full of fresh vegetables from their garden.

"I am old teacher," he said as we sipped tea. "Born on Heigun Tō but teach on Honshu. Now I come back. Many not come back." He shrugged expressively. "My daughter...she is only person under thirty on all Heigun Tō."

Jun took us to the only shop in the village, run by JA, the huge and politically powerful Japan Agriculture cooperative that dominates life in rural parts. We stocked up, and the kindly proprietor presented me with a cold beer and Jenny with a cold orange juice (in the usual way of things). Next day we walked up a steep road to the spine of the island and down to a deserted sand beach looking out over the expanse of the Inland Sea. It was August, the peak of the holiday season. But it looked as if it had been a year or two since anyone had patronized the boarded-up little beach bar. We sat there much of the afternoon, with the cicadas droning in the lush vegetation behind us, enjoying the solitude, the calm seas, the quiet islands on the distant horizon. We spent half an hour gathering driftwood that I would later use to construct a short rope ladder for getting up and down those high harbor walls.

Just before sunset a kayaker rounded the point. He stopped in the water, no doubt as shocked as we were to see somebody else. We helped him pull his heavy red sea kayak up onto the beach.

"Hiroki," he said in good English. "You are the first people I have ever seen on this beach."

He went on to explain that he was from these parts but had moved away ten years earlier to go to University in Tokyo.

"I set off from Yokohama seventeen months ago…" he went on. "I will go all the way through Seto Naikai, maybe to Fukuoka, then we will see…Seto Naikai is very beautiful, I think, it is like old Japan. But it is sad as well."

We didn't need, by now, to ask what he meant.

That night Jun got his three brothers together and prevailed upon his long-suffering wife to cook us a sumptuous dinner at home. One of the brothers, Koji, had been a chef in Australia and Germany before coming back to Heigun Tō, and ran the island's website. Another lived by squid fishing, the third by free diving for oysters. Jun and the travelling brother spoke English, the others none at all. Liberal supplies of alcohol were brought out to break the ice, and toasts were exchanged far into the night. When it was time to leave, Jun walked us through the silent streets, down to *Bosun Bird* and thanked us for coming to his island.

海

We were now at the southwestern edge of the large indentation into the shoreline of Honshu that is Hiroshima Bay. The weather was settled, and generally there was little wind, but as we approached the middle waters of the Inland Sea the currents were becoming stronger, and it was necessary to plan our days' sails carefully. We left Heigun Tō at 5:30 and drifted east in the usual light winds. Then fog set in. Above us the sky seemed bright but ahead we could see almost nothing.

Fishing boats came and went unseen and we forlornly blew our bright-orange foghorn. The GPS showed we must soon cross a major shipping lane, and we started to hear the deeper throb of big ships' engines. The AIS display told us that one would come close, but the chart seemed to dictate that he would need to veer north and miss us comfortably. In a few minutes we could sense him coming. The engines were louder and louder; there were three angry bursts of his own foghorn; he must have seen us on his radar. Panicking, I made a sharp turn and we backed away. Just in time: a wall of black steel slipped rapidly past us, barely fifty meters ahead.

It was so calm and the forecast so good that we anchored for the afternoon and night in the middle of a wide, sand-beached bay called Kodomari Wan. The mist came and went and in the intervals of sunshine it was hot; we swam to cool off. Our Japanese yachting friends, we knew, literally never anchored. The problem, they explained, was that the fishermen were extremely possessive of every stretch of water in and around Japan. If you anchored, you were on someone's patch, and they were more than likely to ask you to move. A couple of fishing boats did come near to us as they tended their nets, but perhaps the Gaijin factor worked again in our favor. Nobody bothered us, and we had a quiet night, our bright white anchor light warning off anyone who might not have expected to find a yacht here.

Another early start, another set of narrows to be negotiated at precisely the right time, and by mid-morning we were in Hiroshima Bay, at a favorite stop of old Australian friends Nick and Jan, of *Yawarra*: Kaze Noko boatyard, on Kurahashi Jima. They'd visited Japan three times over the past decade from their home base in Australia and had sent us a clutch of hand-written notes and diagrams. Kaze Noko was a set of ramshackle floating pontoons, a slipway and a workshop on a peninsula so densely wooded that there was no way through to the main island. Hideto and Matoko welcomed us enthusiastically, with iced coffee and hand towels that had been kept in the fridge (it was a hot day).

"Nick and Jan! Yes, of course, it must be eight, ten years now… I think not much has changed on Kurahashi. Business is OK, not great, now we make electric, hybrid engines for yachts."

Noriko, Hideto's mother, was rustled up and there was much reminiscence of the weeks and months Nick and Jan had spent here. Jenny went off with Matoko to send an email to our old friends, who were now cruising around Australia in *Yawarra 2*, a power boat.

Working our way north towards the city of Hiroshima, we passed one island after another whose sides looked to have been stripped away, leaving great cliffs of bare, yellowish rock and rubble. Large steel barges, laden with rock, were being towed around, and a few otherwise enticing coves were obstructed by barges not in use. This was evidently one of the sources for the limestone that went into all that concrete we found in every Japanese harbor. We'd seen whole islands encircled by concrete wave-barriers and walls. It seemed ironic that while every effort was being made to save some islands from being washed away by the effects of erosion, others were being hacked at on a massive scale to provide the necessary concrete.

Dodging floating rafts where oysters were cultivated, we found a fine haven at a marina on the island of Okinoshima and decided to pause here for a while. We were now in waters so protected that there was hardly a need for encircling walls. It was a relief to tie to a floating pontoon rather than rough concrete on which our fenders would scrape uneasily as the tide rose and fell. We were barely ten or twelve kilometers from Hiroshima, but the setting was bucolic. It was a forty-minute walk up and down steep hills along a quiet and shady road to the nearest settlement at Fukae, where there was a single shop and a bus stop. Where the land was sufficiently flat, little rice paddies had been planted; we would greet the invariably aged men and women who stooped for hours on end to tend their crops, shaded by distinctive conical straw hats. Every twenty or thirty minutes you would hear a dull crack in the distance: automatic crow-scarers, firing off a shotgun round. On very still days, early in the morning and in the evening, you would hear the loudspeaker systems of three or four different villages, slightly out of sync, playing a few sentimental chords of piano music to send children to school or welcome them home.

Here and there, on bends in the road or set back into groves of trees, would be a Buddhist grave or two: meter-high squared-off marble or polished granite pillars artistically incised with kanji characters commemorating the dead. The Japanese O-Bon festival was near: a kind of All Souls', when the souls of the departed return home for three days. They are guided by colorful paper lanterns set on the graves, and at home meals are set for them.

We'd been in Japan for several months now, but we were still keenly attuned to what, in this ostensibly western society, was different. In Fukae I found myself examining the manhole covers. In other places they'd caught my passing attention as well, but now I realized that each municipality had custom cast-iron manhole-covers with a theme or scenes distinctive to the locale. Here it was a few tangerines in the foreground, framing a seascape with a little steamer chugging across. Some were even in color. It was a small thing but perhaps indicative of something bigger: a sense of pride in the community, a touch of artistic sensibility where you would least expect it.

We were impressed in the same way by the little gaggles of old ladies that we would encounter at traffic islands or spaced out along the grass dividers between the two lanes of the road. Their wheeled walking-frames neatly parked to one side, necks and faces shaded by cloths jammed under baseball caps, they would be weeding and troweling the community flower beds, on their knees. Sometimes they would be quietly gossiping to each other or muttering to themselves; usually they gave us a nervous smile as we passed.

We mentioned one morning to Yanuchi, the young marina manager, that we were having problems with our engine control lever. It was slipping and would put the engine in or out of gear at inconvenient times, usually just when we were engaged in a delicate maneuver such as approaching a harbor wall.

"No problem… I bring mechanic. Five minutes is good?"

The two of them spent the entire day struggling over our lever and the control cable while Jenny and I offered occasional advice from the shade of the main cabin. It was eventually determined that a closed unit—it was actually marked "do not open"—on the inner side of the control box was at fault. There was ten minutes of head scratching. We mutely passed the small rectangular box back and forth between each other. The mechanic disappeared without a word; we offered Yanuchi a Coke. Then another.

After an hour, the mechanic was back, a triumphant smile on his face. He brandished a similar Morse-brand control unit that he had evidently just cannibalized from some other vessel; we hoped it was a derelict but our Japanese was not up to asking. He wedged himself once again into the cramped cockpit locker, with one hand dangling outside so Yanuchi could occasionally pass him tools. Another hour later we were back in business; the lever was working perfectly.

"How much?" we asked timidly, North American mechanics' usual fees in mind.

"Is service," said Yanuchi with a small bow.

"Service?"

"Yes...is free."

We protested but there was nothing to be done. Both men went off after another polite bow, refusing even a final drink.

The Naval Academy, Etajima

Yanuchi suggested that as well as visiting Hiroshima we should take the time to go to Etajima, on our own island, and he gave us the bus and walking directions we would need. Formerly known as the Imperial Japanese Naval Academy, but now renamed as the headquarters of the Japanese Maritime Self-Defence Force, Etajima was prior to World War II one of the three great naval academies in the world, after the Britannia Royal Naval College and the US Naval Academy at Annapolis. It is located on spacious, leafy grounds that slope down to an exceptionally well-protected inlet of the sea. Many of the buildings, which date mainly from 1888, are of red brick and have a New England feel about them. But there is a clutch of grand neo-classical structures that are more 1930's Washington.

We signed up for a guided tour that was supposed to be offered in English, but no English-speaker was available that day. So, we tagged along with a group of elderly Japanese gentlemen who were almost old enough to have been veterans and did our best to figure out what was going on.

First, we stopped in a huge marble-floored auditorium in one of the neo-classical buildings, where our footsteps echoed and lowering your voice became instinctive. A young lieutenant in white talked against a background of two crossed flags: the Japanese flag with its red disc on a white background, and the naval ensign of the rising sun. It is the rising sun that is the more evocative to anyone who has seen those images from the war, or any one of a hundred or so American movies where it has inevitably come to be associated with treachery and fanaticism. I wondered what the officer was saying. From his gestures and from the hush in which his audience was listening, we guessed he was conjuring up the war. Maybe one of those mornings when graduating cadets had been assembled here in their finery, perhaps for the last time, to be addressed by some Admiral before being dispatched to join their vessel at the port of Kure.

Nearby, in an equally fine building, was the museum of Naval History. Here was a magnificent larger-than-life painting of medal-bedecked Admiral Togo, who had crushed the Russians at Tsushima in 1905. There were oils, too, of Japanese naval vessels participating in support of the allies in World War I. As we wandered through the museum, it was not difficult to see how the thirties dawned with Japan considering itself an imperial power very much in the same league as Russia, Britain, France, and the USA. Which meant it enjoyed the same rights as those powers had abrogated to themselves: the right to a sphere of influence, the right to overseas markets, the right to colonize. It was a back-handed compliment to Japan that conferred a degree of legitimacy, when in 1922 it signed a treaty with the USA, France, Britain, and Italy, limiting the size of Dreadnoughts each might construct.

When it came to World War II, the attack on Pearl Harbor was here described as The Battle of Hawaii. There was no mention in this museum of the June 1942 Battle of Midway, in which Japan lost four aircraft carriers and a heavy cruiser, and which some historians have described as the most important naval engagement in history. Nor was the April 1945 loss of the *Yamato*, at 73,000 tons the largest battleship ever built, mentioned.

Then there were two rooms dedicated to the Navy's Special Attack Forces, with an enormous bronze plaque listing the names of 2,633 naval personnel who piloted planes, midget submarines, and torpedoes in suicide attacks; another 1,000 died at the wheel of specially designed fast motorboats packed with explosives. There were photos of many, along with their last testaments. Three letters had been translated into English. On his last evening on Earth, Masatoshi Sakai wrote:

"I am honored to have been selected as a member of the kamikaze special attack air corps, and since then I feel my body has been filled with courage and fighting spirit. I promise to make every effort to the maximum extent until my last moment to ensure the everlasting prosperity of our lovely country and people."

As at Chiran, I wasn't sure if the museum was glorifying these deaths. If you half-closed your eyes and knew nothing of the subject matter, you might think that the delicately executed oil that shows six men in a woodland clearing in the sunlight, offering a toast to another man whose back is to the artist, was a sensitive depiction of men answering some high calling, perhaps of a religious nature. In fact, as the card below it indicates, this is the Shikishima Unit of the First Special Attack Corps, about to leave their air base in the Philippines in October 1944 on the first kamikaze mission.

For almost any non-Japanese person, Hiroshima means only one thing. Accordingly, it was a shock to find that this is a bustling, normal city with a modern and efficient tram system that just happens to have a peculiar, ruined building preserved in its center and a large seventies-style museum—that commemorates the dropping of the first atomic bomb.

As at Nagasaki, the experience of visiting this museum was a saddening one, yet it evoked in us even more questions. Was the large board excoriating President Obama for never having visited Hiroshima to "apologize" warranted? What did the Japanese characters engraved in black granite, conventionally translated into English as "May this evil never be repeated again" really mean?

A-Bomb Memorial Dome, Hiroshima

From the context, you had to guess it meant The Bomb. But was it enough to say only that?

Was the idea of a museum appropriate at all? Rather than create a new destination for day-trippers in their sun hats and with their ice-cream cones, might it not have been more appropriate to leave the A-Bomb Memorial Dome—the ruins of an industrial exhibition center that was 150 meters from the hypocenter—standing, without further commentary? As at Nagasaki, we found the account in the museum of Japanese aggression through the thirties and up to Pearl Harbor inadequate, the controversy over school-book accounts of the period glossed over, recognition of Japanese atrocities in China absent.

Outside, as we sat on a bench in the shade of a large jacaranda tree, two friendly looking middle-aged and middle-class Japanese ladies in floral print dresses approached us. In perfect English, they made polite small talk about the weather. Then they asked us what we thought about the bombing of Hiroshima, just as the old man had at Nagasaki. A little uncomfortable, I again made some non-committal response, to which they nodded sympathetically. Then, with a beguiling smile:

"We know the truth. We are in the last days. You can be saved if you join us."

My heart sinking, I took the English-language leaflet that one of the ladies held out to me. In colorful drawings, that looked designed to appeal to an eight-year-old, it showed an earthly paradise in which bearded Caucasian men and flaxen-haired women lived in harmony with donkeys and lions, in a Garden of Eden setting. I was angry for the abuse of my politeness, for the abuse of this location, and also for their having picked on foreigners whom they (correctly) judged would be less likely to brush them away than their compatriots. But of course, I didn't have the heart to be rude.

There's another big attraction near Hiroshima: the huge vermilion-painted Tori (gate) in the shallow waters off the nearby shrine-island of Miyajima. A visit was obligatory but, with O-Bon upon us, the crowds were daunting. At a particular spot on the waterfront, people were posing in front of a small, undistinguished and evidently modern monument, a low marble plinth. Obeying the herd instinct, I began fingering my camera but sent Jenny over to investigate:

"What's it say?" I asked as she tried to read the inscription without appearing in the Yamamotos' family photo.

"It says this—the Tori, not the monument—is one the three most photographed locations in Japan…"

In the exact opposite direction, behind us, was the Tori itself. I snapped a few of the required pictures. It was indeed an evocative sight, apparently floating on the blue waters of the Inland Sea. But I was having one of those existential moments when I wondered if I was impressed for the Tori's own sake, or just because I had so often seen photographs of it as the epitome of Japan. I realized now that you either had to be clever with your focusing or choose quite a special angle so as to avoid having in the background some 1970's apartment blocks. I noticed with surreptitious glee that a little flotilla of Jet Skis was positioning itself so as to be able to ride right through the gate that was meant to be the Gateway for the Gods. Surely there would be an outcry at this sacrilege! But no. Nobody seemed even to notice.

Nor was anyone offended by the commercialism that went right up to the gates of the main shrine. There were dozens of places selling variations on a plain kind of wooden spoon that was allegedly invented centuries ago by a local monk, and that allows for the serving of boiled rice without impairment of its taste. It's said that religion-based commerce of this kind started In Europe at least a thousand years ago, when monks began selling scallop shells (the symbol of St. James) to pilgrims on the route to Santiago; it was certainly still going strong in Japan.

You could actually get away from the holiday crowds very easily. A path worked its way up through quietly buzzing scented pine forests to the summit of Mount Misen, at 530 meters. Normally there was a cableway that saved you most of the climbing; perhaps because this was out of order, we saw almost no one. At the very top was an ordinary looking wooden temple with sensational views over the calm Inland Sea, as far as the great island of Shikoku. In a smaller adjoining temple that was little more than a shed, its interior blackened by smoke, a wood fire burned. A young Japanese hiker in boots and a T-shirt wandered over to explain:

"This flame burns for...what, one thousand two hundred years...bring from China by Kobo Daishi. You know Kobo Daishi? He meditate here for one hundred days."

We didn't yet, but soon we'd be coming across Kobo Daishi's name everywhere. This monk, known before his death as Kukai, was born around 774 CE on the island of Shikoku. In 804, he sailed to China. He was initiated into the "esoteric" strain of Buddhism and a few years later returned to Japan, where he set up what has now become known as the Shingon School of Buddhism. He travelled, meditated, and wrote prolifically. The details of his life are probably better known than of any European figure of that period. His magnum opus, the huge Treatise on the Ten Stages of the Development of the Mind is so long and daunting (dare we say obscure?) that it has yet to be translated out of Japanese into any other language.

It was mesmeric looking at the flame. There was no reason to disbelieve what the young man (and the tourist literature, I found later) said. Certainly, Shingon Buddhism had been going strong for all this time and it was quite plausible that there had always been acolytes at this spot to tend to this very flame. The sense of living history, the feeling that the past lived on, quite comfortably, in the present was something we had not expected to find in this most modern of countries.

Catching the ferry back to Okinoshima among the sunburned holiday crowds, we had what was only our second mildly unpleasant human interaction in Japan. We'd bought a ferry ticket on which the clerk had handwritten the time of sailing: 17:00. But when we presented it at the gangway, the ticket collector firmly pushed us on one side and attended to the next people in the line behind us. We complained in broken Japanese and English. We waved the tickets, we appealed for help from passers-by. But it made no difference. The man would make no eye contact at all. He would give no sign at all that he was even conscious of our angry presence right in front of him. Was it sheer xenophobia? Was there really something wrong with the tickets? Or was it just that he was embarrassed that he couldn't explain the problem to us in English? We couldn't figure it out.

Hiroshima was an officially Open Port, which meant that it was time to obtain another permit from the local branch of the Ministry of Transport, for the next sequence of Closed Ports we'd be visiting. There were so many possible routes from here eastwards, through an ever-more complicated maze of islands and channels, that we listed well over fifty locations. This time there was a significant amount of indrawn breath and concerned chin-stroking; we had the impression that we were the sensation of the day in the office. To an extent that Emi San, the kind English-speaking lady who attended to us, felt she needed to go and consult her superiors.

"But please…while you are waiting…I will give you something to do," she said with a smile.

She took out from under the counter a pile of colored papers cut into 10-centimeter squares. Deftly, her fingers flying, she folded one into the classic shape of a Japanese crane. Then she repeated the process slowly, two or three times, until:

"Now you try, please."

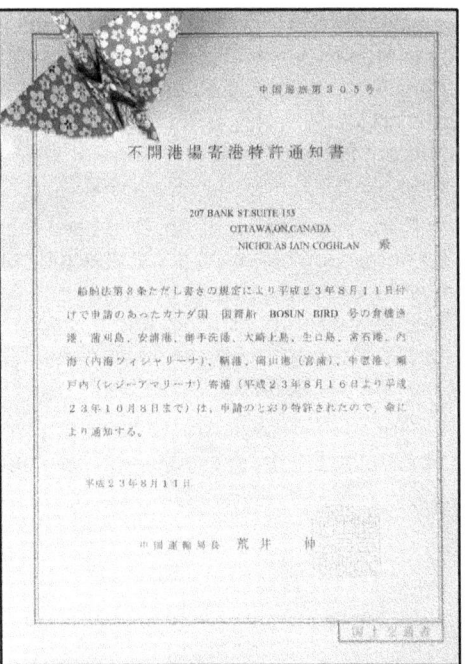

Cruising permit and Origami, Hiroshima

And off she went to the back office. When she eventually came back, smiling with stamped permits in hand, we were still struggling. But with Emi's help we finished three creditable examples of origami, which still sit on a shelf on *Bosun Bird*.

At the marina on Okinoshima we went through the now familiar process of slowly getting to know our neighbors. A couple in their late forties or early fifties owned a very high-quality cruising vessel of a make known as a Hallberg-Rassy 37, named *Sakaura* (a Japanese girl's name) and worth perhaps USD250,000. From what we knew of Japanese sailors we were not too surprised when they introduced themselves:

"This is Miki. She is a black Labrador. I am Yoichi, this is Machiko…we are doctors."

Together, they ran the Shinkai Family Clinic, in Hiroshima. Obviously, they were doing well, this was an expensive boat. We talked frankly over dinner:

"Yes, we have always wanted to go cruising…now we have had *Sakaura* ten years."

"But?"

"But the problem is we never have time to go away for more than two or three days," Machiko sighed. "We cannot close the clinic. We have many patients who depend on us, and we must visit… I cannot see how we can ever get away."

We talked at length about work ethics in Europe, North America, and Japan. It seemed to Jenny and me that in our world, insofar as their savings allowed, there was an ever greater tendency for people to retire from their steady, salaried jobs as early as they possibly could, to live out their dreams—travel, a different job, a complete change of lifestyle—while they were still fit enough to do so.

"Yes," Machiko went on. "We have seen that among our European friends. But here, I don't know, it is still very difficult. Partly, it is the family. In Japan you must take your parents, your in-laws into your home when they become too old. The pressure is very strong. And it is only in the last ten years that people have started to accept they can leave one job and take another. But the economic times are not good for that either."

"For a Japanese person to do this…," Yoichi chimed in, gesturing around our cabin in the flickering candlelight, "you must be very brave."

Chapter Nine:
Of Monks, Prostitutes, and Typhoons
(Mitarai and Onomichi)

We edged our way out of Hiroshima Bay and its oyster rafts, passed the Kaze Noko boatyard again, and nosed into a tiny fishing harbor on the south side of Kurahashi Jima, where Google Earth indicated there was a welcoming floating pontoon. We'd only been tied up ten minutes when a distinguished-looking man with a clean-shaven head knocked politely on the hull:

"Hello, I am Idehata. Would you like to go to lunch?"

Idehata had a number of responsibilities: volunteer tourist promotion officer, curator of the local museum (which had a full-sized replica of the ship in which Kobo Daishi had sailed to China), town councillor, part-time yachtsman, and Buddhist Monk. He had made a lot of money, he said, in an earlier career in Silicon Valley, by developing a Japanese keyboard compatible with regular PCs.

Idehata the Yacht Greeter

Idehata's temple

"Oh yes," he went on in reply to our query. "About five years ago I inherited my temple, which is Shingon sect, from my father. So, I came back from California to take up my responsibilities as a monk."

Once we'd finished our sushi, Idehata took us down to a beach backed by pine trees. This location, he told us, is featured in a poem dated to the 8th century CE (when the island was known as Nagato):

> *I will devote my life to*
> *Pine trees on the shore of Nagato Island.*
> *How many generations did it take*
> *To become such a divine entity, I wonder.*

We walked up a steep hill behind the village to Idehata's temple and his cool, spacious Nordic-style home built on a large rock ledge overlooking the ocean. He pulled aside the sliding doors that hid the temple's statuary and explained some of its history.

"It's probably about 1,100 years old. Maybe founded by Kobo Daishi himself. But I'm not sure about that. Of course, as you know, we constantly rebuild our temples in Japan so there is likely not a single piece of wood that is so old, but it's a safe bet that a temple has been here all this time and that it has looked like this."

Inside a closed cabinet was an ancient Buddha that we were not permitted to see: "We display it every thirty-three years," Idehata said. "I have only seen it once in my lifetime."

We walked a few meters behind the temple to where a small brook tumbled down a dark, mossy gully among the trees. The cicadas were loud. On a slab of polished granite was a short poem, in kanji characters. Idehata said that it was about this very spot, and it described exactly what we could now see and hear: the running of the water, the insects, the summer heat.

"The poem is from a text that has been dated to about 1200 in the Christian era, not as old as the one on the beach."

Idehata left us with a bottle of his temple's proprietary Sake and a pack of equally proprietary joss-sticks. In return, we copied onto his iPod a set of Buddhist chants from Nepal, that we had occasionally found soothing when the going got rough aboard *Bosun Bird*.

Next day the forecast was for winds from the southwest of fifteen to twenty knots, but early in the morning all that helped us along was a strong flood current heading east. A mile or so out we came across a little flotilla of small seabirds that seemed to favor short, abrupt dives and that looked hardly able to fly. After much leafing through our water-stained copy of Peter Harrison's *Seabirds*,[30] we found them: the Japanese Murrelet, or the grand-sounding Synthliboramphus Wumizusume. "Little known and understood," we were interested to read, classed as a Japanese National Treasure and considered an endangered species.

Birding must not be a popular pastime in Japan. Whenever we later mentioned our sighting to friends, with some excitement, we were met with blank looks of incomprehension, even consternation:

"Murrelet, murre…what is murre? Seagull yes, but murre…no I don't think so."

In the afternoon the wind finally picked up. We'd had very little wind in the Inland Sea, and none of it favorable, so we hoisted full sail and pressed on with exhilaration: there were small whitecaps, the sky was cloudless, empty green islands all around; it was a perfect sail.

We were now in a region of the Sea where, between tightly packed islands, the tides that enter from each end of this enormous saltwater lake meet and flow among the islands in complicated patterns, often in counter-intuitive directions. During the centuries when this was the main thoroughfare from China, Korea, and Kyushu to the Japanese heartland and Edo, the settlements on these centrally placed islands prospered as way stations. But, starting a hundred years ago, roads were built on the mainland, the importance of the sea lane declined, and the towns began to empty out.

The process was accelerated when, starting in the 1970's, three sets of multi-span bridges, running north-south, were thrown across from the big

---

30   Harrison, Peter. (1995). *Seabirds; an Identification Guide*. Boston, MA: Houghton Mifflin Harcourt.

island, Honshu, to Shikoku, using the small islands as stepping stones. One by one, local services—doctors, local government, shops—were relocated on the larger islands at each end of the bridges, ferry services were suspended and the island towns became quieter than they have been in perhaps seven hundred years.

One finger on the chart, we edged out of the open waters and into a narrow channel on our left, between two high, wooded islands. In the space of a minute, we were out of the current and the wind, maintaining the faintest amount of leeway on glass-flat and emerald-green water. To port was the island of Osakishimojima. Jenny guided us past the small town of Mitarai, with its hook-like protective harbor wall, to a tiny square basin into which a floating pontoon with two short fingers had been crammed. There was room (just) for four yachts, as long as you were prepared to back out again and not deviate at all from the center of the narrow entrance channel.

For a change, we had company.

"Hello, I am *Olive*," said the suntanned, liver-spotted and rather frail looking man from the neighboring yacht, introducing himself.

We realized after a few minutes that *Olive* was in fact the name of his boat. Mr. *Olive* was well into his eighties. He'd bought his boat twenty-five years ago, he said, and had done a lot of sailing around the Japanese islands.

"Yes, I wanted to sail to America," he said wistfully. "But now is too late. And my wife…yes, she is still alive, but she has never liked to sail. So, I have no crew."

Mitarai's heyday was the eighteenth century. It served then not just as waystation, but as a kind of deluxe resort for the Daimyo of Hiroshima. He would send his retainers here on vacation and entertain senior officials from Edo whose favor he needed to curry. Part of the entertainment, of course, was a plentiful supply of girls.

Mythology has it that the Japanese language has fifty-three words for the English "prostitute." Yet it does not distinguish between "lock" and "key," an interesting commentary on the respective importance to the Japanese of sex and privacy. The girls of Mitarai were known as Oiran (花魁), which literally means "queen of flowers." In *The Inland Sea*, Donald Richie writes at length about the Oiran:

"She turned wanton provocation into an art… She knew all the gossip from the mainland and could tell you just who was with child by the Daimyo of Hiroshima, just why the Daimyo of Satsuma would travel nowhere, not even here, without his little pages… She had a taste for the intrigue that naturally flourished here on this little island, where there was little else to occupy the mind."

Richie, you sense, knows whereof he speaks. His book is delicately written but as well as a travelogue it is an account of slightly mysterious and tantalizing sexual encounters, with prostitutes, schoolgirls, and young men. On an island near Mitarai Richie's long-suffering wife Louise comes to visit him. They speak to each other elliptically, enigmatically. The reader is left with the impression that when she finally gets back on a ferry to Omishima, Richie is deeply relieved and that, in fact, he has decided never to see her again.

Back in the heyday of Mitarai there were four Oiran houses, each home to a dozen or so girls and their servants. Every day they would participate in the "dochu," a Japanese version of the Spanish evening "paseo," a parade on the waterfront. The Oiran would dress up in their finest kimonos and, accompanied by boy umbrella bearers, display themselves to the visiting gentlemen and the gawping townsfolk. One day, one of the girls is reputed to have walked out accompanied by an additional acolyte. Every two or three steps she would find that her three-toed white socks had become muddied; she would call on the boy to bring her another pair from the lacquer box he carried.

One of the most famous Oiran of Mitarai was Yae Murasaki. Every day before meeting her guests she would have her young maid, Shige, help her in blackening her teeth, for thus was the fashion of the day. A special kind of pitch was needed, and it had to be of just the right consistency if it was to cling to damp, shiny teeth. One day, Shige just could not get the mixture right. Clients were calling Murasaki from the next room. In her anger and impatience, the Oiran grabbed the cup of pitch and forced the boiling liquid down Shige's throat. In her death agony, Shige clutched at her chin and throat and brushed the wall with her blood and pitch-soaked palm.

Murasaki was thereafter haunted. Whenever she took up her mirror, there was the face of the dead child looking at her. In penance, she undertook an 88-temple pilgrimage around Shikoku. You can still see Shige's tiny palm print high up on the adobe wall of the Waka Ebisu-Ya, the largest and only one remaining of Mitarai's four teahouses.

It was Lucy, an expatriate American who served as a volunteer guide for the few English-speaking visitors who passed through Mitarai that told us the story. She pointed out a dusty pile of wooden-backed books on a shelf and took one down to show us. Here was the life story of one of the Oiran, from the day she entered the teahouse as a maid; here in these columns were her earnings, the lists of her clients, her debts; here was recorded the day she died. Down at the seawall you could see how some old, engraved stones had been incorporated into the structure:

"Grave markers for Oiran; they weren't exactly outcasts, but they could not be buried in the proper cemetery, they had their own graveyard and over the years it was robbed for stones."

We ambled through the deserted back streets to the old fishing harbor where there were some unusual-looking wooden boats, not very seaman-like, with hard angles and covered-in decks. From the weed on their mooring lines and the flaking white paint, they looked as though they had been unused for many years:

"Orange boats," Lucy explained. "These islands have always been famous for growing mandarin oranges. They still are. You've probably seen those odd little funicular railways that run up and down the hills; those are so that the farmers can reach the steepest slopes. And the boats were designed to be able to pack in the maximum number of wooden orange crates. They didn't have to be seaworthy, they sculled them from island to island with those long, odd-looking hinged oars."

In the fading light of the summer evening Lucy took us home for tea at her rickety old bungalow behind Mitarai. We took turns luxuriating in her cedar hot tub. Her Japanese husband worked during the week and many weekends on the mainland. To our unspoken question, she answered a little wistfully:

"I read a lot. I look after the oranges… I suppose you could call it a Japanese marriage. It's not like a western marriage. I'm not unhappy."

Next day, we assembled our folding bike, rented a second bike (there always seemed to be somewhere that you could cheaply rent a classic sit-up-and-beg bicycle with no gears), and took the ferry to a neighboring island, Osakikamijima. Kinoe, its main town, was another former pleasure town, another that attracted Donald Richie's interest and musing on sex in Japan. Its heyday was a little later than Mitarai's and there survive old sepia photographs

Oiran grave markers, Mitarai

of "honorable prostitute boats," putting out from the Kinoe waterfront to the sailing ships—and by now a few steamships—in the roads.

The prostitutes are long gone, following criminalization in 1958. The local girls had tried to circumvent the law by joining geisha associations, for these were still legal, but the much more refined geishas would have none of it.

There was no one to be seen today in the overhanging streets behind the waterfront, and many of the shops looked as though they had been locked up for years. There were painted signs advertising cigarettes, perfumes, and ladies' fashions. But you could tell from the rust and the designs that they were from the seventies at the latest; in other places they'd have been in a museum. It started to rain heavily so we sought refuge in one of the few lit shops, a barbershop, with old-fashioned red-leather reclining chairs. We had to roust out the barber from a nearby house. While Jenny watched, I had a haircut and an ostensibly cordial conversation without my understanding a word that was being said to me.

A rainy day in Kinoe

But Kinoe was not completely moribund. Cycling a little past the town, we came to a rustic but active shipyard where a 120-foot steel coaster was being assembled on the slipways. Green trees overhung the half-built ship; in an office that was no more than a wooden shack, the construction team was sheltering from the rain over a cup of green tea. This was not exactly how you might imagine the great shipyards of Asia, turning out cookie-cutter supertankers.

On a hillside above the ferry terminal was a bizarre construction: the white prow of a large vessel apparently protruding from the lush undergrowth behind. It was a concrete "ship," a museum to regional shipbuilding. It was well maintained, imaginative, and informative, a worthy idea by the local municipality. But you couldn't help wondering where the tourists were going to come from. Except at Miyajima on the O-Bon holiday, we'd seen scarcely an outsider in the islands, and now was the peak of summer.

Calculating the tidal currents carefully, we edged our way north and east from Mitarai, past more shipyards incongruously located in wooded bays on tiny islands. At one of them, three massive but oddly detached stern sections were under construction. There was no sign of the hull segments to which they would eventually be attached; in fact there would obviously not be room for such segments. Clearly this yard specialized in sterns only and shipped them onwards by barge, one at a time.

We sailed slowly past Omishima and into the mouth of a beautiful wide bay at Miyaura. As always when we are approaching an unfamiliar location, Jenny had the binoculars out and we were moving ahead only very slowly:

"There's a man in a white shirt," she eventually said. "And he's waving at us frantically."

"Waving us in or waving us away?" (this a little impatiently).

"In, I think, yes, definitely in."

Our friend in the white shirt was the municipality's designated yacht welcomer; he'd driven down to our pontoon as soon as he caught sight of us from his office on the top floor of the town hall. He fussed with papers as he chattered on in Japanese and then presented us with what was evidently a bill. After some study I queried it:

"Yes, one yen for one ton." he said, beaming.

"We are four tons…"

"Sou desu ka? Then is four yen."

Last time we had checked, the exchange rate was 80 yen to 1 USD. A night's stay was going to cost us about 5 US cents.

Miyaura is home to the major Shinto shrine called Oyamazumi, one of the three most important in Japan, and dedicated to the gods who protect soldiers and sailors. Notwithstanding its fame, its low wooden buildings, set around a courtyard in a wooded glade with giant camphor trees, were again deserted. On the walls of one corridor were photographs of visiting dignitaries dating back to the earliest days of photography, many of them in military uniform. Although these pictures were not labelled, some were clearly from the thirties and forties when generals were frequent visitors. One appeared to include the thin, bespectacled Tojo and his entourage, undistinguished looking in their rumpled khakis. A monk happily showed us around most of the temple but was mute in front of the photographs. Adjoining the shrine was a museum with Japan's best collection of samurai armor: strange outfits of cloth, bamboo, and leather, some of them 800 years old—like something out of Star Wars. One would have thought them no match for the awesome sword blades on show beside them.

Back on the waterfront, we could see that there was a much smaller but picturesquely located shrine reached along a short coastal path. We walked out in the late evening. A young couple was coming the other way, arm in arm. When they saw us, they looked suddenly embarrassed and shuffled past us, faces averted. We realized why when we reached the shrine and peered into its darkened interior. Here were dozens of vertically aligned stone and wooden penises ranging from a modest 10 cm to 30 cm or more, tastefully arranged in a symmetrical pattern. It was a fertility shrine, a place where couples wishing to conceive come to pray (and perhaps head off into the dark woods behind to have their prayers immediately answered).

Calculating the flood tide carefully, we wove a complicated route from Omishima between green islands, down back channels and under soaring but car-less suspension bridges, to Yuge. We tied up to a long floating pontoon set aside just for yachts.

"Ahaa," said Jenny poring over handwritten notes made months earlier in Kyushu. "It says 'Good Onsen, but expensive.'"

The Onsen, in a large hotel on the hill, with sweeping views east and west over still waters, was indeed on the pricey side at USD12 or so. But we were now well and truly into the culture; we appreciated the different temperatures of its various baths, the option of lounging outside in the slightly cooler air, the dark bracingly cool seaweed tub. Our inhibitions were now long gone, and it seemed the most natural thing in the world to be strolling around naked from pool to pool, exchanging pleasantries with somnolent neighbors with tiny square towels on their head, admiring the ocean views. Before westerners arrived in Japan, we had learned, Onsens were usually mixed. That scene was a bit more difficult to imagine. Can they really have had the anodyne, sexless ambiance of today's baths? Or was that famous self-discipline of the Japanese man so strong that nothing untoward ever transpired?

As the idyllically hot and nearly windless summer wore on, it was sometimes difficult to remember that this was a dangerous time. On Monday August 29th the Joint Typhoon Warning Center (JTWC) in Hawaii indicated two major storms in the offing: Nan-Madol was likely to roll into Taiwan and Talas (Number 12 of the season for Japan) was headed straight for us. Tied to our pontoon at Yuge we had islands all around us. But even a fetch as short as 200 meters could kick up seas that would be dangerous for *Bosun Bird*. The complicated mountain topography could render strong winds lethal. We studied the chart

Onomichi

and all our data carefully and decided to seek refuge a few miles to the North at Onomichi, a port on the big island of Honshu accessed by a river-like channel that promised the best protection for many miles around.

The ten-mile sail on a sunny day took us three hours. Sliding under an ultra-modern suspension bridge, we silently passed shipyards where more half-finished tankers seemed to have their sterns suspended over the water; launches buzzed back and forth; a car ferry crossed our bows; and on both sides now buildings crammed every foot of the waterfront. Onomichi looked to be a grubby, slightly seedy place but as vibrant as anywhere we'd yet been in Japan. With the sails down and the engine on, we eased into a tiny marina that had been improvised behind the shelter of a semi-abandoned ferry dock. We found out that we were only just in time; all the Japanese yachts in the neighborhood (three, that is) had hurried here with the same objective of safe refuge.

Ando San on *Banantem* was a professor of French at Nagoya University so we enjoyed practicing some French with him. Shigeki, on *Sense of Wind*, was intrigued by our self-steering gear, but much more interested in telling us of his grand plans for sailing around the world than in any practical advice we might be able to offer. He did, however, ask how to anchor a yacht; like everyone else, he did not own an anchor. And here as well was the 85-year-old liver-spotted Mr. *Olive* from Mitarai, climbing ever so gingerly on and off his boat but apparently coping well.

We all chatted and helped each other out as we stripped our boats down; the more you can lessen your wind resistance in a typhoon, by taking down sails, stowing everything below and generally lowering your profile, the better. Roller-furling sails are especially at risk: unless they are rolled up exceptionally tight and, ideally, secured along their length with an extra lashing, they risk being forcibly opened by an especially strong gust, starting to unravel, and then whipping themselves to shreds.

That evening we had everyone over for a drink, but our friends brought plenty of liquor of their own. As always, if I was grinningly offered a beer or another glass of whisky, Jenny would be lucky if someone remembered to ask her if maybe she'd like a Coke or a glass of water. It was grudgingly recognized, in front of her, that it might be nice to have someone cook your breakfast aboard.

Donald Richie muses (he happens to be in Onomichi at the time, and spends most of a night in a seedy strip-joint) that:

"In Japan women have things to say only to other women… They can talk forever. With a man the woman tends to become silent. Talking to men, that is the role of the geisha, the bar hostess. It is not the role of the well brought-up traditional Japanese woman. The men of both cultures prefer the conversation of their own sex."

Next morning, with Talas still twenty hours or more away, traffic on the river began to lessen noticeably, and with it the periodic annoying wakes that would rock us from one side to the other. City employees showed up. They worked their way all along the Onomichi waterfront, closing the heavy stainless-steel gates in the sea wall that protected the town from the abnormally high sea levels that could be predicted in either a tsunami or—as a result of extreme low pressure—in the eye of a typhoon. Iron shutters went down over the shop fronts, public transport stopped running. In the evening all but a few of the streetlights were doused.

With the storm approaching land, we could now plot position updates from the JTWC every three hours.

"Sustained 50 knots, gusting to 70," Jenny would read. "CPA for Iwakuni 100 nautical miles, 0600 Zulu."

Iwakuni was one of a number of American bases in Japan that were always listed by the Pearl Harbor-based JTWC as points of reference for approaching typhoons, CPA standing for Closest Point of Approach, Zulu for Greenwich Mean Time.

As evening came on, the sky blackened, and steady rain began. Cloud cover was so heavy that it was difficult to see what the winds were like at higher altitudes, but late at night we started to read reports on the Internet of massive seas hitting the exposed Pacific shores of Shikoku Island, and the Pacific lighthouses reporting 80 to 90 knots of wind. The typhoon's course was unchanged: the eye would pass within twenty or thirty miles.

Our choice had been a good one. Talas came through at about 3:00 a.m. It broke all rainfall records for Japan, and killed seventy-seven people, mostly as a result of catastrophic flooding and landslides. But in Onomichi we hardly felt it. In fact, it was calmer in our little haven with the typhoon warning than it was when boats had been going about their normal business a day or so earlier. After a prudent pause, the great steel gates were reopened in mid-morning and the city got back to work. When the first papers came out after the storm, and in spite of the death toll, Talas merited only a side-column on the front page of the English-language *Japan Times*.

For a moment, this nonchalance seemed surprising to us. But…thousands of typhoons over hundreds of years, how could they have not shaped the national character? Stoicism and pragmatism in the face of inevitable hardship and death, working together in the face of adversity, valuing the community over the individual: this was precisely what was needed when you lived in an environment where natural catastrophe was common, more than performative outrage.

We recalled the weeks after our arrival in Japan in the wake of the Fukushima catastrophe. We'd followed the ongoing saga as best we could, absent regular access to television and newspapers that we could understand. What had struck us at that time, more than anything, was the quiet reaction of the average Japanese person to it all. It was not indifference at all—the Japanese Red Cross was collecting on every street corner and in every shopping mall, and young people volunteered in their hundreds to help the homeless and aged—but there was no massive outpouring of grief. Just stoical acceptance.

To the bewilderment of many western observers however, there was little overt criticism of the incompetence of Fukushima's operator, the massive, monopolistic Tokyo Electric Power Company (TEPCO), or of botched cover-ups by the government. This was another face, not so positive perhaps, of acceptance.

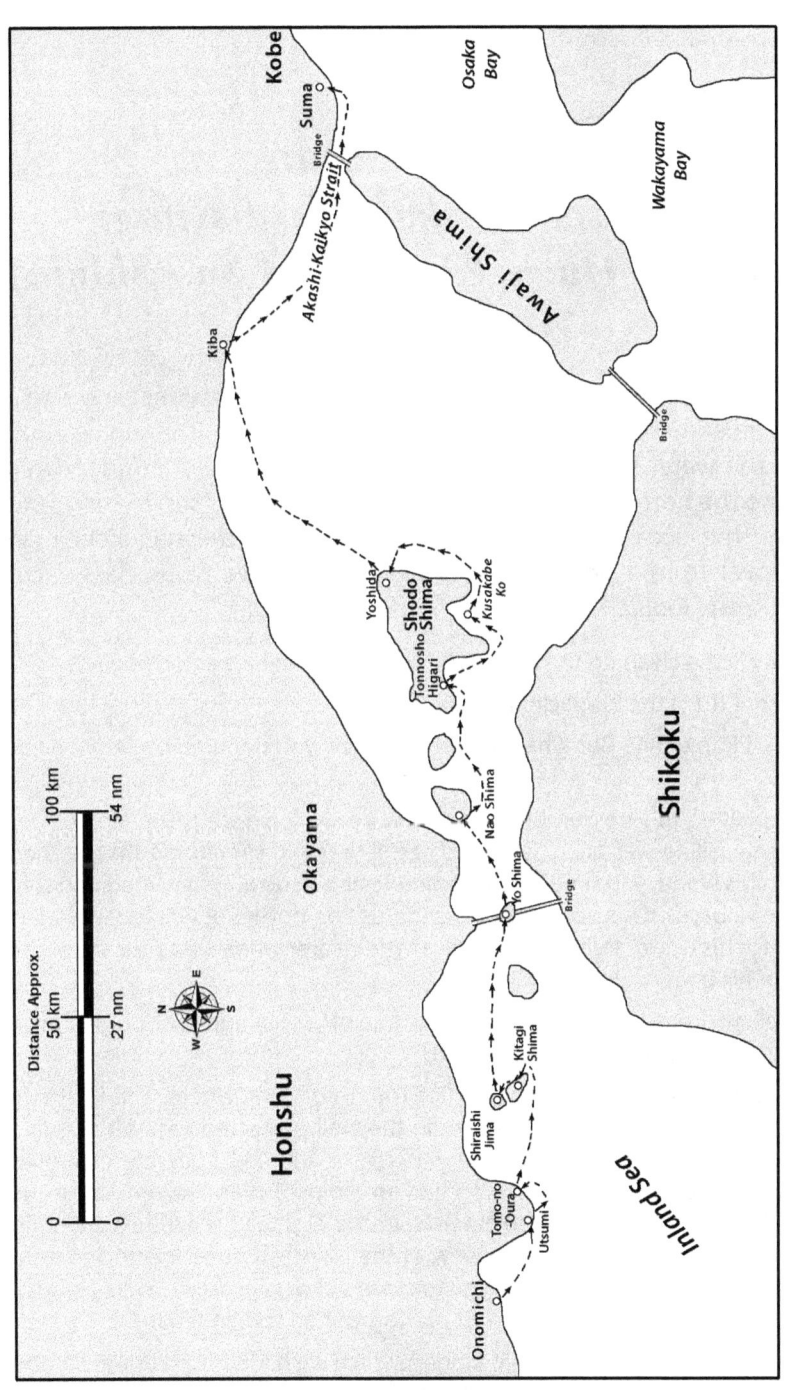

Omonichi to Suma

Chapter Ten:
The Three Musketeers of Kitagi
(Tomo-no-Oura, Kitagi, and Nao Shima)

Once Typhoon Talas was past, we meandered east once more to a quiet marina on another bucolic island: Utsumi. The sun was out, the water was warm, so the crew was set to work underwater, cleaning the bottom. While I was sitting in the cockpit "supervising" and offering the occasional comment, a very smartly dressed older man came over from a neighboring boat, an expensive Baltic-class yacht named *Silver Cloud*.

"Why is she cleaning the bottom?" he asked in well-accented English.

"To get rid of the barnacles and weed."

"Yes, I know that. But what I mean is why do you not employ someone to do this?"

I explained to Hiro San but he was not really convinced. The idea of Do-it-Yourself sailing was alien, we could see. If you had something that needed fixing in his world, you simply paid someone else to do it. Hiro invited us out to lunch and, back on his boat, pressed upon us two bottles of vintage wine. The reason for his way of thinking became a little clearer when we asked about the name of his boat:

"Well, you see, I have a Bentley and some other vintage cars, but my prize possession is a Rolls Royce Silver Cloud."

Next stop was the old port town of Tomo-no-Oura, where, a rarity, there was actually enough space to anchor in the well-protected bay. With houses tumbling down the hillside to the waterfront and the quayside crammed with flag-flying fishing boats, Tomo had an almost Italian feel and, as in the Mediterranean, there were also tourists. In the eighteenth century a visiting Korean delegation described the view of the island-studded Inland Sea from here as "the finest in Japan." Today's Japanese visitors are drawn to that kind of rating, as at Miyajima (the third most photographed spot in Japan…).

We pumped up our inflatable dinghy, which we hadn't used in weeks, and rowed ashore, finding a convenient set of steps in the old harbor wall and a

Tomo-no-Oura; Bosun Bird is lower right

rusting iron ring at its head. From a doorway across the road, a young man smoking a cigarette watched us intently then, throwing down the butt, came over decisively.

"I am pleased to meet you," he said in good English.

He took my arm. My heart sank.

"Like you, I am a Christian. I was saved," and he launched into a long story of how he had come to see the light but had now been rejected by his family.

He was slightly deranged. I was annoyed by the assumption that just because we were westerners, we necessarily shared his faith and wanted to hear all about it. But we kept silent until he concluded:

"Now please you will come to Church with me, and we will pray together."

It was time to make our getaway. I broke away and we muttered some excuse. He followed for more than a hundred meters, lapsing back into evidently angry Japanese before finally slouching back to his doorway. But the man hunted us for the next two days, apparently watching and waiting till we came ashore, then accosting us again, with entreaties and the occasional threat in English:

"If you do not read the Bible you will burn in hell!"

We went in search of what that Korean envoy had in 1711 dubbed "the finest view." Unfortunately, you now have to pay to stand exactly where he stood. But by craning your neck a little at a strategic point on the waterfront you can see more or less what the diplomat saw: a small rocky and wooded island in the strait, with a tiny shrine and red Tori: Benten Jima. It's quaint enough and things cannot have greatly changed in three hundred years. But there was no getting away from the fact that it scarcely lived up to the hype. There is actually a much better view from halfway up the hill to the west of town, but we guessed that Korean Ambassadors did not do hills.

The goddess Benten (or Benzaiten) features in both Buddhism and Shintoism and has an interesting pedigree. She is originally the Hindu goddess Saraswati and represents everything that flows: water, words, speech, music, knowledge. Worship of Benten arrived in Japan from China as early as the sixth century. As time went on, she was grouped together with six other protecting deities (all male) and often shown in a ship with the others; they are known as the Seven Lucky Gods. On account of her nautical associations, you find effigies of and reference to Benten throughout the Inland Sea. The ubiquitous monk Kobo Daishi was a follower of Benten's and wrote at length about her, claiming her rather for Buddhism than Shintoism. Every tourist shop in Tomo-no-Oura had images of Benten and/or her shrine, usually with the Korean envoy in the foreground, admiring the island and stroking his long beard.

More prosaically, we met a Japanese man in a restaurant who had spent four years working at a restaurant in Dutch Harbor, in the Aleutians. His English was more authentic and colloquial than most:

"Yeah, man, fuckin' hard work…but you know fuckin' what? I made a pile o'bucks and now I'm back… Tough town, Dutch. All fishing, ev'ry fuckin' nationality you can think of…but hard drinkers, no shit man, hard fuckin' drinkers."

There were more temples and shrines to be visited and narrow streets to explore, but we liked Tomo less than some of the much quieter island ports we'd visited over the past few weeks. The skyline, ominously, was dominated by a high-rise hotel. There was a plan to drive a four-lane highway right over the harbor so as to ease traffic congestion.

Ten miles to the east of Tomo we came to a comma-shaped island called Kitagi Shima, long known as an island of stonecutters. In a disused stonecutters' warehouse, Canadian Colin Ferrel and his Japanese wife Mika had set up in business as sailmakers and ship's chandlers.

They allowed us to tie up next to their fishing boat, lent us bikes and were our enthusiastic hosts for the next two weeks. While Colin's team of local seamstresses was busy stitching repairs into our tired sails, we explored the island thoroughly, as well as briefly hunkering down for yet another typhoon. Nakamura San and Kinari San, two of Colin's retired friends who had made it their mission to welcome strangers, took us round first by car, arranging private visits to two of the remaining stone factories. Where there used to be sixty, now there are only twenty or so such establishments, all operating at reduced capacity.

"It's the Chinese," the owner of one of the factories told us. "Their granite is cheaper, labor is cheaper, so most of the business has moved offshore; some of our rivals here on Kitagi even find it economical to import Chinese stone, but we still prefer Kitagi stone."

The main business of the factories was fabricating and engraving tombstones. We watched how the granite slabs were cut and polished, and how then with the use of computer-generated stencils, the kanji characters were engraved deep into the granite.

"How much for a complete grave set for the whole family?" we asked.

"Hmm…well this set over here that we are working on would be about US $20,000. But remember that you can put as many sets of ashes inside the tomb as you wish, so it should last you for several generations."

We asked why it was that in cemeteries the engraved characters were usually in black, white, or even gold, but very occasionally red?

"Ah yes. The red is for people who have not died yet. That way, you do not have to engrave the stone again when new sets of ashes are placed there…you just efface the red coloring and replace it with black."

Nakamura and Kinari were both in their late sixties and were not island-born. They were rare exceptions to the outward flow of people from the islands and rural Japan to the cities. They'd decided on retirement to leave their city

The Three Musketeers take us on a tour of Kitagi

lives and their wives behind and live their island dream. It hadn't been, and still wasn't all easy. With Kinari translating for him, Nakamura mused:

"There is a saying about these small communities in Japan. If you have a fire, yes, the villagers will help you put it out, if only because it might spread to their house. And if you die, well they do not want the body to smell, so they will bury you… But apart from that: you will not be accepted."

There were boarded-up, locked houses everywhere. Meanwhile, we knew the population of Japan was aging, more and more people were retiring. In spite of the insularity of the locals, why didn't more city people come?

"It is a good question. More than half the houses in Kitagi are empty. But perhaps you have noticed: there is nothing for sale. In Japan people will never sell their ancestral home, it is too important to them. When they die, they must be buried here. So, we can only rent here, never buy."

Both of them were relaxed about having left their wives on the "mainland" and saw nothing odd about it. It seemed to us to be another example of the different outlook many Japanese had on marriage. Nakamura and Kinari would both shrug.

"They like the city life…shopping on the Ginza. Their friends are in the city. And they do not like the sun, the wind… I think all Japanese ladies like to keep their skin white."

We went one afternoon to Nakamura's for a tea ceremony, with Kinari stepping in to translate when Nakamura's enthusiasm as a stand-in geisha was not matched by his English skills. His cluttered home was a museum of models of sailing ships and tacky nautical memorabilia. On one wall was a large red and white life ring emblazoned with "Welcome! Have Fan!" Packed against another wall were cardboard boxes full of 1950's and 60's collectors' vinyls of Japanese recording stars. On shelves, nooks and piled in the kitchen were coffee-making machines from all over, many of them obtained, Nakamura said gleefully, by rummaging around in 100-yen stores.

Nakamura kept by his door a white board, where international visitors had left photos and messages. Here was a picture of Tom and Vicky on *Sunstone*, who'd preceded us by a year in Japan, and who had been friends ever since we had met them in Patagonia seven years earlier. And here was one from American single-hander Joe on *Risalka*, whom we'd lost touch with since we last saw him in New Zealand. Now he was only a month ahead of us; we copied down his email address.

Kinari, Nakamura, and Colin—as the three outsiders on Kitagi—were an informal, mutual support club and they saw a lot of each other. They called themselves the Three Musketeers. It had been hard for Colin at the beginning, too. He had sailed to Japan many years earlier, spent a few years in the business of importing luxury foreign cars—where he had met his wife Mika—then had spotted an interesting market niche. The sailing community in Japan was small but it was well-moneyed, most of its members living in relatively wealthy retirement. There were yacht chandleries, but these were usually located in premium locations where they paid very high rent and they outsourced their sail-making, taking an excessively high margin. Colin paid almost no rent for a very large space; was strategically located for any and all passing yachts in the Inland Sea; employed local labor; and had started an effective online order business. Mika proudly chipped in:

"Colin has done so well that people from the city council have come to study this model."

Colin and Mika lived in an unusual house on a hilltop, walled in grey-painted corrugated iron, that used to be a helicopter hangar—this from the days when the stone-cutting business was far more lucrative and the Big Men flew in from the mainland. They shared their home with two locally adopted Kitagi cats. Like many of the islands of the Seto Naikai, Kitagi seemed almost to be overrun with cats, who did surprisingly well on the scraps left for them by fishermen, as well as furtive feeding sessions at the hands of ubiquitous Little Old Ladies.

Like many people who have once been to sea, Colin wanted to go again. To this end, he had bought at a bargain basement price a sixty-foot racing yacht that for years had been propped up on land in a Shikoku boatyard. It had a fine pedigree—it had won a TransPac race from San Francisco to Hawaii—but it was set up for a crew of at least twelve. It took four people just to get the mainsail from the shore and onto the boom. You needed a microphone system if you were in the cockpit and you needed to speak to someone in the bows. It would take a huge amount of work to fit it up for cruising with just two people.

Two other island residents were Kiwi yachtie Fenton Hamlin, who worked part-time for Colin, and his Japanese friend Kojima. Kojima, as well as having us over to her home for baths in her cedar tub and a slap-up dinner, bombarded us almost daily with bags of fresh vegetables from her garden. Contrary to the stereotype, Kojima really didn't mind the sun and the wind. So, Fenton, who had already persuaded Kojima to come along with him several times on his beautiful home-built Lyle Hess wooden cutter, *Pateke*, was hopeful that one day they would sail off into the sunset together.

One of the downsides of long-distance sailing is that while you make friends in so many places, you're always saying goodbye. You promise to keep in touch, and for a while you do. Email has helped with that. But the leave-takings can be difficult. When it's time to go, we usually tell friends that we'll be off soon but that we don't know when, and they're not to wait around for us or come and see us off. That way we can slip away quietly and keep our thoughts to ourselves. So it was when we moved on again from Kitagi, only a few miles to the north, to Shiraishi Jima. Half an hour out, we'd only exchanged a few words. Then Jenny remembered:

"This is where Richie tells that long story about the cat."

The writer had come to Kitagi expecting everyone to know a legend about a cat that had long ago been thrown into the water and had resurfaced, to be immortalized in stone. But none of the fishermen knew anything at all about it. They all thought he was an absolute fool to be looking for a cat that had been thrown into the sea hundreds of years earlier. But there it was: a pile of yellowish rocks on the north tip of the island, that if you'd been told and if you half-closed your eyes, you might agree looked like an animal. There is so much history, so many myths and legends in these waters that every rock, tree, and hill has some special association.

At Shiraishi Jima we found a secure berth on a pontoon in the island's otherwise empty New Harbor, a large rectangular walled pool. Immediately, we had new friends from the sailboat on the other side of the pontoon. In a rare exception to the Japanese single handers' rule, Captain Maruo Shuozo, who carefully introduced himself in English as an Aircarrier Airworthiness Engineer, from Osaka, had recruited a friend to crew for him on his yacht. Ryozo ceremonially bowed after he had come aboard and presented to us his card:

"Ryozo Shinohara," it read. "Professor (Baritone)."

As an operatic voice-coach and lover of all things Italian, Ryozo proudly dished up some spaghetti for us that evening. We talked a lot about Japanese culture and music.

"It's odd," I said, "that on the one hand you have preserved ancient cultural traditions virtually intact and unchanged over hundreds of years…".

And I mentioned "Nō" (also written Noh) as an example: a kind of dance drama that is performed on a bare stage and has a small set of roles, players, and plots that have only evolved minimally over hundreds of years. Usually, Nō performers inherit their roles from their parents or grandparents. It's not exactly a popular art form. Japanese friends said to us they could hardly understand Nō plays, which can go on for many hours. But it survives almost as a cultural treasure, in isolation from the modern world. The few performances that are given these days are sold out instantly.

"…but alongside this, you have embraced western culture with huge enthusiasm!"

"Yes," said Ryozo. "You must remember that for many hundreds of years this was the most closed, insular society in the world. Then under the Meiji Emperors, there was this dramatic, very fast opening-up to the world. That's when opera and classical music came in. They were incredibly novel, we had seen nothing like it before…and it became very snob, very cool to know about opera. There was another sudden opening after the war…but the old Japanese art forms never quite died away."

I asked if Japan was now developing its own newer art forms. Ryozo had a brief, animated conversation with Maruo, then turned back to us:

The Moo Bar, Shiraishi Jima

"Well, it's a different medium, but perhaps Anime is something new and Japanese. It started by copying American comics, but I think it's now got a life of its own."

"And J-Pop?" I asked, thinking of the smash-hit group AKB48.

"Oh no," Maruo laughed. "My kids love it. But actually, I think it's rubbish… I don't think it will last."

Shiraishi was the part-time home of expats Amy and Paul (American and Australian), who in the summer season ran the Moo Bar, on Shiraishi's fine sandy beach. It was the last weekend of the season, so we went along to a grand closing barbecue and found ourselves with more foreigners than we had seen in Japan so far, that is to say about a dozen.

We were given a little glimpse into the society through which most English-speaking foreigners, for the past thirty years or so, have come to know Japan: that of ESL (English as a Second Language) teachers. It's a society that has been shrinking in size as the economically strapped Japanese have lost their appetite for the perceived luxury of English classes. Meanwhile the salaries that are offered have become much less attractive. But it's a whole world of its own, replete with bitchiness, gossip, and whining.

We'd respond to the standard inquiry "So how do you like Japan?" with great enthusiasm. But the expression that usually came back said it all: a rueful, sardonic smile that seemed to imply "You don't know the real Japan."

We wondered if this was true. We'd been treated throughout with outstanding kindness and hospitality. Our Japanese friends had been much more open in discussing their culture, warts and all, than we had ever expected. Had we just been lucky? Perhaps, I wondered, it was because we were doing something unusual, something to be considered carefully and with interest by our hosts. And on the other hand, by coming on a boat, we were proclaiming to Japanese sailors that we were members of their club. We had learned that the Japanese are great lovers of clubs, of exclusive sets. Young men who joined a Karate Club at University typically stay in touch with fellow members throughout their lives; Yukio Mishima's novels[31] are full of such references. And there can be no country where more school reunions are held.

But if you arrive on a plane as an ESL teacher then you have no special entrée, no cachet. The young men and women on the beach confessed freely:

"No, I have no Japanese friends…in fact I have never been invited to a Japanese home, and I've been here two years. I've picked up some Japanese, but I can't say I understand them at all. It's like we're from two worlds."

I remembered an anecdote that Tim, a college friend of mine who had come here as just such a teacher in the eighties told me:

"I'd been in Osaka about six months. I used to go to the language school by bike every morning. I was very careful to be polite to my neighbors. I felt after all that time that I was just starting to make some headway with them. We'd moved past Good Morning to a little chit-chat about the weather, or the baseball results. Then abruptly, one day they stopped talking to me, they avoided me, wouldn't say a word. I couldn't figure out what had happened."

"So what was it about?"

"Well, a full three or four months later I told another teacher friend. He thought for a while, then he asked me: 'Did you start to park your bike somewhere else when the rainy season began?'"

"I had… I'd put it under the little shelter between our two houses. Now I realized I'd broken some taboo. I guess it was on their piece of land; but they weren't going to say a thing. I moved the bike out into the rain again, and the neighbors started speaking to me again."

We were also convinced that getting to know the Japanese (to the admittedly limited extent that we had done so) was also a function of doing some homework and showing interest in their culture. Nori from Fukuoka and Nakamura from Kitagi used to chuckle with sheer delight when Jenny or I would ask them some obscure question like why the baby Buddhas wore

---

31   Yukio Mishima (1925 – 1970), author, poet, playwright. His best-known novels include *The Temple of the Golden Pavilion* (1994, New York, NY: Vintage) and *Confessions of a Mask* (2017, London, Penguin). He is controversial for his right-wing, nationalist politics. In November 1970 Mishima entered a military base in central Tokyo, took its commander hostage, and unsuccessfully tried to inspire the army to rise up and terminate the constitution of 1947; when there was no response, he committed ritual seppuku.

red caps or why was it that Japanese houses had no gutters. They often didn't have the answer, but next time we saw them they would have done their own research with friends or on the Internet and proudly explain. It was a benign manifestation of nationalism.

Amy, in contrast to many of the teachers, spoke excellent Japanese and was able to enlighten us on various esoteric questions regarding Buddhism and Shintoism, the result of many years of asking questions like ours. She had recently run the length of a famous pilgrimage circuit on Shikoku Island that takes in 88 shrines (the same one that Yae Murasaki of Mitarai had undertaken in atonement) and was about to publish a book about her experiences.[32]

Ever east. Timing our passage as always to take maximum advantage of the currents, we spent a leisurely day tacking for 16 miles. We were quite close to the shoreline of Honshu now and away to the left you could see, in contrast to the green and largely deserted islands between which we were threading a route, the chimneys of steel mills and the tanks of oil refineries and natural gas farms.

Our stop that night was a strange one. Cut into the side of a small island called Yo Shima was the usual rectangular artificial harbor with a convenient pontoon. Rising from the very center of the island was an enormous vertical pier that supported, 50 meters above our heads, a two-tier bridge, rail and road. For much of the day, trains clattered overhead, from Honshu to Shikoku or vice-versa. For a few minutes as the sun passed, we were in the shadow of the bridge. An off-ramp spiralled down in three or four tight bends to our small island. There was a large car park (with no cars), a video arcade, and a restaurant complex called (in English) Fishermen's Wharf. It had been some time since the place had functioned; we peered in through great plate-glass windows, but all the tables were stacked up and there were dust sheets over the serving counters.

The gaps between the islands here were narrow, the currents stronger than ever. It must be a prime location for shipping accidents, we thought. That night we were briefly disturbed when a large fire-tug with a huge artillery-like water cannon tied up on the other side of the pontoon. It patrolled these waters, up and down, waiting for collisions. The place was eerie, post-apocalyptic, and we weren't sorry to hurry on next morning.

Nao Shima was even more unworldly, but in a more positive way. Richie, of course, had been here as well, forty years earlier. He spent an afternoon flirting with a group of schoolgirls in their cute sailor suits but describes Nao Shima as:

---

32   Chavez, Amy. (2013). *Running the Shikoku Pilgrimage: 900 Miles to Enlightenment.* Volcano, CA: Volcano Press.

In the shadow of the inter-island bridge, Yo Shima

"...a small, beautiful, somehow sad little island... The sadness came perhaps from the loneliness."

This time there were people around. Until twenty or so years ago, this was an island that was dying like so many other islands, with the population—including those now grown-up schoolgirls—leaving in droves. Then the Benesse Foundation, whose wealth is derived from health and education services, decided to make Nao Shima the site of an all-island museum of contemporary art. Monets, Warhols, and Hockneys adorn the interior walls of a modernistic hotel. In the main village six houses have been taken over and restored as stand-alone exhibits. One has a Statue of Liberty breaking through two floors; another has submerged and colored LED displays ticking over the numbers one to nine in a pool in a darkened room, while a third has you sit in apparently total darkness for ten minutes before the faintest of visions appears eerily before your straining eyes. On a jetty stands an enormous yellow and black pumpkin, the work of Yayoi Kusama; while at the ferry terminal there's a similar black and red squash inside which you can shelter from the rain.

Nao Shima's traditional Japanese Sento, in the village behind the harbor, has been given a makeover. Outside it is lit up with red and purple neon like an Art Deco movie theater. There is the usual grandma in John Lennon glasses who eyes you as you get undressed, and inside there is the same high dividing wall, with the classic blue ceramic paintings at either end. But this is a Sento with a difference. Striding along the center wall, its back grazing the ceiling, is a near life-size African elephant. The taps at the stalls that line both sides have pictures of Marilyn Monroe set into their clear plastic controls. Disconcertingly, as you step gingerly into the piping hot bath in the middle of the room (on the men's side…), you notice that the floor is a mosaic of old postcards, pictures of 50's movie stars and—wait!—pornographic woodcuts from sixteenth century tomes of Edo erotica. Erotica in a public bath? I averted my gaze to the elephant on the dividing wall.

When we came out and were putting our shoes on beneath the gaze of grandma, I asked Jenny to describe the floor of the bath on the ladies' side:

"Well, I don't know really…just a few old postcards of the Eiffel Tower, I think."

Yayoi Kusama's pumpkin, Nao Shima

Chapter Eleven: Twenty-Four Eyes (Shodo Shima and Kiba)

We were now nearing the eastern end of the Seto Naikai, and approaching its second largest island, Shodo Shima. Here the theme wasn't modern art, but olives, introduced from the USA a hundred years ago. But California hasn't quite the aura of Greece and Italy. So, the Welcome to Shodo Shima sign at the main ferry port was executed in Greek characters, there was a fake Greek windmill nearby, and Greek and Italian flags flew. The stores sold everything from olive-flavored chocolate and ice cream to olive-shaped Hello Kitties, olive-colored bathroom linen and olive soap.

"But you can't actually buy any olives anywhere," Jenny complained after an hour or two wandering around town.

With autumn approaching and just the slightest hint of yellow and red in the leaves, we took a long hike one clear day to the 800-meter-high summit of Shodo Shima. The next day, with the first rain in months teeming down, we made an interesting literary pilgrimage. Not, this time, in memory of Donald Richie and his enigmatic encounters, but of the much more homely Sakae Tsuboi.

Ms. Tsuboi (1899-1967) was a poet and novelist born on Shodo Shima, the fifth daughter of a maker of soy sauce barrels. Her most famous work, and the only one translated into English, is *Twenty-Four Eyes*,[33] set over an eighteen-year span starting in 1928. It tells the stories of an untried woman teacher and her twelve charges at a tiny rural school on the island. After they move on to high school, they keep in touch but then the war intervenes; few of the boys return. The book was made into an award-winning black and white movie in 1954 and re-made in color in the eighties. It remains a firm favorite with the older generation in Japan:

---

33 Tsuboi, Sakae. (2007). *Twenty-Four Eyes*. North Clarendon, VT: Tuttle Publishing.

Sakae Tsuboi's old school, Shodo Shima

"The village numbered only slightly more than a hundred families and was situated at the tip of a long cape that made the bay appear to be a lake..." the story begins.

With just the one bike between us and no public transport around to the cape on the far side of the bay, I set off two hours in advance of Jenny, on foot. After twenty minutes, the light drizzle had intensified, and I was soaked. But with my shoes squelching, we arrived within a few minutes of each other at Tanoura, on the end of the peninsula. This is where the author went to school and the place she said was in her mind when she wrote. In spite of the pouring rain there were tour buses parked outside the reconstructed wooden village that was used as a set for the color re-make and where there was, predictably, a steep entry fee. But the old one-room schoolhouse, the real one where she had taught, still stood, a kilometer or so away.

The cedar-shake walls were dark from the blowing rain, which was running in waves down small-paned windows of thick, old glass. The school was built in 1902 and was used right through to 1972. Everything had been left as it was on the last day of term. There were ten or so infant-sized desks, with their chairs built in, facing the teacher's much more imposing desk, set on a platform. There was a box full of giant wooden geometrical instruments for teaching: a large set square, an outsize compass that took chalk. On the walls were world maps from the 1960s; there was a harmonium on one corner; curling charts of kanji characters flanked the blackboard. Stacked neatly on the windowsill was a set of slates. I felt old; I recalled using a slate myself when six years old, and they seemed so antiquated now. But modern times were already coming in the seventies; in a cardboard box were exercise books from the very last class of boys and girls to graduate from here.

You could see the appeal of the place for any Japanese in their sixties or seventies who grew up in rural Japan. This is how it was for them, or at least how they would have liked it to be. The novel is in itself an exercise in nostalgia as Miss Kobayashi, after a sequence of never-ending Indian summers at Tanoura, strives to keep contact with her former charges. The years pass; the war takes its toll.

As for the black-and-white movie of Twenty-Four Eyes, it was a smash hit in the austere fifties as the hardship-inured Japanese, still rebuilding after the devastation of the war, reveled in remembering more sunny, innocent pre-war times. If you were of that age and sentimental, now you could come back yet again: nostalgia for nostalgia. Conveniently, the anti-war message of Twenty-Four Eyes was quiet and melancholic, not an angry one. Not much blame is assigned. One time the teacher is moved to tears as, picking up on the obvious reference to death in the mention of cherry blossoms (obvious to a Japanese, that is), she hears the boys sing:

> *Navy officers' coats*
> *All have seven buttons.*
> *Cherry blossoms and anchors*
> *Are marked on all of them.*

There was one final island group to the east of Shodo Shima, where we intended to stop before touching the shore of Honshu again at Himeji and making the run east into Osaka Bay. But Ie Jima and its neighbors were now little more than vast open-air quarries, the once-wooded steep mountainsides stripped bare and zigzagged with precipitous tracks from which limestone was quarried and then dumped into ships that tied up directly to the shoreline. By this time of year, too, the seaweed-cultivation industry was replacing fishing as the mainstay. This meant that nearly all of the most enticing-looking bays on the chart were blocked with complicated arrangements of floating rafts and ropes, with strange flat-bottomed craft that harvested the kelp buzzing back and forth at all hours.

So, we bypassed Ie Jima. After a long-day's sail in near calm winds, we tied up at a small marina on the industrial waterfront of Honshu, called Kiba. The sunset that evening over the adjoining petrochemical plant was especially spectacular:

"Particles in the atmosphere," Jenny dryly commented.

At the Matsuri, Kiba

After we had moored, a workman in a boiler suit, who was painting the bottom of a boat on the slipway, came over. In shy and halting English he told us:

"Tomorrow…Matsuri…interesting, I think… I show you?"

We took our friend's hand-drawn directions and next morning hopped onto the Sanyo Electric Railway line in the direction of Himeji. In a tight side street by the suburban station he had named, we found great throngs of men assembling, many in those jockstraps and loose brightly colored jackets, others in the traditional baggy pantaloons of rural Japan. All wore the colors and symbols of one of the twelve city wards, and their rallying points were enormous bamboo poles topped in the same colors by artificial flowers made of crepe paper. Around the fringes were the camp-followers: proud girlfriends giggling in their skin-tight jeans or mini-skirts, small children chasing each other between the legs of the adults.

The focal point of each contingent was their dazzlingly ornate gilded float, built around a large, canopied drum. Four seated drummers in the gaudy garb of Shinto acolytes, their leader in a strange dunce-like conical hat, maintained a steady rhythm. But the floats were so ornately decorated with gold thread flaps and cushions that you could not see how they could see their partners to keep time. At some unseen signal the men belonging to the first float began to gather and position themselves around its long wooden carrying arms, while the camp followers lined up ahead and astern. With a violent fore-and-aft rocking motion and rhythmic grunting, the float was lifted onto the shoulders of thirty or so men, their naked buttocks tensing visibly as they took the strain.

Then they were off. Some of the men were not in the best of shape; they were sweating profusely and stumbling after only a minute as they propelled the 2,000 kg weight of the float along the street. But there were eager volunteers always ready to spell them off. One by one, each with a slightly different chant and with many pauses for recovery, the floats followed each other on a complicated route through the narrow streets; anyone who had a balcony was leaning out lending encouragement. Young boys with long poles were ready to lift overhead electrical cables when a conflagration looked imminent. Lengthy pauses were necessary as and when the level-crossing on the railway line was reached and, with the usual siren and bells, barriers came down to halt the entire affair and allow the frequent suburban trains to clatter past. Other boys followed with carts full of drinking water and emergency supplies (including Sake).

We watched for more than two hours. I asked a friendly looking bystander:

"So what is this about? It is Shinto, yes?"

He shrugged and smiled.

"Yes, it is Shinto, I suppose. Maybe Buddhist too, I don't really know. But this is tradition, it is culture, it is not religion. The young men? They just want to belong."

Among the float carriers were overweight and bespectacled businessmen and punks with wild hairdos, who would make the most of breathing spaces to check their smartphones and hang out with their girlfriends. It was quite clear as well that this parade was not mounted for tourists: we were the only evident outsiders in sight, and there was little publicity for the event.

Not counting Nara and Kyoto (which were never bombed) Japan does not actually have much in the way of genuinely old historic buildings. Like the castle at Hirado, the most beautiful and authentic looking of structures have been repeatedly restored and rebuilt over the years. This is usually because they have been destroyed by fire. An exception was Himeji Castle, which was two stops further along the line from our matsuri. It was, we read, largely unchanged since the sixteenth century and had been used as a set for Tom Cruise's *The Last Samurai*.

Unfortunately, when we got there, the great donjon (or keep) was entirely swathed in tarpaulins and scaffolding (and would be so for several years more, signboards told us). I had to be very creative in photographing the building's few protruding and intact sections in such a way that the covered-up parts did not show. I'd eaten something deep-fried at the matsuri that didn't agree with

Sailing under the Akashi Kaikyo suspension bridge

me, and anyway spent much of the afternoon looking for washrooms while Jenny sat impatiently on benches, earnestly reading tourist leaflets. I consoled myself by taking pictures of the space-age toilets with their control panels. These allowed for music, hot air, jets of warm or cold water and a number of intriguing options that could only be guessed at from the lazy-W symbols that appeared to indicate a person's buttocks.

Leaving Kiba by sea, we now headed for the narrow gap that separates the large island of Awaji Shima from Honshu, and which is crossed by what was at the time the longest single span (1991m) in the world, the Akashi Kaikyo Bridge. On the old paper chart that Nozaki had given us back in Takashima a few months earlier, the bridge—finished in 1998—wasn't shown: we had spent a careful fifteen minutes penciling it in from Google Earth photos.

To our left the shoreline was ever-more industrialized, yet fringed with fish and seaweed farms, which meant that the water could not be as polluted as we had thought. To our right ships of all sizes and shapes converged on the narrows. With 90 meters to spare above our heads, and with a favorable current rushing us through at nearly seven knots, we surged into Osaka Bay, those ships now complemented by low-flying aircraft bound for Kansai International. With the Inland Sea and its quiet bucolic beauty all but behind us, we tied up at Suma, a suburb to the west of the mega-city of Kobe.

To our great pleasure, the beaming Taizo Ishii of *Skal*, last met at rainy Hirado four months earlier, was there to greet us with a warm Japanese welcome to his home port…and a large bottle of Shochu.

Chapter Twelve:
There at Sumahama
(Suma, Kobe)

Suma has ancient history. Lady Murasaki Shikibu's monumental *The Tale of Genji*[34] is a biographical novel centered on the real-life figure of Prince Hikaru Genji, an aristocratic courtier from the Heian period. Completed around 1021 CE, this 54-chapter saga recounts political intrigues and the love-life of its eponymous hero, who spends much of his time sending wistful poems to his diverse and equally aristocratic ladies. His affairs become so complicated that at one point he is obliged to exile himself from Kyoto to the seacoast at Suma. When he first sights the sea he sadly and enigmatically recites:

> *The waves roll back, but unlike me*
> *They come again.*

Genji and his entourage install themselves in thatched cottages behind the beach. They spend their days mournfully contemplating nature, painting watercolors. One day the sight of geese making their autumn migration through Akashi Kaikyo—the Strait now spanned by that massive bridge—has Genji hum to himself:

> *The wandering birds above us flying,*
> *Do they our far-off friends resemble.*
> *With their voices of plaintive crying*
> *Make us full of thoughtful sighing.*

Nearly a thousand years and many haikus later, the beach at Suma ("hama" in Japanese) was still inspiring poetry, or at least songs. A Japanese girl asks her mother:

> *Tell me tell me mama*
> *Will you ever go again to Sumahama*

---

34   Shikibu, Murasaki. (2018). *The Tale of Genji*. North Clarendon, VT: Tuttle Publishing.

> *Perhaps you'll find love there*
> *Somewhere between the Earth the sky and water*
> *There at Sumahama.*

The songwriter is Mike Love, and it's from the Beach Boys' *L.A. (Light Album)*, which came out in 1979.[35] Local rumor in Suma had it that Love still had a Japanese girlfriend and was occasionally to be seen strolling on the beach with her. We were never able to vouch for that.

Suma's beautiful sand beach is one of the few remaining on the shores of the Inland Sea; but it is backed by a multi-lane highway and residential high-rises that serve as expensive dormitories for the mega-city of Kobe. There were signs every hundred meters or so along the beach telling you, by the use of symbols, what you could and could not do. These showed, among other prohibitions, a man's bare back with a tattoo and the conventional large "X" sign across it. We recalled Mel's having nearly been branded as a Mafiosi, on account of her tiny tattoo. A similar set of signs at our local supermarket in Suma had a fizzing bomb with the red "X." Did the general public really need to be warned that bomb-throwing in crowded spaces was illegal?

Often, walking along the beach, we would meet little gaggles of senior citizens working as volunteers, picking up garbage and putting it into colorful bags provided by the municipality, adorned with its logo: a laughing aubergine. They would invariably present us with an empty bag as a gift, bow politely, and hesitantly murmur a welcome in broken English.

The marina was at the east of end the beach: a rectangle of concrete walls jutting out into the usually still waters of the Inland Sea. From here on further eastwards, it was miles and miles of dockland and industrial waterfront, with artificial islands of reclaimed land creating protected inner channels. On one such island was Kobe Airport; Kansai International was on a much larger island still further around. Adjoining the marina was an aquarium that attracted busloads of tourists and schoolchildren on the weekends. We'd often see the schoolchildren, following their visit and in their uniforms and regulation caps (different colors for different grades), being led down to the beach by their flag-carrying guides for a class photograph with the aquarium and marina behind.

On Saturday and Sunday mornings, the local little league softball teams would come and practice on the beach below the aquarium, in their old-style baggy softball uniforms. It was always very disciplined, with the coach calling out instructions, the boys taking their turns at bat or in the field. In their way, they were clearly having fun, but it didn't involve any running around, shouting or laughing. You could hear from the aquarium a catchy little theme tune that played on an endless loop during the daylight hours: a children's performer

---
35 The Beach Boys. (1979). *Sumahama* from L.A. YouTube. https://www.youtube.com/watch?v=R8OujIRLXuc.

would cheerily list the cuddly sea mammals you could see here, concluding triumphantly with the Japanese for:

"You can see them all at Suma!!"

海

Soon we were installed for the long term in Suma's marina, on our own pontoon bearing a plaque with the name *Bosun Bird*. Ishii had immediately adopted us and made all sorts of arrangements, introducing us to the initially bemused but later very friendly harbor master, Miyazaki, and a host of his sailing friends.

A month or so after our arrival, we were kindly invited as guests of honor to the annual dinner of the Owners' Club. This took place on a cool autumn evening at the British-style Kobe Club, set in wooded grounds on the exclusive upper slopes that back the city. Wood-paneled rooms and hallways were lined with black and white photographs of members and the Club Committee, going back to the twenties. Though the years and as black and white turned to color, more and more of the European faces on the Committee were replaced by Japanese, although the expatriate community in Kobe, focused largely on shipping, was still sizeable.

There was a convivial dinner at which even in our best clothes we were greatly under-dressed; the men wore traditional black dinner jackets, the women long evening gowns. And then things became even more lively. A band had been engaged for the evening. Its members were all in their fifties or older; the lead singer sported Bono-like sunglasses and clearly considered himself very cool. They played a non-stop series of fifties and sixties hits, all in passable but slightly accented English that had us cracking up to the bewilderment of our friends. Then came the star turn, introduced in what was obviously meant to be an American accent:

"Ladies an gennelmen…pliz welcome…fresh from his latest tour to Australia…Elvis Presley!"

The crowd had clearly been waiting for him: we all rose to our feet. In a red velvet jumpsuit and pasted-on sideburns that repeatedly came unglued, Japan's Official Number Two Elvis Impersonator launched into an energetic version of *Blue Suede Shoes*. Looking around at our new friends as they smiled at each other and swayed along with the music in a slightly embarrassed fashion, it struck me that they were of the Elvis Age. Born in the late forties and early fifties, they had lived the Japanese economic miracle and bought their yachts in middle age, just before the economy ground to a halt.

And how odd it was that their generation, growing up in the shadow of the war, under the American occupation, had so enthusiastically embraced Americana. Later I would read more about that occupation, how—notwithstanding the bloody fighting in the islands that preceded the horror of the two atomic bombs—once the Emperor delivered by radio his message to his people, simultaneously renouncing his divinity and instructing them to surrender, they had done so with apparent placidity. With some sixth sense, even that old redneck Douglas MacArthur had known that the occupation did not need military enforcement. When he first set foot on the soil of Honshu on August 30, 1945, he did not carry a side arm, he had no escort, and he drove himself by jeep from Atsugi air force base to Yokohama.

"Not exactly placidity…," said one of our new friends, Suzuki San. "But pragmatism, yes pragmatism… We had lost the war. We knew we had to rebuild."

Protest came later. As a student Suzuki had demonstrated against the American bases in Japan,

"But it was the sixties," he smiled.

Anti-Americanism in those days, he admitted, came from both the left and the right: the left was dutifully ant-imperialist, the right (as personified by Yukio Mishima) predictably nationalist. We talked one day about Japanese aggression before the war.

"I don't condone in any way the conduct of particular Japanese commanders in, say Nanjing…" he insisted. "But the idea of having our own empire: well, everyone that we admired had one too…and mostly taken by force… Did you never find it ironic that after the war the British wanted Malaya back again? Of course, the Americans weren't going to have that."

Guilt was often the sub-text of our conversations with Suzuki. I mentioned how Germany had virtually embraced its guilt these past fifty years; there were monuments to the Holocaust, Holocaust denial was illegal, German leaders routinely and repeatedly apologized. But it seemed to me that among many older Japanese there lingered not so much guilt as, still, a very slight sense of having been wronged.

"You may be right… MacArthur understood us quite well. But the decision he made not to purge the entire Japanese establishment and rule directly—as the allies did in Germany—made us think that since we were not being obviously punished, we had not done anything so wrong. In some ways it was wise to let Hirohito live. It made governing easy."

"But was he a war criminal?"

"By the standards of Nuremberg, if you believe in victors' justice, yes, he was, no less than Tojo. He knew what was going on and he played a major role in it. Still, you see, he was allowed to sit on his Chrysanthemum throne, to visit Europe. He was received by the Queen. To us Japanese it didn't look as though you thought he was a criminal at all."

On a lighter note, Suzuki warned me not to over-analyze the Japanese:

"You know, many people say that a Japanese person is like an onion: you keep peeling back layers, and you find another layer. But you know what?" I waited. "At the center of an onion…there's nothing!"

And he laughed.

By October, the nights were getting chilly. Living on a boat in winter, even in a marina, has special challenges. Unless you're able to close most sections of the boat off and live in one small and well-insulated compartment, it is difficult to keep warm: *Bosun Bird* only had two compartments. Even with an adequate heater—we had a powerful kerosene heater, but it was more practical to use a two-bar electric heater a friend gave us—the heat rises in such a way that your face can be sweating while your feet feel like blocks of ice.

It's also very difficult to arrest condensation: everything acquires a sensation of damp, the windows stream with moisture and your paperback books start slowly to swell in size. Only by placing them in the oven or blasting them with a hairdryer can you restore them to their correct size.

None of our new friends in Suma had much advice to offer. Living on board was such a strange thing for them that it was weeks before many of our frequent visitors realized that we actually ate and slept here; everyone seemed to assume we went ashore at night. Oddly, to us, on the rare occasions when very heavy weather threatened and it was advisable to strip the boat down and

The Kobe waterfront

double up on mooring lines, they could not understand that we wanted to be aboard so as to keep an eye on things, rather than in a hotel:

"But it will be much more comfortable and quieter…all the fishermen go home when there is a storm. Why do you not stay with us?"

Ishii took us out on trips in Osaka Bay, aboard *Skal*. He was touchingly anxious that we should not feel pressured to stay in "his" marina, so one day we did a sea-borne tour of the major yachting facilities in the area. Another weekend when we had another marine outing with Ishii planned, there was a gale warning, which would have made us surely stay at home had it been *Bosun Bird* that we were risking. But a Japanese yachtsman with a schedule is not easily deterred. Sure enough, by the time we had made the 20-mile crossing of the Bay and were preparing to enter a new marina for the night, through a narrow gap in the rock breakwaters, the wind had kicked up to 40 knots and we had to spend a couple of hours meandering around under power in the lee of the massive artificial island of Kansai International. The situation was not reassuring. Ishii admitted his engine had of late been giving him some problems, it was getting dark and of course *Skal* carried no anchor. Ishii must have misunderstood the shadow that passed over my face:

"Ah, Coghlan San, another beer?"

Ishii takes us on a tour of Osaka Bay

We soon got to know Ishii's best friends: Akihara, who was an abstract artist and whom we'd briefly met with Ishii back in Hirado, months earlier, and Naito. Like Ishii, both were happily married: we did meet Ishii's wife but not Akihara's, and Naito's only briefly. Like our retired friends on Kitagi Shima, the men had their lives and friends, the women theirs. Ishii, Naito, and Akihara had been friends from decades before, when they were members of the Okayama University Sailing Club; although they now lived about 100 km from each other, rarely would two or three weeks go by without their meeting up, often for a well-lubricated party aboard *Skal*.

As well as whisky, Japanese beer, Sake, and Shochu, exotic snacks would be prepared for such events; our new Musketeers liked observing our reaction when they offered us fried potatoes coated in sugar or long chewy tendrils of dried squid. They would chortle gleefully when we obligingly grimaced. Sometimes the smiling and long-suffering Mrs. Ishii would appear to retrieve Ishii from these gatherings; other times, he would wisely have been dispatched from home to the marina on his bicycle; still more wisely, he would sleep things off on board before going home in the morning.

Our friends took us everywhere: to ancient Kyoto and its temples, to the great castle of Osaka, to the other imperial capital, Nara. We were not allowed to pay our way on these trips. We would meet Ishii at our nearest station, Sumakaihinkoen, and find that he had bought our train tickets for us already. We would go out to lunch at one of their favorite neighborhood bars and, when it was nearly time to leave, we'd find that the bill had mysteriously been paid in advance. They delighted in our questions on Japanese history and culture and would often hold intense, whispered conversations in Japanese with each other when we asked some particularly perplexing matter. If they could not immediately come up with an answer, then by next time one of the three would have researched it all.

Another good friend was Captain Onishi who, quite unusually, did go around with his wife Mikiko, a former cabin crew member for JAL and ANA. They had a yacht, but Onishi spent most of his time working as a pilot on foreign ships traversing the Inland Sea. Jenny and I had met in the UK when Abba were in their heyday; Mikiko was of the same age. Like her we knew every Abba song, however embarrassing an admission that might be. So when the musical *Mamma Mia* came to Kyoto, and Mikiko and a girlfriend suggested we go, we leapt at it.

The massive modern theatre in the Kyoto station complex was packed, mainly with women of a certain age, but also with businessmen in their fifties, in suits and ties, who must have been taking the afternoon off from the office. I don't know why, but I had expected the show to be in English. With the exception of the odd line such as *Money, money, money…*, it was all in Japanese. It was the strangest of experiences to listen to *I Have a Dream* being sung by a petite Japanese girl, to know exactly what each line must mean, yet not to understand any of the individual words or phrases. It was truly a cross-cultural experience, in Kyoto of all places. In the grand finale, when all the biggest hits are played at a frantic pace—*Dancing Queen* merging with *Thank You for the Music*—all those men in rumpled suits were on their feet, waving their faintly illuminated smartphones in time with the music.

We enjoyed talking to Onishi about his years guiding ships from Osaka to Kanmon Kaikyo; he knew every nook and cranny, every tidal pass. He was not complimentary about Japanese fishermen, whom he said had a habit of stubbornly enforcing what they saw as their ownership of the sea by not moving out of the way of large vessels until the last possible moment. But Onishi worried that we must be missing fellow Anglo Saxons:

"I think you must go to see Father John," he kept saying. "I will telephone him, so he is expecting you."

Father John was a sprightly Englishman with a trim white beard, who ran the Kobe Mission to Seafarers (formerly Seamen, the mission is now unisex) in a small building just off covered Motomachi Street in downtown Kobe. He welcomed us warmly, courteously, not pushily, and showed us the small chapel at the back of the building, the bar, and the lounge. Over the weeks, we became frequent visitors, often dropping in to swap books or have a coffee after a day doing business of some sort in Kobe. The place was popular with Filipino merchant sailors who would be skyping back to their wives or girlfriends in Manila or earnestly discussing in Tagalog.

Another regular stop recommended by Captain Onishi was the International Center of Hyogo (the prefecture of which Kobe was the capital). This occupied two very spacious and well-appointed floors of a fifteen-year-old high-rise: there was a library of books in English, leaflets and brochures for foreign visitors and residents, a large bulletin board for those in search of or offering English teaching. It was a beautiful facility but barely frequented. After fifteen years or more of economic stagnation, how could Japan afford to keep such places running and fully staffed? It was the same when we visited the various government offices that we needed to see so as to keep our paperwork in order: the service was polite, but much of the bureaucracy made no sense and the staff were visibly underemployed.

The library allowed us glimpses into a Japan that, cocooned in our own rather special world and spoiled by friendship, we could otherwise only guess at. I read, in English, more dark and intense novels of Mishima; a gothic novel by Natsuo Kirino titled *Out*,[36] in which four women co-workers at a lunchbox-packing factory get into the business of cutting up bodies; Miyuke Miyabe's *All She Was Worth*,[37] in which a woman disappears so as to avoid the clutches of

---

36   Kirino, Natsuo. (2005). *Out*. New York, NY: Vintage Books
37   Miyabe, Miyuke. (1999). *All She Was Worth*. Boston, MA: Mariner Books.

the consumer-crazed Japan of the eighties; Murakami's *Norwegian Wood*,[38] a bleak story of tragic love and suicide.

You would have to live here a long time, I thought, to sense this Japan personally. We could only see the occasional, disconcerting manifestation of alienation: the "wanted" posters at the train stations; glassy-eyed young men spending their days in smoky, cacophonous Pachinko parlors; those ghostly figures encountered in passing at the Internet cafés that doubled as manga libraries; brief accounts in the newspaper of teen suicides coordinated through the Internet. There was a sense, above all, of the younger generation being held in a still-tight grip by the older, but resenting it. Jenny put it well one day:

"I love it in Japan, but I'm glad I didn't grow up here."

We would travel back and forth on the efficient and clean suburban train system: it was five or six stops from Sumakaihinkoen to downtown Kobe. Initially bewildered, we soon learned to interpret the electronic signboards that, in kanji and Romaji, indicated which train was arriving at which platform, and the ritual announcements over the loudspeaker. Arriving trains would be signaled ten or fifteen seconds in advance by little musical jingles and you would line up at the exact location on the platform that corresponded to the class of incoming train: triangles or circles corresponded with Express, Local, and so on. There were usually schoolchildren on board. Middle and high school girls wore the well-known sailor-suit uniforms or English-style plaid kilts with white blouses, the boys high-necked black tunics with brass buttons that must have been impossibly hot in summer.

Like kids everywhere, they would spend most of their time on the train texting their friends or fiddling to find some favorite tune. The girls' satchels were always festooned with little felt toys or trinkets; Hello Kitty was alive and well, a subset of Japanese teenagers' addiction to everything that is "kawaii" (愛い; approximate translation: cute). Travelling on public transit in Sydney, London, Toronto—almost anywhere in the west—you would these days expect to see people of every culture and facial characteristic. But it was rare for us to see non-Japanese-looking features on Japanese public transit.

Above the windows, inside the clean compartments, were the usual diagrammatic maps of the rail system, ads, and various public service exhortations. Many of the ads featured the English language, but just didn't quite ring true. Two cell phone companies had the slogans, respectively:

"Why not interact?" and "Inspire the next!"

Some of the Japanese public service announcements were quite mystifying. Many featured a stern, even angry-looking teddy bear who was clearly

---

38   Murakami, Haruki. (2010). *Norwegian Wood*. New York, NY: Vintage Books.

delivering a message to children to not make a noise or leave garbage on the trains. But he might be festooned, for example, with a garland of green grapes.

"What's it all about?" we would ask Ishii or Naito. And they would go to work.

The explanations were often quite complex. Usually, they revolved around the ambiguity of kanji script. In this particular instance, what the teddy bear had to say, so Naito patiently explained, included a sound like "Muscatel." In fact, it was the kanji character combination used to describe muscatel grapes, hence the visual pun of the teddy bear's garland.

Ishii had an easier time explaining the 15-meter-high statue of grey steel that we would see on our right every day we clattered into Kobe, as we approached Shin Nagata station. His eyes lit up:

"Ah yes, is Iron Man Number Twenty-Eight!"

Iron Man was a comic book hero of Ishii's childhood. He first came to life in mangas in 1956 and then earned his own cartoon series on TV. Ishii told us Iron Man's story. During the final days of World War II, the Japanese military is secretly developing a weapon intended to defeat the USA: a massive, all-powerful robot. But when, after twenty-seven attempts, mad scientist Dr. Kaneda finally succeeds, the war is almost over. The Doctor dies in frustration at seeing his work wasted. Iron Man 28 is given to Dr. Kaneda's ten-year-old son Shotaro and, under Shotaro's control, is put to work stopping criminals and enemy robots. Ishii pointed me to various websites, and I read up on Iron Man's creator, Mitsuteru Yokoyama.

"When I was a fifth-grader," Yokoyama had written, "the war ended and I returned home from Tottori Prefecture, where I had been evacuated. The city of Kobe had been totally flattened, reduced to ashes. People said it was because of the B-29 bombers…as a child, I was astonished by their terrifying, destructive power.[39]"

Yokoyama listed as other inspirations his viewing of Frankenstein and his reading up of the last months of the war, when the Nazis pinned their hope successively on various secret weapons of great power that would reverse the tide of war. The genesis of Iron Man would be recalled in the wake of the terrible earthquake of January 1995 (the Great Hanshin Earthquake) that killed 5,000 and that destroyed much of Kobe, including the Shin Nagata district. A public subscription was raised, and this enormous statue erected as a symbol of strength and rebirth in the home of Kobe Steel.

The Japanese love their comic-book heroes and, of course, the manga has now become a modern art or literature form in its own right. A common sight on swaying trains would be a middle-aged "salaryman" in dark suit and tie,

---

39   Mitsuteru Yokoyama. (1956). Tetsujin 28-go. Wikiwand. https://en.wikipedia.org/wiki/Tetsujin_28-go

Iron Man #28, Kobe

clutching a hanging strap in one hand, eyes glued to a manga awkwardly held in another. Or you might find the same man slurping his noodles loudly in a neighborhood noodle shop, a manga propped up behind his bowl. Many of the manga heroes were benign: another favorite of Ishii's was Doraemon, the blue-coated and smiling robotic cat who has travelled back to the present from the twenty-second century to help a bullied little boy named Sewashi Nobi.

But not all are so child friendly. There is now a phenomenon best described as porno manga, that we'd first glimpsed back in Kagoshima: cartoon stories featuring girls with short, spiky hair, doe eyes that cry at the slightest pretext, and enormous breasts that escape their covering with no provocation at all. The classic Japanese vision of a beautiful woman is one that is virtually cylindrical, with breasts so small or flattened as to be unnoticeable; a kimono's undergarments seem designed to bind the chest flat, in fact. And yet these comics betray a yearning for enormous breasts, while still pandering to that preference for short women with black hair and large black eyes.

"So what's it all about?" I asked one of our friends, who had better remain nameless.

"Well, pornography... I've heard that western men like little Japanese girls," he answered. "Isn't it always about the exotic, the different?"

Porno mangas could be found at the ubiquitous "konbini" (convenience stores), firmly wrapped up in cellophane to discourage browsing. But while Jenny wandered the aisles of 7-Eleven, Family Mart, or Lawson (the selection of goods and the internal geography was always identical, no matter what the name of the store), I would leaf through more accessible magazines. Their covers did not necessarily offer clues as to what was inside. Like on those infamous sweatshirts that carry meaningless groupings of English words and that have come to be synonymous with Japan, the titles looked to have been plucked at random from a dictionary. I took to carrying a notebook around. Enigmatic entries included:

Blenda

Mens Egg – Hairs

Potato

Used Mix.

Elsewhere on the shelves were products that might experience marketing issues in the west: a brand of powdered milk called *Creap*, bottled water labelled *Pocari Sweat* and *Calpis*. In the pastry section you could buy a *Cream Sand* but if you wanted something more substantial, the Copenhagen Hot Dog Bar In Suma temptingly had on its menu *Christian Dog* and *Marist Dog*. Even more enticing, a sign that caught our attention every time we neared Motomachi Station advertised the delights of the *Clap Café*; a Pachinko parlor was called *Tomato de Tomato*.

I guessed it was all because of the exoticism of English, the hint of sophistication that its use implied. But it was frustrating to walk over to a big signboard at the station that was headed *Information*, and then to find out that everything was in kanji characters.

Back at the marina there was work to be done. We were diffidently asked if we might be prepared to do a pair of illustrated talks on our adventures. It was the least we could do to repay the hospitality we were being offered. The talks, delivered in a large room above the marina office, went down well. There was great and genuine interest in the idea of offshore cruising, we sensed, and yet... Nobody seemed truly ready to take the most important and most difficult step, which is to cut your ties with family, friends, jobs: the land in all senses. Once you've done that, the sailing is easy.

Part of the problem, we realized by degrees, was that as our Japanese friends (nearly always men) listened to us, they knew that they would not in fact be doing what we were doing. They would be doing it alone, single handing; indeed, the small but distinguished pantheon of famous Japanese sailors consists almost exclusively of loners who, like most of their breed, are slightly unhinged. Their wives would never come.

We had practical tasks to get on with as well; on an old boat such as ours there are always items that need repairing, maintaining, or replacing. As the winter went on, I occasionally noticed small white gobs of some gummy substance rising to the surface just astern of the boat. Reluctantly, I deduced that this was engine oil that had somehow combined with seawater. The seawater must have made its way up the propeller shaft and into the supposedly sealed-off rubber sleeve, full of oil, that simultaneously blocks the entry of water up the rotating shaft and lubricates its movement. We would have to haul the boat out of the water to replace the seal.

Of course—again often the case with older boats—the requisite spares were no longer manufactured. We became a fixture, propped up on dry land in the boatyard with a ladder up against one side, as correspondence went back and forth between Japan, the USA, and the UK in search of a new kind of shaft seal. Living in a boat on "the hard" is more complicated than on the water, because you cannot allow water to drain down the sink, you cannot draw in seawater for washing up, and you cannot pee over the side. The prospect of getting up at 3:00 a.m. after a night of too much beer, to climb into the frosty air of the cockpit, down a rickety ladder and a hundred meters across the darkened boatyard to the washrooms was not always welcome.

Waiting for parts allowed us time once again to do the rounds of offices in Kobe with our list of Closed Ports that we wished to be able to visit on our way further east along the Pacific Coast of Honshu. Our friends had many suggestions for interesting stopping places, albeit sometimes the fruit of land-based visits. We were soon supplementing folders of Google Earth photos with photocopies of fragments of their large charts and miscellaneous information about tourist sights and hot springs.

We were particularly interested in being able to track the Kurushio, the Black Current that sidles up against Honshu then makes its way out into the Pacific en route for North America. If we could locate and ride this current, it would give us a powerful lift. The Coastguard directed us to their useful websites that gave daily animations of the current. But when we asked them if, on our way to Alaska, we were likely to encounter debris from the previous year's catastrophe at Fukushima, the answer was frustratingly bureaucratic:

"Very sorry, we do not follow. Mandate ends 200 miles east."

We turned to NOAA, the American oceanic and weather agency, for more help. Their website had a model that showed that most of the debris—a lot of

Hauled out for work on the propeller shaft, Suma

it would be house-sized—should be approximately halfway across by now. But it was not actually tracking things and, perplexingly, reports were already in the newspapers of items as diverse as an abandoned 120-meter-long fishing boat, a container full of Kawasaki motorbikes and a soccer ball having already reached the North American mainland.

Our replacement shaft seal arrived. We soon had it installed, repainted the bottom and were back in the water by April. As the days drew out and the temperature slowly rose, so a trickle of farewell gifts from our friends grew to a flood: a large blue, red, and white flag of the Suma Yacht Owners' Association, a book on Japanese etiquette from Captain Onishi (a bit late, we thought as we mentally listed the many faux pas we had made over the year, but the gesture was kind), many bottles of Shochu, Sake and very expensive whisky, a large tin of shortbread biscuits baked by Naito's wife. There were various lucky charms as well: a small stuffed toy cat to bring good luck, amulets to protect fishermen, a bulbous black plush fish from Hokkaido with a bandanna round its head, with some unknown exhortation in Japanese (it was probably another difficult-to-explain pun, we were sure).

Adachi, one of our neighbors, gave us a set of CDs for us to listen to on the long night watches: Kate Bush, John Lennon. Yes he was of that vintage too. For two weeks, we had farewell tea parties, lunches, and dinners. Those whom we sadly missed left us gifts in the cockpit, with notes. We still have the message that Captain Onishi and Mikiko left along with a large, expensive melon and a tin of exotic pastries:

"Dear Jenny and Nick: Thanks for having a good and enjoy time. We have come habor and sailed off Suma, and call *Bosun Bird*. Please eat now. We hope your safe and enjoy sailing for Alaska. Bon Voyage."

Just as we preferred, it was unnoticed that on April 17th, at 6:00 a.m. we quietly slipped out. We said a silent goodbye to Suma.

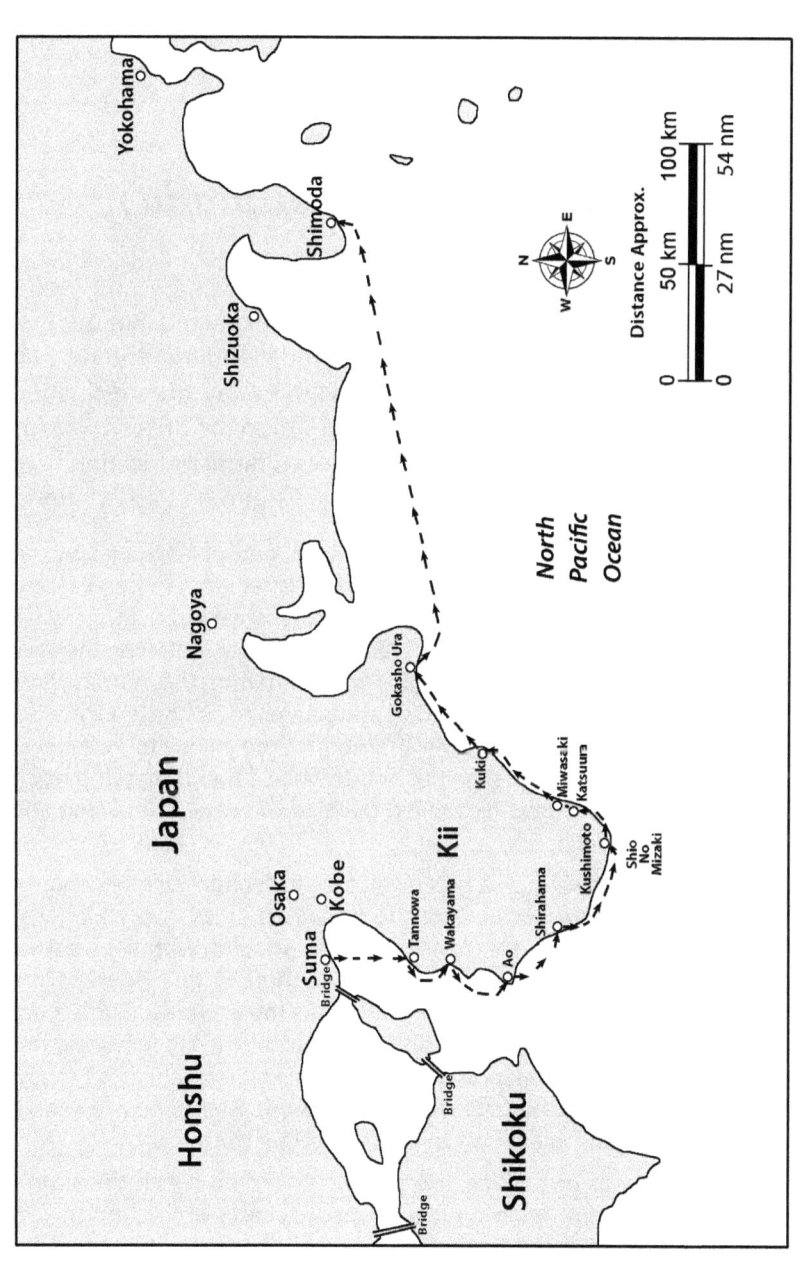

Suma to Shimoda

Chapter Thirteen: The Black Ships (Kii Peninsula and Shimoda)

Winter had lingered longer than we had expected. But our first day out from Suma was hot, still, and cloudless, and we had to motor much of the way across Osaka Bay, our destination Tannowa, on its south side. Plumb in the middle, forcing dozens of ships out of their way, was a two-square-mile seaweed farm, its location here a testimony to the power and influence of the fishermen's associations.

Setting out after a long layup usually leads to one or two unexpected problems on board, and today was no exception. After we had been sailing along for a couple of hours and had the Tannowa breakwater in view, we started the engine. We were greeted by complete silence, not even the click of the starter motor. Fortunately, the engine was warm from the morning and, at 20 HP, is small enough (with the help of adrenaline) to be started by hand. But it took Jenny much of the rest of the afternoon at the marina to track down the faulty wire leading from the ignition. Meanwhile, I found myself getting my hands dirty when the head (i.e., toilet) decided to cease functioning and demanded a messy rebuild.

We knew that Tannowa gave a great welcome to foreign yachties, and we had considered wintering over here. But today was Tuesday, everything was closed, and we could not even leave the gated compound. With the weather set fair, we decided not to linger. Next day, after three or four hours sailing beneath the Kansai International flight path, with the morning flights from Europe coasting in one after another, we reached the narrow gap that separates Osaka Bay from more open waters and thus constitutes the southeasterly-most entrance to the Inland Sea. Here funneling winds from astern and a favorable tide had us zipping along at over seven knots, in bright sunshine.

Our destination was one which, like the vast island on which the airport is located, simply did not figure on the old paper charts we had borrowed: a large rectangle of reclaimed land containing two marinas, a funfair, and a mock European village, known collectively as Wakayama Marina City. We had an early visitor who was typically blunt:

"I am Tomoko San. Please, you come to dinner tonight."

Tomoko, small, dark, and lively, worked at the marina and knew Ishii from Suma. She drove us that evening to her home, where we met her three equally lively children, her diving instructor husband (Buddy) and her best friend, who loaded us down with bags full of home baking. There then arrived another family friend who managed to explain, by expressive hand signals, that he was a serious mountain biker. After he had put away four beers, I asked him through Tomoko:

Dinner at Koya San

"Is that good for your health?"

"Ah...," he smiled and pointed to another half dozen cans of Asahi beer. "Special Japanese energy drink. Very good!"

Jenny learned origami (again), and Tomoko San's friend's teenage daughter did us the great honor of presiding over a formal Japanese tea ceremony for us. The meal was of course sumptuous and many-coursed; the difficulty as always was knowing how much to eat, without being sure how much more was going to be produced.

We were still on the track of the ubiquitous and itinerant monk, Kobo Daishi, who had seemed last summer and autumn to have beaten us to every island and mountain top in the Inland Sea. So, we took advantage of a spate of poor weather to make a train trip away from Wakayama and up into the remote hills of the Kii peninsula. A combination of three ever more local trains, followed by a brief spell on a funicular railway, took us to Koya San, the headquarters of the Shingon School of Esoteric Buddhism: a monastery town and Kobo's resting place.

As is habitual here, we stayed the night in a Buddhist temple. The rooms, though Japanese-style (i.e., you sleep on the tatami floor) were not spartan in the least and the temple also had a very pleasant Onsen. Dinner (strictly vegan) was eight separate courses served in our own private dining room. In the morning we were invited to attend the dawn service in the temple's candle-lit

Great Hall. We did not understand a great deal—much chanting and turning of ancient pages—so we asked a fellow pilgrim who spoke English, and who had also got up early to hear the Abbott. He looked immediately vague:

"Ah...well...you know Japanese Sakura?[40] It is beautiful but, how can I say? It dies... Life is short and, how you say, all that shit?"

Our friend tailed off. But we had got the general idea.

The highlight of Koya San is the Oku-no-in cemetery and mausoleum: thousands of tombs and grave markers scattered alongside a path that meanders through centuries-old cedars. It was mournful, sinister in the late afternoon mist. There were grand tombstones and sponsored enclaves, the most famous of which was constructed by a pesticide company in expiation of the billions of ants whose death it had caused. The UCC coffee company had put up a massive granite coffee cup engraved with its logo, and there was a rocket commemorating a Japanese rocket scientist.

Scattered around everywhere were tiny Jizos—those miniature sculptures of the Buddha as a child, often coiffed in a red woolly hat and/or a red apron, although the red had usually turned to green with years of fog and rain. At the end of the gradually climbing trail was the vast Lantern Hall, where two particular lanterns were said to have been burning for 900 years, and behind it (no cameras allowed) the mausoleum of Kobo Daishi himself.

A monk in a white robe slowly walked over to us, bowed, and began an explanation, "Here is mausoleum of Kukai,[41]" he started. "Is 1,200 years old. But actually, Kukai is not dead. He is inside, waiting the return of the Lord Buddha."

"Oh yes...," the monk added when the shadow of a doubt must have crossed our faces. "He is just meditating. We take him food two times each day."

We said goodbye to Tomoko and, sailing ever south, we stopped next at the quiet fishing village of Ao (pronounced Ow). After so long in marinas it took us time to get back into the special routine of tying to barnacle-encrusted harbor walls, with a tidal range of up to two meters. But the weather was peaceful, the fishing harbor still. We wandered around town and were touched when, as we later sat in the cockpit to watch the sun go down, an elderly couple drew up in their car and, with no fuss at all and waving away our thanks, presented us with two cold beers and a bag full of cakes.

Eighteen miles on, with the great island of Shikoku now barely visible over our starboard quarter, the Pacific opening up, we came to Shirahama. Entry here required some caution: there were many rocks in the bay and seaweed and

---

40 Sakura=Cherry blossom. The Sakura is widely seen in Japan as the symbol of hope and renewal, but also of the brevity of life; in World War II, kamikaze aircraft were painted with the Sakura symbol.

41 Kobo Daishi: the posthumous name of Kukai.

oyster farms blocking most of the obvious channels. But Sho, a sailing contact we had made through email, had given us a set of precise GPS waypoints and we were able to work our way in to a very secure and tranquil corner, tying up to a pontoon literally at the foot of an Onsen. In season Shirahama was a very popular resort town but, like everything else and as we'd found in Fukuoka, the season in Shirahama was highly regulated: July and August. Although the temperature was well into the 20s (centigrade) and the pristine sand beach looked tempting, there was not a tourist to be seen.

Actually the beach was not entirely pristine. It was being groomed by a pair of bulldozers, which were redistributing sand blown into inconvenient locations by winter storms. *Lonely Planet* added:

"…if the beach reminds you of Australia, don't be surprised; the town has to import sand from Down Under."

Everywhere there were Onsens. We favored one outdoors, with a fine view over the ocean. A series of pools of gradually decreasing heat descended through the rocks towards the sea, the ladies' side discreetly boarded off but the men's openly visible from a pair of cliff top hotels. I wondered if Japan suffered from Peeping Toms. You would think that every society in which clothes are worn would do so, but maybe not. There was a convention here that if women wished to cross from their side into the men's, they were welcome. In fact, there was a one-way door in the fence for this purpose. But the reverse was not allowed. I turned to my wallowing neighbor in the Onsen, who was as usual wearing his tiny towel on the top of his head and asked him why this was so. He thought hard and I wondered if he had understood me. Then he slowly nodded:

"I think is because…is because Japanese man drink. Woman no drink. So better give woman choice; not let man to choose."

At the pontoon, meanwhile, there was socializing: with the intrepid single-handed captain of *Joanna*, making the annual pilgrimage many Japanese yachties undertake from Yokohama to the more scenic Inland Sea, and with various passers-by. One had barely introduced himself when he was urgently dialing on his cell phone. He said a few words, listened intently, then thrust the phone at me:

"Is my friend Ken San. He speak very good English. Help all Yotto people. You speak now!"

Ken was indeed very friendly and after two or three minutes' conversation he had committed to make all sorts of arrangements for us to be visited and hosted further down the road.

The weather pattern was by now typical for Spring: two or three days of drizzly but warm easterlies (i.e., contrary winds) followed by the same period of westerlies (favorable) with brilliant sunshine. The forecast called for the next spell of westerlies to start at thirty knots; it was hard work powering out of Shirahama into the seas these winds generated, with rocks and seaweed farms lurking on all sides. But once we were able to turn the corner, we romped down the Pacific swells and put in over forty miles at speeds of up to seven knots, turning past the great cape at the south of the Kii peninsula: Shio-No-Misaki.

"Cape of Currents," Jenny informed me briskly after checking the dictionary.

The Kurushio Current is supposed to strike the headland at speeds of up to four knots, but we experienced no current at all. Instead, we found ourselves dodging a hundred ships of all sizes during the course of the day, all converging on this, the southernmost tip of the great island of Honshu. Sunburned, but pleased with our mileage, we turned into the quiet lee of Shio-no-Misaki, passed below the elegant white arch of a high road bridge and spent the night wall-tied at the perfect natural anchorage of Kushimoto. The shelter was so good that we could just as well have anchored in the open bay.

Next day, with the coastline to port becoming ever more rugged, we turned to the northeast but, having lost the wind, had to motor most of the sixteen miles on to Katsuura (Bonito Harbor). Oddly, I was at this time reading a rather tired paperback version of Francis Chichester's *The Lonely Sea and the Sky*,[42] picked up at the Seafarers' Mission book-swap in Kobe. Chichester is famous above all for his circumnavigation of the globe under sail from 1966 to 1967. I remembered as a boy being enthralled by the grainy black and white pictures the BBC had shown of him rounding Cape Horn flying just a spitfire jib. But I'd forgotten he'd had an earlier, even more illustrious career as a flyer. An attempt by Chichester to become the first person to fly around the world alone ended when his tiny float plane hit a cable when taking off from Katsuura on August 15, 1931. The plane was a write-off and Chichester was lucky to live. My paperback even had a picture of the wrecked aircraft being hauled out of the water.

This was another well-protected location: an inlet running north-south, closed off at its northern head with a natural pool, and protected to seawards by a line of rugged pinnacles, atop one of which there incongruously sat a large hotel. Several high-tension cables ran high across the inlet: these presumably were what Chichester had hit.

It was only two hundred meters from our quiet wall (where Jenny thought the street lamp shining into the cabin all night was the moon) to the nearest of many Sentos. This was one of the older-style establishments. Unusually, both sides were busy. The men were polite but taciturn, the easily heard women on the other side far more gossipy and giggly. I could tell by the way the men

---

42   Chichester, Francis. (2002). *The Lonely Sea and the Sky*. Chichester, U K: Summersdale Publishers.

started to look at me out of the corner of their eye that the women were all talking, if not to, then about Jenny.

Tourist posters for Katsuura featured young girls riding dolphins, and friendly whale logos abounded. But within sight of the town to the south was the small bay of Taiji, infamous worldwide for the annual killing of dolphins and pilot whales that takes place here, literally turning the bay red. Japanese friends were aware of the controversy caused by this and by the country's international whaling fleets. They were aware too, that the idea that Japanese whaling was for "scientific purposes" was a fiction; whale meat was freely available, and children were often served it for school lunch.

When I'd asked Suzuki San his thoughts, he'd shrugged and asked back:

"How is it different from killing cows?"

And he launched into a slightly tongue-in-cheek discourse on what he termed as "arbitrary western sentimentality."

A short run north took us next to the fishing port of Miwasaki. As we had been throughout Japan, we were relying largely on word-of-mouth, combined with Google Earth photos, for an idea of places that were good for yachts to tie up: either a pontoon or a non-overhanging wall with a reasonable amount of space. Here word-of-mouth failed us. The reported owner of a pontoon had passed away and his pontoon was no more; we spent an hour or so on one wall, then moved further in when some swell seemed to be working its way in.

We'd only been tied up for a couple of hours, when one of Ken San's friends, Hamabata, showed up: his yacht, *Adventurers*, was moored a few miles away. He spoke little English, but the still invisible Ken San had clearly given him strict marching orders. Hamabata seemed a little afraid of us:

"Plis, you come now!" he said with a nervous smile. He kindly took Jenny shopping and then took us both out to his own favorite rustic Onsen, a family affair tucked away in the hills near Katsuura. We were finding by now that you can meet interesting, if undressed people in these places. Jenny's tub-mate was a woman who had come with her husband all the way from Tokyo to pray at a nearby shrine.

"Oh…," said Jenny with concern. "You must have lost someone. I'm sorry to hear that."

"Oh no, is just our dog," she laughed. "He wery old. We bury him in shrine so he go to dog heaven straight-way."

With a major and very wet front coming our way, we lingered in Miwasaki but took a day off for some tourism. We took a train and bus into the hills behind Nachi and, in gradually intensifying mist and drizzle, hiked up a magnificent ancient trail called the Daimon-zaka: a paved way, lined with enormous cedars, up to Nachi Taisha, one of the three great shrines of the Kii peninsula. Its location is on account of the Nachi-no-Taki falls, the highest—at 133 meters—in Japan. We had learned that remarkable natural features such as waterfalls or conspicuous trees are said, in Shinto, to embody "Kami," or gods. Painted in the classic bright vermilion and ornamented with gold, the shrine was busy even on this increasingly wet day, with the usual sellers of amulets and fortunes doing brisk business. Next door—in a manifestation of that Japanese instinct to take Pascal's wager and bet on every possible option—was a much less gaudy Buddhist temple of ancient, unpainted timber, its interior smoke-blackened. But even here there were semi-official personages ensconced on thrones, taking in large quantities of yen in return for dispensing hand-written fortunes.

The temple at Nachi Taisha

Once the front had passed, we had a gusty sail northeast up the peninsula to the very snug, tree-lined, and tranquil inlet of Kuki. A nearby inlet was Kata; the neighborhood was thus called Kuki-Kata, approximately pronounced Cookie Cutter. We had a recommendation for Kuki that dated back nearly forty years, to when the Roths cruised these waters in their yacht *Whisper*. The women no longer wore kimonos, they probably bathed more than once a week and the local runabouts now had outboards, but we sensed the place could not otherwise have changed that much. We were waved in to tie up at a pontoon cluttered with nets and obscure fishing paraphernalia, and spent a couple of days here. Unusually, we had the company of several Japanese yachts, for it was again Golden Week, one of Japan's major holiday periods. We recalled that exactly a year earlier we were just starting our adventure in Japan; we'd passed a rainy Golden Week on the southern tip of Kyushu.

There was one small shop where the friendly owner, who had spied our Canadian flag, spoke to us:

"So where are you from?"

"British Columbia…"

"Maybe Prince Rupert?" he asked to our surprise.

He informed us that his municipality was twinned with the remote BC town. The fishing connection was obvious. But there had also once been a great deal of logging on the Kii peninsula. All of the substantial trees were long gone, but shiploads of trees and wood chips still came in from Canada and Chile (respectively) to unload at mills on this coast. We now realized what that distinctive smell was: paper milling.

"It is to make jobs," the shop owner said. I immediately recalled the smug answer that British Columbians would give visitors who wrinkled their noses at the same odor: "That's the smell of money."

It seemed very short-sighted on the part of Canada to be shipping raw materials all the way across the Pacific for Japanese mills to process them; surely the labor could not be that much cheaper here in Japan, if at all.

Leaving Kuki Jenny snagged her palm on a small fishhook that had become caught in a mooring line. Looking carefully at the line, and the distance from it to the nearest pile of fishing gear on the dock, I had a sneaking suspicion that we were facing another of those rare instances of passive aggression, and that the hook had been deliberately placed. Had we offended someone or broken some rule by tying up in this particular location? I looked around; there was a man at the wharf-head, watching, but he said nothing and soon walked away.

Meanwhile, too squeamish to pull the hook out, Jenny declared herself hors de combat for the rest of the day. This left the captain to single-hand to Gokasho Ura and the Vivre Ocean Club (VOC) marina, about thirty miles on. Approaching the fine, multi-armed inlet inside which VOC is snugly located, squalls of thunder, lightning, and hail had us alternately becalmed and rail-under, the wind direction switching 180 degrees in a few seconds. Later we learned that the line of squalls had travelled onwards to Tokyo and inflicted severe tornado-like damage, which is most unusual for Japan.

By email, we had alerted Ken San to the hook dangling from Jenny's hand, and he had kindly arranged already for Tommy, the marina manager, to run her into the local hospital by car and have the hook removed. Ken was starting to seem like some invisible God, presiding over our travels but never manifesting himself directly.

With such a warm welcome and in another very tranquil setting where the only sounds were the twittering of birds and the buzz of cicadas—a sign of another approaching summer—we decided to stay a few days and get on with preparations for our impending trans-Pacific passage. As always, there was a shrine handy, this time the most important of all: Ise-Jingu. Tommy investigated the bus timetables for us, ran us into town, and we made the one-hour ride to the city of Ise, on the large bay of the same name.

The shrine (or shrines: there are dozens) of Ise-Jingu dates back to the third century CE and is the most venerated in the Shinto tradition. Every twenty years, the main buildings are taken down and replicas built on specially designated adjoining sites: 2013 would be the 62nd time this would happen, and the new shrines were already taking shape under vast all-concealing white canvas canopies. The shrines are in two main groupings, Geku and Naiku, both in beautiful ancient forest land. Unlike so many Shinto shrines, which can border on the gaudy, these are austere and unpainted, the only ornamentation being the golden tips of the roof timbers. As far as you can see, that is. For the main shrine compounds are all fenced off behind two-meter-high wooden fences and are accessible only to the Emperor and other very senior dignitaries.

Shinto must be the only major world religion whose holiest place is thus made so inaccessible to its adherents.

Ise was atmospheric, there was no doubt, perhaps as much for its sylvan setting as anything. And it seemed refreshing to us that, in Shinto, the age of physical structures was considered to be irrelevant. Fires, earthquakes, and other catastrophic natural phenomena with which Japan had always been plagued had made a virtue of necessity: what was treasured was the age of the tradition or practice, not its physical manifestation.

Although the VOC marina was in the quietest of settings, we made two sets of friends. Nakashima and his Romanian-born wife Lily were the proud owners of a near sister ship of ours, a Vancouver 28. They worked so hard that they barely had any time left for cruising, the more so in that they ran their own business of setting up shop displays in Nagoya, and often needed to work at night or on weekends. In a decade, they had never left the bay. Although Nakashima was in his early fifties he estimated he was the youngest yacht-owner at this marina.

Maruyama San and Shigeko San, meanwhile, were of that older generation. They owned a condo at the marina and a Cabo Rico 38 ketch but by their own confession had now probably left it too late for long distance cruising. Well into his seventies, Maruyama San continued to work as a GP part-time. As we sat drinking tea in their condo, a photo of Maruyama with a buxom, raven-haired woman caught my eye:

"Sarah Brightman!" he said triumphantly. "I am Number One fan in Japan! Have all the records, I go to New York just to see her in The Phantom; we meet backstage; I think I am in love!!"

Shigeko shrugged theatrically and sipped her tea with no comment.

Maruyama and Shigeko took us to a spectacular Onsen nearby where, from steaming hot exterior pools, on a clear but cool evening, we watched the sun sink behind the mountains of the Kii peninsula. It was a perfect end to the night when, on our way home, we stopped at their favorite sushi bar. The chef dazzled us with knife-work so fast his hands were a blur and gave Jenny lessons on how to make sticky rice.

East of Gokasho Ura is a long stretch of barren, exposed coastline with no secure harbors so, for the first time in nearly a year, we were forced to make an overnight passage, of 125 miles. I had spent some time studying the requirements for haiku composition, which can be boiled down as follows: three lines of five, seven, and five syllables respectively; a juxtaposition of two images; a seasonal reference. I spent the night hours composing two very bad haikus that nevertheless sum up this passage:

> *Shimoda by sail:*
> *All those ships, how black the night,*
> *My hair turned quite white*

> *By yacht past Fuji:*
> *Alas it was all hazy,*
> *With nothing to see*

Aficionados of Japanese culture and history might appreciate the punning of the first haiku. Shimoda, our destination, was famous in Japanese history for what is known as the episode of the Black Ships. In 1854, US Commodore Matthew Perry, much to the consternation of the Shogun in nearby Edo, appeared at Shimoda literally out of the blue, with several powerful, modern warships. He demanded that Japan end its 200-year-old policy of isolation and permit commerce with the USA. Subsequently, a Treaty of Amity was signed at Shimoda and the first western consul of the modern era, Townsend Harris, was installed in a convenient Buddhist Temple.

Fortuitously, we tied up at the very location where Perry had first landed and even more luckily, we found that we had arrived at the start of the annual three-day Black Ship Festival. There were Japanese and American warships at anchor and the place was flooded with shore-leave sailors in their best whites. American and Japanese flags festooned the streets; there were marching bands and majorettes; parading Boy Scout troops from American forces high schools; and a civic delegation from Newport (Rhode Island), Perry's hometown.

It was very Japanese that the local people had no qualms about celebrating an outrageous act of gunboat diplomacy by America. But bearing in mind what was happening seventy years before our visit in this part of the world, it was moving to see the Stars and Stripes being hoisted by Japanese sailors and the once-ominous Rising Sun ensign of the Japanese Navy saluted by Americans.

But the Black Ship Festival was much more than this. We were already coming into another matsuri season, and this was the excuse for the annual bash that every Japanese community loves to have. One night there was a spectacular fireworks display that we watched from the cockpit of *Bosun Bird*, and the next a different display of traditional (Edo era) fireworks. Macho young men dressed only in loincloths rushed around madly in the dark with what looked like outsize fire extinguishers, but which gushed great showers of sparks over them for two or three minutes apiece. In the streets, traditional dancers from many parts of Japan paraded and performed daily.

Drummers at the Black Ships festival, Shimoda

Most evocative of all were two ethereal women from Okinawa who wore ungainly lampshade-like hats and gyrated in slow-motion to plink-plink notes from an accompanying stringed instrument. And a quite different and awesome nighttime display of drumming, that was not just music but theatre, with the powerfully muscled young performers moving in synch like trained gymnasts. There was a Japanese-Brazilian samba school troupe from nearby Shizuoka with the customary extravagant, and sometimes very skimpy, costumes; and a Brazilian-Japanese man singing live samba as they gyrated around downtown.

I remembered from my reading of *Out*—the noir story of the four women who carve up bodies—how substantial the Brazilian-Japanese community is; it is quite old and is mirrored by similar communities in Brazil itself. Other than the Koreans, who are visibly indistinguishable from Japanese, this is the main immigrant population. Alienation seemed to us to be the predominant theme in modern Japanese writing; we wondered how the stereotypically outgoing and flamboyant Brazilians were doing in such a tight society.

On our pontoon we made more friends: Dutch/Japanese couple Sytze and Sae, and a pair of young reporters from *Kazi* sailing magazine, who travelled here from Tokyo to interview us. And we had lunch with Australian/Japanese Graeme and Kazumi, who lived one hour north of Shimoda by train, and sustained seven stray cats. By chance, as we came close to the end of our

Dancer at the Black Ships festival, Shimoda

stay in Japan, we seemed to be meeting more and more expats doing business here. Partly it was because we were now close to Tokyo; in fact, Shimoda was almost a resort area for the metropolis, where those who could afford it had second homes. Few were positive about the economic situation. Sytze and Sae gathered together observations we had made ourselves:

"It's a kind of perfect storm... The work force is ageing and getting smaller: Japan has one of the lowest birth rates in the west, what with young people getting married later and later on account of the economy... You must have seen all those empty islands. So, there's less tax coming in, more money going out on health care and pensions. There's very high internal debt, and of course when the immediate economic competition is China and Korea, it's very hard..."

Rationally, it was time for them to move on. But, like us, they were finding it difficult.

A long stretch of contrary easterly winds set in. There were two early-season typhoons that passed to the south of us and made us glad that we had not rushed to sea. They wrecked the separate attempts of two British adventurers respectively to kayak and row across the North Pacific; both had to be rescued by the Japan Coastguard, whose vessels were usually moored just astern of *Bosun Bird* in Shimoda.

What we were now waiting for was the annual phenomenon by which the Baiu or Tsuyu ("Plum Rain," a wet front that arrives around the time that plums ripen) is pushed northwards by the expanding Pacific High, reaches the Japanese archipelago and gradually drifts up over it. The front brings three weeks or so of rain with it before summer proper arrives. As long as the front remains to the south it provides a convenient low-pressure alley for typhoons to wheel to the northeast, directly across our path. Once north of us it would (in theory) give us more southerly and westerly winds that would help us on our way.

The delay enforced by the weather meant we had to make a three-hour trip by rail to Shizuoka, to renew our about-to-expire visas with a Mr. Hamada at the regional immigration office. But our friends Ishii and Naito conveniently had a close friend here—Terao San, a City Councillor for the Communist Party—so we made a day of it. With him, we dutifully "oohed" and "aahed" at an ethereal Mount Fuji and paid a quick visit to the marina at Shimizu to see the yacht that Terao proudly co-owned. As we poked around below, Terao coughed theatrically and shyly indicated a patch of bare fiberglass. It had been autographed in felt-tip-pen by New Zealand yachting legend Peter Gilmour when he had once visited Japan to advise the Japanese sailing team.

"Mundai..." said Terai. ("Problem").

"What do you mean...?"

"Yotto old, I want to sell. But I cannot sell. Writing too important," and he laughed.

Terao and a friend took us up into the mountains to the spectacular Toshogu Shrine, where one of the great Tokugawa Shoguns is buried. Just restored, this was a riot of gold leaf and vermilion, with many intricate wooden carvings of dragons and less mythical beasts. As a departure present, they shyly gave us a Hagoita, an implement in a traditional game of shuttlecock, consisting of a beautifully embroidered and decorated paddle. The more successfully you play this game, they say, the greater protection you will have against mosquitoes: the shuttlecocks used in Hagoita games are said to resemble dragonflies in flight; and dragonflies eat mosquitoes.

Back in Shimoda, Itoh, who ran Shimoda Yacht Services and was one of the City Fathers, plied us with many cups of green tea as we mused over the weather. Every day he would print off the day's meteorological chart and we would ponder it together. Every day it seemed to be the same:

"Low," he would say, tapping with his pen at the low pressure to the south of us. "Need low here," and he would move the pen upwards.

"High here," he'd add, unnecessarily.

"Maybe tomorrow," Itoh would conclude with a big toothy smile.

No doubt sensing we needed someone to communicate with in a more substantive manner, he introduced us to one of his good friends. Nakamura San ran a coffee shop called Okawaya Fruits, that had been in Shimoda since 1811. But she was also an accomplished translator/interpreter and elementary school teacher. Mrs. Nakamura introduced us to her Grade 5 and 6 English students (English had only just been brought in at this level) and we gave a number of talks about our sailing experience. Mostly, the questions were what you would have expected of North American Grade 5s:

"Did you see any monsters?"

"How many pirates did you meet?"

The most thrilling picture was one we showed of a coral snake that had come on board up our cockpit drains in Vanuatu: one of the little girls screamed. As Grade 5s typically are, they were also interested in earthy matters such as how the marine toilet worked and how we showered (standing out in the rain); in embarrassment, Nakamura San had to shush them up. We were impressed with the careful preparations made by the teachers in case of natural disasters. Tsunami and earthquake drills were held regularly, and the children must always have their white helmets at hand. In one of the schools, the Grade 5s were responsible for looking after the school's rice paddy, seeing the whole cultivation process right through from planting to the annual production of some 60 kg of prime rice.

At all the schools (as elsewhere in Japan), cleaning of the premises, including the bathrooms, was done by the children themselves with only minimal adult supervision. School lunches, at least around Shimoda, were centrally cooked then distributed by van. The children ate at their desks and took responsibility for serving and cleaning up, as well as saying prayers before and after; white smocks and hair-caps were obligatory at lunch time (to which we were invited).

At Ogamo Elementary the Principal, Tonoka San, insisted on breaking his busy schedule to take us for an afternoon drive in the nearby countryside, complete with a treat of Wasabi (horseradish) ice cream. Next day, as rain and wind lashed *Bosun Bird*, one of the young teachers from Ogamo knocked tentatively on our hull. He had brought a carefully lettered Thank You poster for us, with whales, sharks, and dolphins drawn around tiny pictures of a little yacht en route to Alaska.

Another evening, Nakamura San's mother gave Jenny a lesson on how to make sashimi (more work still required: the rice stuck to everything but itself) and we all then enjoyed a sumptuous Japanese dinner. While Japanese sushi and sashimi are justly famous, what impressed us as much was the enormous care taken to present the food in an attractive, colorful manner; you almost feel guilty when you break the symmetry by taking that first piece of sashimi. One afternoon we went around for a talk with Nakamura San's aged and infirm father. He insisted on standing up, bowed to us and, through his daughter, said:

"You honor us by visiting our home."

We chatted about his life.

Dinner with Nakamura San and Family

"Yes, I was in Manchuria before the war. I was a private, not an officer. We were not from an officer family, you see. It was terribly cold; I never knew anything like that winter. So many of us died."

And he tailed off. Jenny lightened the tone by asking Mrs Nakamura senior the secret to making sticky rice. She thought carefully, put a finger to her lower lip, then said enigmatically:

"Old Japanese secret…"

Her daughter interrupted with a laugh:

"Special electric sticky rice cooker!"

Whenever we were in port, we were in search of Wi-Fi. In many towns, there was free Wi-Fi at the train stations. McDonald's was another option. One evening we walked home to *Bosun Bird* late, after an hour of reading and sending email and a couple of Big Macs. Hours after we had gone to bed—it was past two o'clock in the morning—there was a very tentative knock on the hull and the even more tentative call:

"Police, please!"

In alarm, I grabbed some clothes and climbed out into the cockpit. A young female officer in uniform apologized profusely for waking us. She held out her hand, with Jenny's wallet. It had been found at McDonald's and handed in, she said.

"But how did you know to find us?" I asked.

"Oh, is very easy." She opened the wallet to show us.

"I find card inside. It has address and telephone of Mr. Ishii San, from Kobe. I think he your friend so I call him. He tell me two Gaijin on Yotto, so I come to find only Yotto in Shimoda... Everyone know you are here."

Of course, there was nothing missing. But we felt sorry for Ishii who must have been woken up at home with this strange request from the Shimoda police.

More friends we made included the Director of the Shimoda History Museum and his colleague, another Sensei, whom we met at the Gasshou Folk Museum that the Sensei ran. This was a giant four-story A-frame house of wood and thatch transferred here from the Gifu region of Japan in 1964. It was used in its heyday, some 200 years earlier, for the raising of silkworms and was now packed with a fascinating clutter of smoke-encrusted farm and domestic junk. Chatting in the eye-watering and dark interior, the polymath master corrected our impression that tranquil Shimoda must have escaped the horrors of the war:

"You see, the B29s went for Tokyo. But sometimes they could not find their target. We were the only place on their way home to Guam, so they would drop their bombs here... I lost both my parents in the bombings, here in Shimoda. Everything was wooden in those days; everything burned."

We'd met lots of wannabe cruisers in Japan, but few who had actually been out there and done it, let alone as a couple. So, we were delighted to be approached in the street one day by Shu, who had seen our boat and found herself immediately nostalgic for the time she and her husband Hiro went cruising fifteen years earlier to Australia and New Caledonia aboard . She showed us fading color prints of their adventures. Over a hot foot bath and cups of tea we encouraged her to set off again, before it was too late.

Shu, who had an air of the hippie about her and spoke excellent English with a slightly American twang, was sanguine. Hiro kept getting absorbed by new projects, she said; he'd already built three houses and she didn't think he was focused enough to get his act together and go sailing. She was disarmingly frank and mused aloud:

"I have told him to stop sleeping with me. Maybe one day soon I will leave him... I don't know. What do you think?"

Shimoda still would not let us go. Twice, three times a day now, we would get out our chart for the North Pacific, measure out the curving route to Alaska, plot the weather systems that lay in our path, the ones that were lurking over near Taiwan and that might still come our way. Our nervousness grew. In the evenings, to pass the time, we often watched movies on our laptop. We'd copied these from friends over the past two to three years and often their titles meant little to us. One evening we cranked up a movie called *The Guardian*.

The dramatic opening sequence has a sailboat foundering in rough, cold seas as a red and white rescue helicopter clatters overhead. The husband and wife jump overboard. Then the desperate husband fights the wife to be the first into the rescue basket that has been lowered. The chopper finally gets under way, with both of the shivering yacht crew aboard, while Navy diver Kevin Costner glowers at the un-chivalrous and sniveling husband. The first words of the movie are spoken by the pilot, into his radio:

"Kodiak base, Kodiak base; we're on our way…"

We were not reassured. Kodiak was our precise destination.

Quiver, a Canadian Vancouver 27 that, the previous year, had sailed from Japan to British Columbia, had a good weather window in early June. But in 2012 all of May and most of June passed. The Pacific High, which we were hoping would strengthen sufficiently so as to graze Japan and give us those favorable westerly winds, remained weak and distant.

Then came word that a Super Typhoon named Guchol was on its way.[43] Fishing boats from all over south-central Honshu streamed into Shimoda, for the tight, safe river moorings it provided. For two or three days the place was a hive of activity as lines were led across the river in huge spiders' webs, in such a way that when arrangements were finally complete, you could not have left if you had wanted to. An air of tension filled the town. Everything went eerily quiet as the skies darkened, the rain began and the winds built up. The fishermen all went home to watch TV and see where Guchol would make landfall, leaving every vessel except ours deserted, left to fend for itself. There was nobody on the streets, everything was closed.

The storm struck early on the evening of June 19th at Kushimoto, one of the favorite stops we had made on the Kii peninsula. It was the first typhoon to hit Honshu in June in a decade. But in Shimoda we dodged the eye by seventy miles. The winds rose to 60 knots for several hours, causing the pontoon to which we were lashed to snake uneasily from side to side and, as swells in the outer bay increased, to begin undulating gently. We didn't sleep much as our lines strained and creaked, the wind howled and we heeled violently from one side to the other. Even the town street lamps briefly went out, adding to the sense of doom.

By morning all was quiet, the river turbid and full of debris. A second storm (Talim) followed two or three days later. We reconsidered our options. The Pacific High was still distant. We would face moderate easterlies for several days after we left Japan, but it looked as though we now had at least a week to

---

43   The World Meteorological Organization maintains a roster of potential names for storms, from submissions by regional member countries; Guchol means Turmeric in the language of Yap.

spare before another typhoon might start cartwheeling towards us. It would be sufficient time, we hoped, to cross the typical southwest to northeast paths the storms follow. It was time to take the plunge before another Guchol came our way.

Our friends were reluctant to let us go. Nakamura San took us to a special private tea ceremony at one of the town's oldest temples, where the wife of the temple priest presided. Here, the Shogun himself had once rested while waiting for a fair wind to take him to Edo (modern day Tokyo). We were presented with a beautiful hand-made tea bowl in memory of our own visit.

On Friday June 22nd, we hopped on to the first available train for the three-hour ride to see our friend Hamada San at the Immigration Office again. We were worried he was going to be difficult; he had let us know that the rules said that once he had stamped our passports, we had only 24 hours to leave. But he took them off to the back room, came back a few moments later, and said:

"Here are passports. Please open on train. Not now. Please have safe sail."

We were mystified and opened the passports in the down elevator. He'd given us four extra days of leeway, quite against the regulations.

The weather window remained open. We said sad goodbyes to Nakamura San, to Itoh, and to his wife. A week or so earlier, when we had had a false start, we had given Itoh a fine bottle of Ballantyne's whisky. We now saw he'd put it in a display case along with much memorabilia associated with Japan's long-ago America's Cup bid, in which he'd had a hand. Itoh's wife saw our puzzlement and took us on one side:

"I think it is best if Mr. Itoh not drink this… Last elementary school reunion…," and she graphically demonstrated a human being falling flat on the floor. "So, I tell him to put whisky in museum instead."

I wrestled with a last-minute problem that inconveniently made the head (toilet) unusable again, Jenny bought up half the fresh produce section of the MaxValu supermarket and…we were more or less ready. On a grey Saturday morning, we motored out into the open Pacific, across the wide mouth of Tokyo Bay. Destination: Alaska, 3,500 miles away.

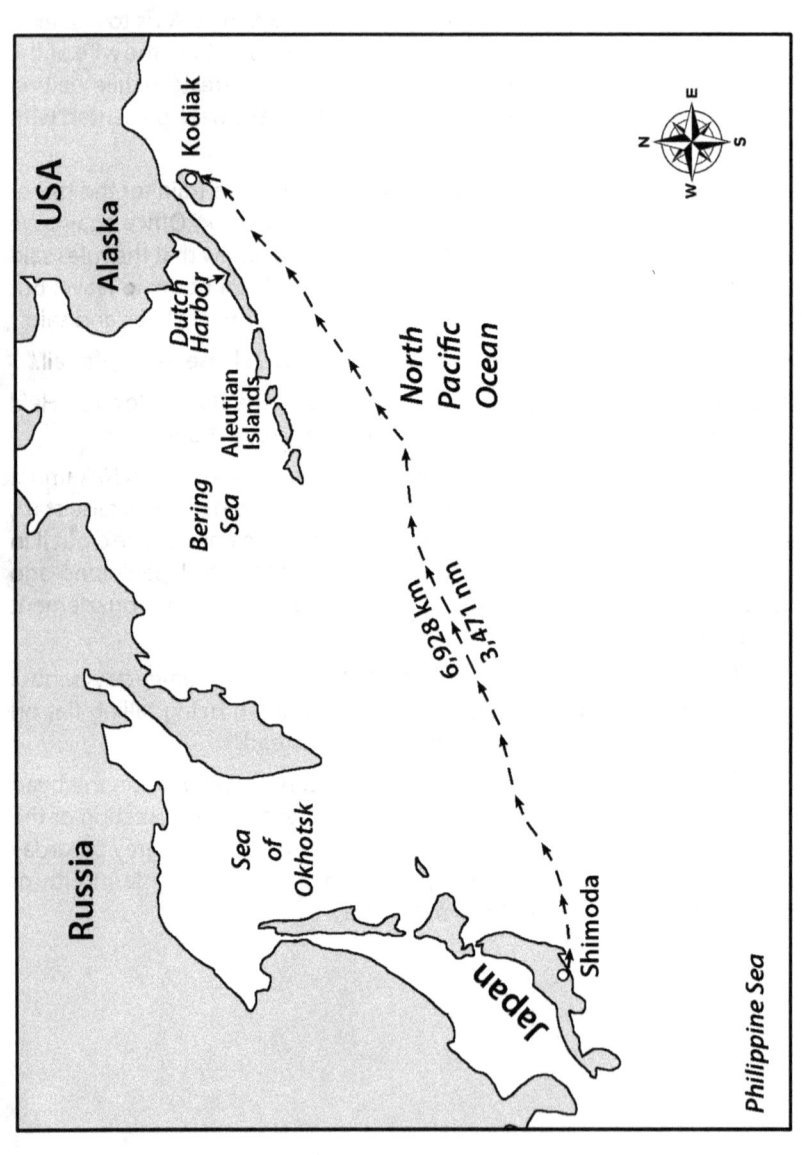

Shimoda to Kodiak

Epilogue:
Kodiak, Alaska

The forecast on our laptop said easterly winds, the Japanese Navy northwesterly. The laptop was unfortunately right.

We made our way between two big, high islands: O Shima (another one) and Tō Shima, grey-blue in the haze, like those old Japanese watercolors. They were the last land we saw for weeks. Under overcast skies, day after day, we tacked first to one side then the other, looking for a more favorable angle on the wind and occasionally picking up a boost from the current.

Our second night out, the loom of the vast metropolis that is Tokyo and Yokohama faded slowly away, leaving us lonely. But fishing boats were a worry for another three or four days. After that, almost the only company was the flashing red lights of long-haul aircraft far above us and heading for North America. It was odd to think of the passengers, five miles up, settling down for their evening meal, maybe a movie; by morning they'd be in Seattle or San Francisco.

It is the opening days of these long passages that are usually the most difficult. The distance to be run seems almost insuperable. On our chart, which had the Philippines on the left and North America on the right, the little "x" marks we made every evening to show our progress could hardly be separated. We knew that we could have easily stayed back a few days and right now could be enjoying a walk on shore or a meal at a restaurant. And we knew that sooner or later we would get hit with some bad weather.

Four days and 200 miles out, a large white fishing or research vessel slowly came over to have a look at us. Under its bow, floating and somehow secured to the vessel, was unmistakably the carcass of a whale; some men were peering over the side at it. What was the ship doing? We called up the captain but there was no answer.

And the winds stayed invariably in the east, northeast, or southeast There was just one very uncomfortable period of 40 knot southerlies that pushed us onwards; but it made for a couple of unpleasant, rain-lashed nights.

Beating en route to Alaska

As the wind rose, we would progressively reduce sail until we reached the extremity of running under bare poles, that is to say maintaining forward motion just from the pressure of the wind on the hull and bare rigging. The routine was always the same. The crew member who was below would start uneasily to sense that *Bosun Bird* was heeling more and more, that we were rushing down the waves, crashing and shuddering as we hit oncoming seas. Occasionally there would be a loud machine-gun clatter as the sail luffed in the strengthening wind. Then would come the call from outside:

"Time to put a reef in…"

Out of the warm and dry sleeping bag, stumble to the wet-weather locker while holding on, put on damp and musty-smelling wet-weather gear. Next the rubber boots; it was easy in the dark to put these on the wrong foot; and it was awkward bending down on the slightly slippery cabin sole while trying not to fall as the boat lurched. All the time, the movement would be getting more violent.

Then came the safety harness; its seatbelt-like straps would invariably twist so that it was too tight to put on, while the person in the cockpit muttered ever more impatiently. Finally, the life jacket, with its whistle, strobe light, and knife all attached. Unzip the companionway cover, feel around in the dark to find a U-bolt to snap in the safety harness's snap-link. Stumble out into the blackness and rain, to be greeted by:

"What took you so long?"

While Jenny minded the tiller or the automatic wind vane, I'd turn on my headlamp and organize the multitude of color coded reefing lines and halyards that were coiled up under the dodger, either side of the companionway. Usually, they had become tangled as the boat had pitched and lurched. As I took each step in the reefing process, I'd then call out what I was doing, and Jenny would confirm.

More times than not, as the sail came down the track on the mast, a slug would jam and prevent the process from being completed. When this occurred, Jenny would have to unclip her safety line, reach around carefully to clip it onto one of the stainless steel jack-lines that ran up each side deck; then cautiously make the step out of the cockpit and onto the windward side-deck, which was usually being swept with waves. Making her way forward, she'd unjam the slug by hand, and retreat to the safety of the cockpit again.

It was a complicated procedure but with practice we could do it in a few minutes. The reward was invariably a gentler, less violent motion. The duty crew would huddle once again out of the worst of the spray, behind the dodger. The off-duty member would retreat below, undress, and get back into the same, still warm sleeping bag—after checking to see how much time remained to the end of the watch.

After one moderately sunny day at the start, with a glorious sunset, the fog set in. It stayed with us almost all the way to Alaska. Day upon day would pass with visibility at no more than 100 meters, often accompanied by a fine, chill-inducing drizzle. We had hoped to spend many of the night watches listening to our iPod; but in these conditions, it was wiser to be listening for ship's engines and/or for the alarm on our AIS that would indicate a ship on a converging course with ours. Jenny got more nervous than I did about approaching ships. If I was in my bunk off watch, I'd hear the AIS beeping. She'd come down to have a look at the screen, turn off the alarm, then go out again. This would happen two or three times. I would brace myself. Then:

"Would you mind getting up to have a look?"

Ten days out, steering to the east-northeast, we were on the route that the Japanese fleet—six aircraft carriers, under the command of Vice-Admiral Chuichi Nagumo—had taken in the winter of 1941. The ships had assembled at Etorofu, off Hokkaido, and set sail for a point far to the north-northwest of Hawaii (whence they would turn south) on November 26th. A combination of strict radio silence and signals deception meant that until the moment the attack began at dawn on December 7th, US intelligence was convinced that the carriers were still in home waters.

The fog that hangs over the North Pacific for much of the year, broken up in winter by heavy gales, hid the fleet from the curious eyes of aircraft but it must have made keeping the carriers in line a massive challenge. The radio silence meant that none of the ships could speak with each other, they showed no running lights and Nagumo also prohibited signaling with lights. It would have been almost as tense for Admiral Yamamoto, waiting at home for news of the attack. In code he could signal political developments, including the last-minute declaration of war (that arrived late) but he could receive no word back of his ships' progress.

As little *Bosun Bird* felt her way onwards over the same waters, we were reminded almost daily of that time. Among the various weather-related items, we'd download every morning via our satellite phone, the key forecast was always from Pearl Harbor.

Most days there were boat chores to be done. Both of our sheet winches developed a worrying propensity to lift off their cylindrical mounts when in use. Dismantling, cleaning, and reassembling these devices is delicate at the best of times, involving carefully prying out with a small screwdriver, tiny little springs that are all too liable to ping away (and over the side) during extraction. Performing the job while the boat pitches and rolls, with the occasional burst of cold seawater spray thrown in, is testing. Every so often we would have moments of perplexity. Our Aries wind vane gave excellent service to the point of indispensability, but I'd find myself saying to Jenny as I leaned anxiously over the stern:

"See this bolt here? It's angled upwards. You can't tighten it at all; it's bottomed out. But if it falls out the whole vane falls into the water… How could anyone have designed something this way?"

A cable tie and generous application of insulating tape did the trick in this instance, but then you were left worrying about other as-yet-undetected disasters that could be waiting to happen.

When it wasn't raining or blowing so hard that we were likely to get soaked by spray, we'd read on day watches. We had assembled a motley collection of paperbacks courtesy of Shelley's English-language School in Shimoda but as the days drew on and it became evident that it was not going to be a fast passage, we'd both find ourselves eyeing our dwindling supply, dreading the moment when there would be nothing for it but to open some heavy Penguin Classic. I lingered for days over Joyce Carol Oates' *We Were the Mulvaneys*, deliberately rationing myself to two or three pages at a time, not looking forward to the next tome on the shelf. Figuring out my tactics, Jenny would scold:

"There's no getting away with it. No more serial killers. Next you have to read that book of essays by Clive James."

The damp got everywhere. Woolen sweaters still kept us warm but started to smell, the inside of our wet-weather gear was always clammy. And the paperbacks swelled by the day. A few started to develop large patches of mold on the inner pages, close to the binding, and we got into the habit of placing the worst-affected books inside or on top of the oven for half an hour a day. Jenny's glasses were permanently fogged, our hair never dry-feeling, the pillows cold and damp.

We munched through our supplies steadily. Several loaves of white bread were still quite edible after two weeks, a comment on the quantities of chemical preservatives that Japanese bakers use. It was a particularly sad day when we ate the last Chocolate Chip Melon Pan.

So as to break the routine, we had celebrations. The most important of these was on July 20th, over 2,000 miles and a month out from Shimoda, when we crossed the 180-degree meridian. We carefully set the camera up to record the instant when we passed from the eastern to the western hemisphere, capturing the reading 180.00.000 W, but we were not quick enough to catch the corresponding numbers for E (exactly the same position…). It was the usual drizzly afternoon, but we got out a Suma Yacht Owners' flag that had been presented to us, and a pennant of Shimoda Yacht Services, given by Itoh San; we drank a small bottle of vintage Sake. Ceremonially we adjusted our watches to Midway/Samoa Time, which must be the most under-populated time zone on Earth. The log records that we lived Friday July 20th twice.

We were not lonely. On this passage we were never without the company of birds, including a solitary Laysan Albatross and a much rarer Black-footed Albatross, whom we named respectively Albert and Black Albert. At night tiny storm petrels fluttered around the stern, by day dancing in the foam of our bow waves. For several days running, a squadron of porpoises came by to give us company, two or three times a day. Contrary to expectations, we saw very little garbage. Every two or three days we might glimpse a plastic water bottle tossing on a wave-top, or a small piece of Styrofoam. But there was much less junk on this route than we had found in 1989 when edging around the Pacific High, bound from Hawaii to British Columbia on our earlier yacht. Sadly, this time around there were no glass fishing floats to pick up; they had gone out of use years ago.

Friday August 3rd and we were exactly six weeks out from Shimoda, but 43 days of elapsed time. As dusk fell, I picked up the binoculars, trained them over the port beam and adjusted the focus back and forth. At last, I was sure. I called down to Jenny:

"Crew on deck…"

"Do I have to? I've just put the spaghetti on…"

"Yes you have to."

Faint but unmistakable in the evening haze was the whaleback outline of Sitkinak Island, one of Kodiak's outliers. Soon we were starting to pick up Kodiak Coastguard Radio, for local weather forecasts. We checked the FM radio: three religious stations, two Country and Western.

Remains of wartime coastal guns, near Kodiak (Alaska)

Next day the weather gods were generous: brilliant sunshine, pleasant following winds, the first time we had had such a combination on this crossing. There to port were the jagged snow-capped peaks of Kodiak itself. Albert and Black Albert were joined by puffins, fulmars, and dozens of juvenile Black-footed Albatrosses. A Humpback whale surfaced, sighed, and sank again. For twenty minutes or so a squadron of killer whales went about their business 100 meters away from us.

For the first time in weeks were able to strip off the top layer of our cumbersome foul weather gear and feel a semblance of warmth. A red and white helicopter from the massive US Coastguard Base on the island briefly disturbed the peace by buzzing us. Jenny craned her neck to look upwards:

"I can't see Kevin Costner in the cockpit."

The sun set late, the moon came up, the Humpbacks returned. By dawn of our final morning, we were negotiating the entrance channel to Chiniak Bay, Kodiak, comparing perplexing green, white, and red flashes with the notations on the chart. Chunky fishing boats chugged outwards, their lights still blazing.

As we drew near to port my finger wandered over the chart to a small notation just north of the bay:

"Coastal guns (ruins)."

I recalled that sunny headland we'd walked out to near Christchurch, New Zealand, the coastal guns. And the old tin trunk that had started us on this adventure. I'd have a few things to tell my Dad about Japan now, I thought. I might even change his mind about visiting.

From below, Jenny called out:

"I've set the last waypoint, for St Paul Harbor. Two miles."

Appendix: Cruising Notes for Japan

A – General
B – Kyushu: Kagoshima to Nagasaki
C – Kyushu: The Goto Retto Archipelago
D – Kyushu: Goto Retto to Fukuoka
E – Inland Sea: General
F – The Inland Sea: Fukuoka to Hiroshima
G – Inland Sea: Central
H – Inland Sea: Osaka area
I – South/Central Honshu

A – General

Ports of Entry (Open Ports). Entry by sailboat can only be made at designated Ports of Entry ("Open Ports") Ports. In southwestern Japan these include Okinawa, Chichijima, Kagoshima, Nagasaki, and Fukuoka (the last three all on the island of Kyushu). While the island of Amami-o-Shima might be a tempting landfall for yachts approaching from the south, there are no immigration officials based here.

For the full list of Open Ports, see:

https://www.mlit.go.jp/common/001257673.pdf.

Application forms for entry should be sent in advance from your last port of departure to the appropriate office of the Japan Coast Guard (which is affiliated with the Ministry of Land, Infrastructure, Transport, and Tourism - MLIT). You should update your arrival information no later than one working day before your actual arrival. More information and the necessary form can be found at https://www.kaiho.mlit.go.jp/ope/apply/hoan00-e.html.

Some contacts:
- Kagoshima (Kyushu) jcgakagoshimakotsu1-2c2a@mlit.go.jp
- Naha (Okinawa) jcgbnahakq3-8f5m@mlit.go.jp

- Chichijima (Ogasawara) jcg3ogasawara-9q3p@mlit.go.jp
- Wakayama (Osaka Bay) jcg5wakayamakotsu2-7g2d@mlit.go.jp
- Shimoda, (Shizuoka) jcg3shimodakq1-9t8x@mlit.go.jp

For more on entry procedures, see:

https://100r.co/site/sailing_in_japan.html#entry_procedures

Check-in procedures are lengthy; you can expect up to ten officials (from Immigration, Customs, Coastguard/Transport, Agriculture, and possibly Police), most of whom will wish to come aboard and have you fill in multiple forms. In the case of Kagoshima, staff at Kagoshima Marine Services (at the marina at Taniyama; see below) summoned all the officials on our behalf; Immigration had us come with them to their downtown office, half an hour away.

You can expect a polite but formal official scolding if your date/time of arrival differ greatly from your forecast; you may be required to post, within your boat, an official notice of reprimand.

Onward formalities. All ports in Japan are deemed to be either "Open" or "Closed." Until recently, cruisers had to apply at an Open Port with the Maritime Bureau of MLIT for permission to visit each and every Closed Port on their subsequent itinerary. This process has now been greatly simplified and a single Cruising Permit can be issued at the Port of Entry. A minimum of one week's notice is required.

See: https://www.mlit.go.jp/en/maritime/specialpermission.html but see https://www.mlit.go.jp/common/001420113.pdf which explains that you do not need to list every Closed Port.

Radio contact. Very few Japanese sailboats or fishing boats have VHF radio; the fishing boats use their own version of Citizens' Band. However, the Coastguard and large commercial vessels monitor VHF Channel 16. You should not necessarily expect your interlocutor to speak English.

Accessing information on the internet. For a visitor to Japan, it is relatively easy to buy a data SIM card but currently not so easy to obtain a voice SIM card. A number of websites describe the complications, for example: https://trulytokyo.com/how-to-buy-a-sim-card-in-tokyo/.

Although many of the websites listed are in Japanese only, we found Google Translate does a reasonable job.

Boats approaching Japan from offshore with low bandwidth internet access (for example by satellite phone), who wish to access weather/current information, will need to use their current method of internet access. Traditionally this has involved two services:

- an email service that minimizes the amount of data in an email message
- a service that allows you to request information on the internet that is delivered by email. It could be from a library maintained by the service

or a web page. Typically, you can make a one-time request or subscribe to receive the information at specified intervals. https://saildocs.com/ is one example of such as service.

While in Japan, if the signal from our data SIM card was poor or non-existent, we would use this method. For more ideas see: https://www.practical-sailor.com/marine-electronics/ocean-tested-must-have-software-for-cruisers.

Approach to Kyushu from the south. It is useful to have, in advance, a chart of the usual track of the Kurushio Current and its various offshoots and countercurrents; the Pilot Charts are inadequate for this purpose. For an overview, see: https://bluejapan.org/geography/currents-of-japan/.

When it is still more than 100 miles from Kyushu, the northeast trending Kurushio begins to turn to east and southeast; it runs at speeds of 2 to 3 knots. For boats with reasonable bandwidth internet access, estimates of the present location of the current (updated every weekday) can be found at: https://www1.kaiho.mlit.go.jp/KANKYO/KAIYO/qboc/index_E.html.

General notes on cruising. Japan's coastline is exceptionally indented and long but virtually every tempting-looking nook, however unlikely, has a harbor installation of some sort and/or floating fish/seaweed farms. The amount of harbor infrastructure is staggering, with even small ports having hundreds of meters of built-up inner seawalls and off-lying breakwaters.

Small local fishing boats usually moor Med-style, bows to the wall, the stern held off by an anchor or mooring; unoccupied moorings that you may see in fishing harbors are usually private.

Sailboats have three choices:

a) The Med-mooring pattern, in which case it may be necessary to launch a dinghy to run lines ashore; there is some risk of fouling an anchor as harbor floors are typically crisscrossed with mooring lines.

b) Side-tie to the wall. You need to find a relatively smooth wall with no overhang and use either a fender board and/or the large foam fenders favored by the fishermen (which can be purchased locally). Getting on and off at low tide may be a challenge, and line adjustment will be necessary as the tide moves up and down. In theory, wall areas for visitors are marked in black and yellow paint. Some Japanese yachtsmen carry rigid ladders so as to be able to scale high walls.

c) Find a floating pontoon to tie to (or barge/boat to raft). Most harbors have pontoons, but you may be required to move at short notice should a local ferry arrive and/or fishboats wish to use the pontoon for loading/unloading.

Few local yachts ever anchor at all; many consider their anchors as emergency-use only and are unpracticed. The local fishing boats do sometimes anchor and at great depth, but on light ground tackle and only for a few hours at a time.

The relationship between Japanese yachtsmen and fishermen is occasionally antagonistic. As a foreigner, and provided you observe all the usual courtesies (avoiding nets, asking permission to side-tie etc.), you will likely be given considerable leeway. But few fishermen are likely to speak English; if you unwittingly break some taboo, displeasure may occasionally be manifested in silent passive-aggression.

Weather. Common wisdom has it that the best time to approach Japan from the South Pacific or equatorial zones is mid-March to late April, when the winter trades have begun to ease but before the risk of typhoons[44] has begun to crank up.

We arrived in Kagoshima in mid-April to find that it was still cool (but sunny). By mid-May the rainy season was beginning and the daily temperatures rising, with many days of overcast, light rain, some fog and light winds from round the clock. On May 25th the first typhoon of the season manifested itself: a "Super" typhoon (winds of 100 knots plus) that hit Okinawa hard but that only brushed Kyushu. The second typhoon came a month later.

Weather forecasting. We generally accessed English-language weather forecasts at http://www.jma.go.jp/en/seafcst/ using our data SIM card.

So as to be ready for poor internet access, before setting off we would save this page on our laptop. In case of no signal, we would then use our satellite phone (see Accessing information on the internet above). Using the saved page, we could see the marine weather forecast areas used by the Japanese Meteorological Agency (JMA) and the corresponding text web page. We would then request/subscribe to that web page.

For typhoon tracking, see https://www.metoc.navy.mil/jtwc/jtwc.html.

As above, in the case of no signal we used our satellite phone and requested/subscribed to: https://www.metoc.navy.mil/jtwc/products/abpwweb.txt.

This web page of the Joint Typhoon Warning Centre (JTWC) is updated daily. It lists any typhoons/cyclones developing and developed in the northwestern North Pacific (180 degrees longitude to Malay Peninsula), and also in the South Pacific, from the coast of South America to 135º E. As and when a typhoon/cyclone develops, the site gives you the reference to more detailed information (it says SEE REF near the end); to obtain the more detailed information, request/subscribe to: https://tgftp.nws.noaa.gov/data/raw/wt/xxxxxx.pgtw..txt, where xxxxxx is the reference (4 letters plus 2 digits) you obtained from abpwweb. Note the two periods after "pgtw." Usually, you have three to seven days' notice of a typhoon.

---

[44] "Typhoon" is the term used for tropical cyclones occurring in the northwestern Pacific; "Hurricane" for the Atlantic and northeastern Pacific; "Cyclone" for elsewhere. Typhoons account for one third of all tropical cyclones.

If you have a good Internet connection then the websites of both JMA (http://www.jma.go.jp/jma/indexe.html) and JTWC (https://www.metoc.navy.mil/jtwc/jtwc.html) have a host of useful information, including graphic representations of projected typhoon tracks.

Charts. Virtually every cove in Japan has an artificial harbor at its head. Many of these are shown in only very sketchy detail on C-Map; the situation is complicated by the fact that new construction is constantly going on. Ideally one should buy all the relevant paper charts, but that could be prohibitively expensive.

A compromise option is the 12-volume "S-Guide" of chartlets, numbered H800-W to H812-W. These are now out of print; but pdf versions of the same books are available (for a fee); each volume contains fifty or more harbor Chartlets. For online sales, volumes are divided into groups of ten to fifteen Chartlets: https://www.jha.or.jp/en/shop/products/smallcraft/index.html.

The Chartlets are in color and have excellent detail, the usual international symbols (for lights etc.) are used and they have exact latitudes and longitudes indicated. However, most of the script is Japanese (kanji characters), so one of the first things you need to do is have a friend transliterate the harbor names into western script. An "S" inside a red circle indicates areas/walls considered particularly suitable for small craft. The books also have a chart showing the meaning of the complex arrays of lights that Japanese fishing boats display (again, translation is necessary) and a small but useful chart of typical typhoon tracks.

We found it useful to supplement these Chartlets with Google Earth/Maps; the rate of construction is such that recent developments are much more likely to show on Google than on the charts.

The books are by no means comprehensive; many harbors we visited were not in the books. For this reason, it was useful to consult Japanese yachtsmen for their recommendations, in particular regarding the availability of pontoons.

The Japan Nautical Chart Web Shop at https://www.jha.or.jp/shop/index.php?main_page=index lists some of the newer possibilities:
- paper charts specially for small craft (Y charts);
- various formats of electronic charts.

List of marinas ("Sea Stations"). https://www.umi-eki.jp/en/. This list is not comprehensive and includes a number of locations suitable only for dinghies. It is in English and has telephone numbers. Some marinas maintain websites, often in Japanese only, but Google Translate helps and the photos are useful. The fax machine is still in widespread use.

Hospitality. The artificial nature of cruising in Japan (virtually no anchoring, nearly always in harbors) is more than compensated by the hospitality that is customarily offered to the few foreign yachts that venture to these waters (ten to twelve annually, it is thought). Reciprocating can be a problem, but in our experience, acquaintances greatly appreciate simply being invited on board for a cup of tea or a drink. A supply of small gifts such as flag pins is useful.

When visiting Japanese friends' homes or boats, be wary of expressing too much admiration for items on view as they may be pressed upon you. Learning at least a few words of Japanese is a good idea; you may be surprised by how little English your hosts have, this notwithstanding the fact that English has long been a compulsory subject at school. In our experience, only those who have lived/worked abroad are likely to be fluent. A preparedness to sample the local cuisine, however odd or mysterious it may initially seem, will enrich your stay; basic chopstick-handling is essential.

Should you base yourself in a single location for a significant amount of time, know that when Japanese people go travelling away from their homes for more than a day or two, they customarily bring back gift items—often the "typical" confectionery of the place—for friends and colleagues. You will win many friends if you observe this practice.

Some useful nautical terms:

Sailboat – ヨット – Yotto

Fishing boat – 漁船 – Gyosen

Marina – マリーナ – Marina

Harbor/port – 港 – Minato

Bay/inlet – 浦 – Ura (or (Oura)

Beach – 浜 – Hama

Large bay – 湾 – Wan

Island – 島 – Shima, Jima, Tō

North – 北 – Kita

South – 南 – Minami

East – 東 – Azuma

West – 西 – Nishi

Prices. At the time of our visit (2011-2012) the exchange rate was approximately 1USD to 80¥ (yen). By late 2023, the exchange rate was approximately 1USD to 145¥. Accordingly, all quoted prices should be taken as extremely approximate.

B – Kyushu: Kagoshima to Nagasaki

GPS positions/distances. All positions listed are in degrees and decimal minutes. Distances at sea are given in nautical miles.

Kagoshima. This is a modern city of 600,000 on the western shore of Kagoshima Wan (Wan = Bay), where the long and wide bay is forced to narrow by the imposing, invariably smoking Sakurajima volcano on the eastern shore. There are several miles of built-up docks/waterfront, which are used not only by freighters but by large ferries that ply to Okinawa and elsewhere, and fast jetfoils that run to Yakushima Island. Incoming yachts are asked to tie up at Taniyama, a suburb of Kagoshima proper, eight kilometers to the south of the center. Officials will travel from downtown to meet you there, so there is no need to find a mooring space in the main dock area.

Kagoshima Marine Services (KMS) at Taniyama consists of an office and a yard for the dry storage of yachts; it formerly had responsibility for the "marina" adjoining, but at the time of our arrival the relationship between KMS and the marina was cloudy, and no charge was levied for our tying up.

Yachts moor in a well-protected cut off the main harbor; mooring is bow or stern-to the wall (tide is 2 to 3 meters), using buoys, mooring lines, and foam fenders that are already in place. Each mooring slot has its own tiny raft on which you pull yourself to the nearest ladder in the harbor wall. Our position: **31° 29.665' N, 130° 30.910' E** (Chartlet book H-809W, p. 72). The location is well-protected, the only downside being some wash from small passing fishing launches that come and go from their moorings further up the cut. Twenty or thirty yachts are moored here, with the same number on land; KMS owns a large crane and hauls yachts in and out on a daily basis; the local racers keep their boats on land and have them put in the water only for a few hours at a time.

There are showers at KMS (available in working hours) and a washing machine; there is no charge for either. The loan of bicycles may be possible. Water is available close to the office but not at the quayside. Diesel can be easily arranged through KMS (a truck comes regularly to fill the crane); alternatively, it is ten minutes' walk to the nearest gas station. The owner of KMS (who is also the crane driver) has a reputation as an excellent mechanic and all-round Mr. Fix-it for yachts. Hauling and long-term storage are possible.

There are two or three restaurants within a five-minute walk, and large supermarkets to the north and south, but a little further (20-minute walk, 10 by bike). Local currency (¥; yen) can be obtained via the ATM at the post office (fifteen minutes' walk, up the hill behind Taniyama) during normal working hours. There are suburban trains to Kagoshima proper, leaving from Sakanoue station, close to the post office, usually three per hour, ¥280/USD3.50 one way. It is also possible to take a bus from Sakanoue.

Yamagawa (Chartlet book H-809W, pp. 66-67) is a small fishing harbor in the southwest of Kagoshima Bay, usefully located for vessels heading up either the east or the west coast of Kyushu; it is 24 miles south of Taniyama (Kagoshima). There are three pontoons on the east shore of the bay; we tied up at the southernmost, which is pale green; our position: **31° 12.193' N, 130°**

38.028' E. No fee was charged. There is also a small inner enclosure behind walls in the southeast corner of the bay; a side-tie would be possible. As in many of these fishing villages, there is less and less fishing and the population is dwindling. And as in most, the starting and finishing hours for the working day are signaled with chimes of popular tunes (*Edelweiss*, *Love is Blue*) on the village loudspeakers. On shore there are one or two small shops and a covered market area; the small town is very quiet. A local train line runs to Kagoshima.

Makurazaki (Chartlet book H-809W, p. 62), 27 miles west of Yamagawa, is a medium-sized fishing town and harbor towards the south-southwest tip of Kyushu, approached via a series of L-bends between claustrophobically high harbor walls. Unlike most of the smaller ports in Kyushu, it is classed as an "Open" port. Compared to other harbors we visited, Makurazaki was relatively lively but still by no means busy. Exposed as it is to the Pacific, Makurazaki gets more than its fair share of very heavy seas from passing typhoons. But deep inside, this would be a good typhoon shelter. We tied to a pale green pontoon on the north shore at **31° 16.146' N, 130° 17.433' E**; no fee was charged; a municipal worker indicated that this would be acceptable, but for one night only. Wall tying would also be possible, notably in the enclosure in the extreme northwest corner. There is a large supermarket in town, also a Sento. Local train to Kagoshima.

Kasasa, 23 miles onwards to the west and then north along a rugged and spectacular coastline, is in a narrow but very well-protected inlet three miles east-southeast of Nomo Misaki. It does not appear in the book of Chartlets, and it may be helpful to Google Earth/Map it. As you approach, beware the fish havens in the lee of the northern breakwater; on the southern shore are the landmark buildings, red brick, of the large luxury Ebisu Hotel. The Ebisu has its own pontoon. Although there would be room for a medium-sized yacht on either side and at the end, one side of the pontoon is semi-permanently occupied by a much-travelled but modern Yamaha sailboat that is here as a museum piece (another such yacht is permanently installed on shore). The end of the pontoon may be occupied by a local whale-watching craft; either side-tie to it or to the free side. There is a fee of ¥2,000/USD25 plus ¥600/USD7.50 for the crew. This is a very secure and interesting location. Our position: **31° 24.916' N, 130° 08.046' E**. Your fee entitles you to a free printed weather forecast and free use of the hotel's luxurious Onsen, with a fine view over the East China Sea. You can also visit the hotel museum; this has miscellaneous exhibits on fishing (including two full-scale reconstructions of traditional wooden craft) and one room dedicated to the voyages of a locally well-known long-distance cruiser. There is a large wind farm on Nomo Misaki Cape, and you can visit, free of charge, a wind farm "museum" on the edge of town; there is a path to the lighthouse, but the vegetation is dense and there is no view to speak of from the light. There are a couple of small shops in the village.

Sato Ne (or Sato One) (Chartlet book H-809W, p. 59A) is towards the north end of the Koshiki Shima archipelago, 29 miles north of Kasasa. This picturesque group of islands was reportedly used by the Japanese navy when rehearsing for the attack on Pearl Harbor. When we visited there was a white and blue pontoon at **31° 50.510' N, 129° 55.287' E**, close by a very prominent, large hotel; but by late 2022 the pontoon had been removed. There would be plenty of other spaces for side-tying to walls (colorfully painted with murals), as commercial fishing here seems almost to have ended. There is a small supermarket five minutes' walk to the south. The town is very quiet but is reportedly busier in high summer. Behind the town, to the northwest, is another beach and small harbor. There is a Buddhist temple and, on top of the hill at the south end of town, the ruins of an old castle.

Akune (Chartlet book H-809W, pp. 50-51), 19 miles to the northeast from Sato Ne and back on the big island of Kyushu, is a large harbor with several mooring options. There is a pontoon in the southeast corner, marked on the chart, but this was occupied so we tied to another one in the northern sector, at **32° 01.738' N, 130° 11.443' E**. One side is used by a tourist boat/ferry; there was no fee. This is quite a big (but dying) town; there are good shopping options. Many of the shops' shutters are enlivened by imaginative mural paintings.

Ushibuka (Chartlet book H-809W, pp. 48-49) is a complex of harbors 18 miles to the north, including some tightly boxed pools with high typhoon fencing (perforated fencing that adds another 5 to 7 meters to the already substantial walls). Although pontoons are in short supply at Ushibuka this might be a good place to seek shelter in case of an advancing storm. We side-tied to the inner side of a wall protecting the final pool in the northwest extreme of the harbor but, when approaching, passed two other enclosures on our right that looked to be very snug as well. Our position: **32° 12.031' N, 130° 00.623' E**. As along most of this coastline the tidal range is 2 to 3 meters; it is advantageous to arrive close to high tide so that you can easily climb ashore; a fender board is useful against the very gnarly barnacles that encrust all the walls here. Ushibuka is picturesque; the small fishing boats in our pool tied up directly in front of their own combined stalls/sheds. They also seemed well-organized; when the weather forecast called for 25 to 30 knots, a red flag flew and nobody went out (the only place we observed this).

Nomo Ko (Chartlet book H-808W, p. 75—note new volume if proceeding from the south), 35 miles north, is a superbly protected harbor in an inlet on Nagasaki Hanto, the long peninsula that juts into the East China Sea to the south of Nagasaki. Although the 50-meter-wide entrance between the cliffs, with 5 meters of depth, could be intimidating in a strong northwester, once inside you are safe from almost any wind and sea. The inlet is about half a mile in length and its shores are entirely walled. There are at least three pontoon options. We tied up to one on the end of the small peninsula that divides the bay into two arms, near its head, at **32° 35.014' N, 129° 45.222' E**. We asked permission at the office just behind; there was no fee. Walk through the town at the head of the bay and you come to another, south-facing, harbor. Nomo Ko was very quiet in the prevailing rain and mist, and it would be harder to imagine a safer anchorage. There are one or two small shops.

Sailing north towards Nagasaki on a gloomy morning with fog and drizzle, we were startled when an eerie sight loomed up from the mist: what seemed to be an enormous grey-black battleship at its moorings. This is **Gunkanjima**, an Alcatraz-sized black rock crowded with decaying buildings and structures that give it a ghostly air. For a hundred years this was a colliery, its shafts and galleries extending deep under the ocean, with a small city of miners and their families crammed onto the top of the rock; it has been abandoned since 1970; on a calm day it would surely repay a visit; tour boats visit from Nagasaki.

Nagasaki is approached along a steadily narrowing channel lined by the huge Mitsubishi dockyards and with houses tumbling down the steep green slopes on either side. An elegant grey-silver suspension bridge crosses the inlet and about a mile further on, to starboard, is the small, artificially indented rectangle of water called Dejima Wharf.

Two T-shaped floating pontoons, each with three 15-meter fingers on each side, are reserved for passing yachts and, provided you approach slowly enough, the marina manager may hurry down from his office and direct you to a space. The pontoons are new and well-maintained, and access from the land is controlled by gates that require passkeys, ¥500/USD6. For foreign yachts, mooring is free for the first week, but ¥2,100/USD26 per day thereafter; local yachts pay for each and every day. Our position: **32° 44.642' N, 129° 52.209' E**. There is an alternative location at Sunset Marina, five miles away and under the same ownership, but there is no deal for foreign yachts there. Sunset Marina is less accessible to and from town.

The only downside of Dejima is that it adjoins the ferry terminal, which is busy with comings and goings and whose announcements punctuate the day. Ferries leaving and arriving set up some wake, but as long as space permits (and it usually does) you are encouraged to lay lines across the marina slip to hold yourself off your finger; the problem is not a major one. At Dejima you are five minutes' walk from a major shopping complex and supermarket, called the You-Me Saito; and fifteen minutes from the main train station. Restaurants line the waterfront above the marina, which is lit at night with fairy lights. The main line of the city's excellent tram system passes very close by; it is twenty minutes' walk (or five minutes on the tram) to the nearest Sento, the same to the closest Internet option. There is a chart agent in Nagasaki, perhaps best contacted via the Coastguard; they hand-delivered to us a chart we especially wanted, as their office is some way out of town.

Nagasaki is famous for one terrible moment in August 1945, and a visit to the site of the atomic bomb blast is on most visitors' itinerary. The area is now a leafy, middle-class suburb. The point above which the bomb detonated (the "hypocenter") is marked by a simple black obelisk in a park; close by is the larger Peace Park with a set of sculptures, a memorial hall and a Peace Museum. The Museum documents the day of the blast and also has exhibits on the build-up to the war and the postwar nuclear arms race.

There is more to Nagasaki than The Bomb. This was the location through which, after millennia of isolation, Japan first entered into contact with the west. Immediately behind the marina is a full-scale reconstruction, on its actual site, of the original trading post of the Dutch East India Company. In several locations there are Christian churches—the largest Christian church in Asia was destroyed by the atomic bomb (it has since been reconstructed). Across the other side of the harbor from Dejima is the Foreign Cemetery. Here there is a tiny onion-domed Russian Orthodox Church surrounded by dozens of graves with the distinctive crooked cross of that church; many of these commemorate Russian sailors who died in the naval engagement in nearby Tsushima Strait in 1905, which saw the Russian Grand Fleet annihilated by Japan.

C – Kyushu: The Goto Retto Archipelago

It is a 50-mile sail west from Nagasaki to the southern end of the Goto Retto archipelago. Although night-sailing in Japanese waters is not generally recommended, this stretch is relatively free of fishing floats and nets.

Fukue (Chartlet book H-808W, pp. 136-7) is the main town, on the largest island (of the same name). There are two ferry pontoons, not counting a third that is used by the Jetfoil. At the inshore end of one of the pontoons—on the town side and immediately opposite the four-story building that houses the Coastguard and Customs—a space is reserved for yachts at **32° 41.786' N, 128° 51.020' E**. A modest fee (about ¥120/USD1.50 daily, depending on size) is payable at the office on the first floor of the very modern adjacent ferry terminal. Wi-Fi (free) and garbage disposal are available in the ferry terminal. It is five minutes' walk to a large supermarket. Tourist information is available inside the ferry terminal; there is a bus stop immediately outside it. This corner of the harbor is well-protected; we rode out the fringes of a typhoon here. Customs and Police visited us here. There are a couple of yachts based at Fukue and their friendly owners may well introduce themselves.

Arakawa (Chartlet book H808-W, p. 141B), an inlet on the west side of Fukue with a well-protected artificial harbor, would be an interesting and safe place to visit. **Omoura** (northeast side), reached under a high bridge, is reported to be calm in almost any condition. There are a number of interesting old Christian churches to visit on the island, notably at Dozaki and Mizunoura (near Kishuku). There is an Onsen at Arakawa (reachable by bus from Fukue) and another inside a clinic near Kishuku, also reachable by bus; there is an Onsen inside the Campana Hotel, Fukue.

Eight miles northeast of Fukue is the quiet, beautiful island of **Kabashima** (not featured in the Chartlet book). There are two villages of about 200 persons each, each with an artificial harbor. The best place to stay for a yacht is on the large pontoon in the central bay that almost bisects the island, with the white buildings of an Elementary School and a Junior High at its head. Our position: **32° 45.491' N, 128° 59.317' E**. This could be exposed in a heavy northeaster. The school staff welcome visitors. This island is a classic example of rural depopulation; apart from the teachers and the few school children, almost everyone else is in their seventies.

A further ten miles to the northeast is Narao (Chartlet book H-808W, p. 134) with two adjacent harbors split by a hill. We tied up to the pontoon on the southwest wall in the almost deserted northern harbor, at **32° 50.810' N, 129° 03.482' E** (pontoon not shown on the Chartlet, although the Jetfoil pontoon on the southwest wall is). Wi-Fi (free) is available at the Jetfoil terminal. (Note re Chartlet: the outer, detached, breakwater is straight—there is no bend at the north end—and has no green light; the southern inner wall has two green lights at its north end, not one). Narao used to be a very busy purse-seining port but now sees little if any fishing movement. The southern harbor would be snugger in heavy weather but is tight; it has a couple of small, rickety pontoons. There is an Onsen in the red hotel on top of the hill. There are one or two small shops; the place is very quiet.

The passage north from **Narao** needs to be timed: thirteen miles to the north, a stretch with reversing current of up to 5 knots is traversed; there are no current tables, but slack appears very roughly to coincide with high/low water.

On the island of **Uku Shima**, the northernmost large island of the archipelago, there is a safe modern marina (Chartlet book H-808W, p. 129), behind high walls, with about 40 slips; water on the pontoons; fee of ¥1,100/ USD14. Our position: **33° 15.377' N, 129° 07.737' E**. Fifteen minutes' walk into town there are two small supermarkets and one restaurant. Free Internet is available inside the large yellow-brick municipal building on the waterfront, which is where you also pay for the marina. The marina makes a good, safe base to visit the neighborhood, which is quiet, bucolic, and rapidly depopulating.

From Uku Shima—both the main port and the smaller southern port of **Konoura**, reachable in ten minutes by bus—there are frequent ferries to nearby **Ojika** Island, which has a large artificial harbor with several pontoons. From here you can in turn visit Nozaki Island, by a ferry combination that leaves you on **Nozaki** for about six hours.

High and wooded, **Nozaki** has been uninhabited since 2002 and is now overrun by deer. There is a beautiful Christian Church to visit, and you can walk on trails through the forest to either end of the island; at one end is the abandoned village of Funamori, and at the other, deep in the woods, an eerie abandoned Jinja (shrine). There is a wide sandy bay in the middle of the island, which in steady conditions would be a fine anchorage; there is a tiny, snug artificial harbor in the north corner of this bay, where it would be possible to tie either to the wall or the small pontoon (but the ferry needs the pontoon twice a day). There are no shops. In spring and summer there is a caretaker at the old school, which operates as a hostel.

D – Kyushu: Goto Retto to Fukuoka

The approach to historic **Hirado** (Chartlet pp. 56, 58 in H808-W), on the large island of the same name just off the northwest tip of Kyushu, needs to take account of tides/current. There are current tables available for Hirado Seto, where the maximum current is about 5 knots. The current runs fastest under the Golden Gate-lookalike bridge a mile or two south of the town, and in the immediate approach to the harbor (which is, however, current-free). Contrary to what the Chartlet shows (three), there are only two pontoons, both on the north shore; tie up on east side of the innermost pontoon, with the cream-painted tin roof. Our position: **33° 22.287' N, 129° 33.290' E.** Check in at the small municipal tourist office in the nearby bus-park; they will ask you to fill in a form, but no fee is payable. Another small office in the bus-park is most helpful with tourist information, and free green tea and free Wi-Fi in working hours. Most of the time this is a secure location, but should any swell enter the harbor (or should a ferry leave a particularly large wake), your shrouds/spreaders could be in danger of striking the pontoon roof; use your thickest possible fenders so as to keep your distance. Coastguard and the Police visited us here. There are two large supermarkets; a gas station (diesel available) is about ten minutes' walk from the pontoon.

There is a lot to see and do in Hirado, the first location where Japan had contact with the west, in the 16th century. William "Anjin" Adams, the model for James Clavell's Anjin-San, is buried on the hillside behind the town. There are lots of restaurants (including one that serves whale-meat). There are Onsens in the two largest hotels in town; one of them is below sea-level; turtles watch you idly through the plate glass as you sit naked in the steaming pool. A short bus-ride to the south, on the shores of Hirado Seto, is the ancient, quaint fishing village of Kawachi, where the notorious pirate Coxinga was born.

Six miles to the north of Hirado is the island of **Azuchi-o-Shima** (not to be confused with O-Shima, northeast of Fukuoka). There are three harbors on this island; we spent several days in the smallest, which is in the southeast (Chartlet book H808-W, p. 53). Our position, tied to a wall: **33° 28.471' N, 129° 33.429' E.** There is a pontoon used by the (surprisingly large) ferry, that calls four times a day, but the unused side of this pontoon looked very shallow. There is one shop in the village, which is quaint with narrow streets and overhanging wooden houses. On top of the hill behind town is a red-roofed hotel with an Onsen; this can be reached via a stiff 20-minute walk that cuts off the hairpin bends of the road. Also above the village are a number of wind-generating turbines; if you visit the municipal building at the far end of town, an electronic display will tell you the wind strength "outside."

To the north again from Azuchi-o-Shima is the much larger island of **Iki Shima**, which has several harbors. Uncertain as to which was the most suitable, we had randomly listed **Intuuji** (Chartlet book H-808W, p. 105) as our intended destination. However, after talking to locals and other yachties we discovered that **Gonoura**, on the southwest corner (Chartlet book H-808W, p. 107) is much more suitable, with three pontoons set aside for visitors; the position quoted to us was **33° 44.8584' N, 129° 40.7448' E** (checked on Goggle Earth/Maps). We did not take this up; the Coastguard are present in Gonoura and we judged it likely that they would have inspected us and, finding we had not listed Gonoura, asked us to move on.

Instead, we moved east, passing a nuclear power station, to **Yobuko**. This is an important squid-fishing center and is a large and busy port. There are various harbors within a small, well-protected area; a spectacular suspension bridge joins the big island to an offshore island and separates the two principal harbors from each other. We moved under the bridge and found a wall-spot at **33° 32.610' N, 129° 53.479' E** (Chartlet book H-808W, p. 47), in one of the two "L" shaped enclosures that jut out from the eastern shore. This was not entirely satisfactory; the wall has an unpleasant overhang that becomes evident at mid-tide; the harbor was also very busy through much of the night, with squid boats coming, going, and setting up wakes.

With a personal recommendation, we moved to the small, hat-shaped and wooded island of **Takashima**, which is a mile off the large commercial port of **Karatsu**, but a world away in terms of tranquility. Karatsu can be identified from many miles away by two prominent and very tall chimneys, supported by steel frames, and, from closer, by a reconstruction of a mediaeval castle. There are two adjacent harbors on the south-facing shore of Takashima. The easternmost (now protected by an additional free-standing breakwater not shown on the Chartlet, but visible on Google Earth/Maps) is the quieter, but it may be the shallower, with Low Water Springs depths barely exceeding 2 meters. We tied briefly to the small ferry pontoon (longer term stays on the pontoon not welcome), then (with permission) rafted to a fishing boat: our position: **33° 28.373' N, 129° 59.431' E** (Chartlet book H-808W, p. 45).

There are no cars or shops on the island, but there are frequent ferries to Karatsu. It is a thirty-minute walk around the perimeter, another thirty minutes to the summit. The island is locally famous for its shrine, to which people bring their lottery tickets and cash to be "blessed," and also for a legion of cats.

At **Fukuoka**, the largest city in Kyushu, there are two popular marinas, close to each other: Odo (the municipal marina; https://fyh.jp/) and Marinoa (https://sasaki-corp.jp/offices/marine/nfmarinoa/), located adjacent to a modern shopping complex and identifiable from a distance by a large Ferris wheel.

Odo seems to offer the best rates and is by far the fuller, although its installations are not as modern; our position: **33° 35.463' N, 130° 18.704' E** (Chartlet book H-808W, p. 42C). The approach is straightforward; tie up on the west side of one of the three long north-south running visitors' fingers before enquiring at the office for a berth further in (where there is greater protection). Neither marina any longer offers free moorage to foreigners. Odo charged ¥34,800/USD435 for one month or ¥2,900/USD36 per day—this assumes a length of 8 meters, which is what we are. But we were told informally that the 8 meter length is applied, as a concession, to all foreign boats. Water fee of ¥400/USD5 if the marina hose is used. Coin-op showers. Free Wi-Fi is available on the ground floor of the marina office building. It is a five minute walk to a large food supermarket; the same to a big hardware store; ten minutes to a coin-op laundry; fifteen/twenty minutes to the nearest subway stop, whence central Fukuoka is another twenty minute ride.

Fukuoka is a vibrant modern city with all imaginable services available and is a good place from which to make a visa run to Korea (Jetfoil, ferry, or flights). A small marine supplies shop opens within the main marina office building on most days; there is an active dinghy racing scene. The marina will phone Customs if required; they will then come and visit you on board.

E – Inland Sea: General

Weather. Japanese weather forecasts cover the entire Inland Sea (Seto Naikai) a single zone. This may be of limited use in that so many local effects apply. The only lighthouse reports are from Kobe (at the east end) and on the outer (Pacific) coast of Shikoku Island, where things are usually a lot windier than inside.

From our experience in the Inland Sea (July-October) and also in Kyushu (April-July) we offer the following observations:

- The rainy season ran from May until July 10th; the finish of the rainy season was quite abrupt.
- The prevailing summer winds in the Inland Sea are easterly, generally less than 10 knots, but higher near Kanmon Kaikyo; calms are common.
- We experienced two mornings of fog, in late July. Moving about close to the shipping lanes in fog is not advisable.
- By October 19th there had been twenty-three tropical depressions/storms/typhoons in the NW Pacific. This was a slightly less-than-average year. Only nine approached or hit Japanese territory; the most affected areas were Okinawa, Amami-o-Shima, the south coasts of Kyushu and Shikoku, and Honshu from Wakayama to Nagoya. In Honshu over 100 people were killed in one typhoon, but this was almost entirely due to avalanches, mudslides, and flooding.

- The first typhoon was in late May; by early October the season was virtually over.
- The island of Shikoku shelters the Inland Sea from the worst effects of typhoons.
- Most marinas would serve in case of a typhoon. We sat out one typhoon in Onimichi and felt no wind, even though in open waters in the Inland Sea readings were 50 knots. The only drawback here could be the wake of passing ships, but during a storm warning there are no ships moving in any case.
- It was hot and humid during the summer (over 33 degrees centigrade); temperatures began to drop in early October.

Current animations. An important factor in route planning is current; the circulation of currents within the Inland Sea is complex and can be strong. The Japanese Coast Guard provides useful current animations for the whole of the Inland Sea and other locations (including western Kyuhu, Ise Wan, and Tokyo Bay) at https://www1.kaiho.mlit.go.jp/TIDE/pred2/CurrPred/iCurrPred.htm.

F – The Inland Sea: Fukuoka to Hiroshima

From Odo Marina in **Fukuoka**, it is approximately 50 miles to Kanmon Kaikyo, the tidal narrows between Honshu and Kyushu that are the western entrance to the Inland Sea. Kanmon Kaikyo means "Barrier Strait" and the narrows need to be approached with caution and close attention to the state of the tidal current. Twenty-three miles NNE of Odo, the island of **O-Shima** is a good staging place for the approach to Kanmon Kaikyo from the Sea of Japan. There is a Chartlet of O-Shima's main port (Chartlet book H-808W, p.36), but in April 2011 a new harbor was constructed immediately to the south of the existing harbors; this may not show in the Chartlet but is seen on Google Earth/Maps. Parallel to the new harbor's northern wall is a floating pontoon which is set aside for visiting pleasure craft. The idea is that you Med-moor to it, but as long as there is no-one else there, side-tying is possible. There is a fee of ¥3,000/USD37, payable at the fishing store at the inshore end of the wall; there are showers and toilets in the same building. Our position: **33° 53.633' N, 130° 26.015' E**. Much of the rest of this harbor is taken up with a semi-permanent fish-farm where tourists are invited to try their luck. The adjoining harbor to the north has two ferry docks, the easternmost of which is a pontoon, and which may also be available for yachts. North again of the ferry harbor is the fishing harbor, which was tightly packed when we visited. And a mile north of this set of three harbors is a fourth harbor, which looked a lot quieter and where there is a sizable pontoon. The island is a holiday destination, with sandy beaches and small shops. Note that O-Shima means Big Island and is a very common name hereabouts.

As you approach **Kanmon Kaikyo** from the west, the Kyushu shoreline becomes steadily more industrialized; the last mile or two are marked by wind turbines. Inshore on the Kyushu shore is the large (population 1 million) industrial city of **Kitakyushu**, which was originally the Number One target for the second atomic bomb; on the Honshu side is the smaller city of **Simoneseki**. A suspension bridge joins the two cities at the eastern end of the Strait and there are also road and railway tunnels.

The strait is in the form of a lazy "U" and is about half a mile wide at its narrowest point. At either end, illuminated boards indicate the present direction of current flow (east or west), with the speed, and an arrow shows whether the speed is increasing or decreasing. Current tables are available for Kanmon Kaikyo and it is a good idea to have these on hand. The area of strongest current is close to the bridge, where a strong east-going current that meets the chop raised by the prevailing easterly winds in the Inland Sea can create unpleasant, even dangerous turbulence. Generally speaking, the current is stronger on the Honshu side. The Japan Hydrographic Association provides a useful animation of the current at various stages of the tide: http://www.mirc.jha.or.jp/cgi-bin/w/w-tcp?AREA=kanmon.

Vessels are required to maintain a watch on VHF Channel 16. The traffic control center is called Kanmon Martis and operators speak English; on SSB 2019khz at 0015 and 0045 every hour there are local weather reports in English and warnings of movements of large ships. Kanmon Martis provides a useful summary in English of navigation rules and tidal current information at https://www.mlit.go.jp/jtsb/bunseki-kankoubutu/jtsbnewsletter/jtsbnewsletter_FINo4/FINo4_pdf/jtsbnlE-FI04_1417.pdf.

Small vessels are not required to check in.

There is room for yachts to move without straying into the marked shipping channel. Ideally you should time your passage to begin at the last of the contrary current, and then have favorable current wash you through; the current turns quickly and attains maximum speed in about an hour. Note however that very large vessels also make the most of slack to maneuver in and out of the many commercial and industrial berths that line both sides of the Strait. You may find your path temporarily blocked by a large tanker and its tugs. Small fishing boats weave in and among the heavy shipping as well; in this area our AIS maxed out at 50-plus targets. A detailed paper chart is advisable; C-Map is poor; Chartlet book H-804W covers the Strait adequately.

This is not a scenic location in which to anchor or moor. If caught by the tide or poor light, it may be possible to anchor close to the entrance of **Wakamatsu** inlet at **33° 56.250' N, 130° 51.000' E**, which is to your starboard if you enter the Strait from the Sea of Japan, but this is exposed. Several miles down the same inlet, under a high bridge and then into a cut to port, there used to be an abandoned pontoon favored by Japanese yachts: **33° 52.736' N, 130° 48.514' E** (Chartlet book H-804W, pp. 120-121); across the way is a 24-hour container-loading facility. With the pontoon gone, anchorage is still possible (but hardly desirable) in the northeast part of the bay. The channel is lit almost all the way in.

At the eastern end of Kanmon Kaikyo, notwithstanding a weather forecast for the Inland Sea that called for westerlies, we found that the wind was just south of east, making it impossible to lay a course to **Ube**, where there is another free pontoon. Local sailors later confirmed that in the western end of the Inland Sea easterlies are prevalent.

Accordingly, we peeled off south for about five miles, to the marina at **Shin Moji**. Approaching the marina, you need to take care to avoid large floating oyster farms and associated moorings; at low tide we saw a rusty steel pole sticking up from a patch of otherwise open water. The protected marina has two well-maintained fingers, with about thirty slips, most of which are usually vacant; there is a haul-out facility and a large modern yacht club with adjoining restaurant and wedding chapel; our position: **33° 53.441' N, 131° 00.158' E** (Chartlet book H-804W, pp. 122, 135B). Electricity and water are available on the pontoons; showers (free) in the Yacht Club. Expensive: ¥4400/USD55 for our 27-footer. The marina is on reclaimed dockland; it is a thirty-minute walk to the nearest shops (two convenience stores). Ferries from Osaka dock at the nearby commercial port, two or three miles south. Also on reclaimed land is Kitakyushu airport (not shown on our older paper chart).

Thirty-five miles to the east is a favored stop for yachties: the island of **Himeshima**. We tied to the east side of a south-southeast aligned wall at **33° 43.286' N, 131° 38.820' E** (Chartlet book H-804W, p. 130A). No fees/officials. There are one or two small shops in the quiet, attractive town. At the east end of the island, about forty-five minute walk, is an Onsen with fine views over the Inland Sea. Although there is still some fishing here—the fishing boats come and go in the night, to/from an unloading point close to the place we tied—the island's main industry now is the raising of shrimp, in large saltwater pools through which seawater is circulated artificially.

A further thirty-five miles to the east-northeast is **Heigun Tō** (or Heigun Shima), a very beautiful, high, quiet island well-worth a stop. It is not in the Chartlet book; our position: **33° 46.731' N, 132° 15.849' E**. As you enter the harbor steering approximately west you pass on your starboard the location where the ferry docks (otherwise a tempting location) and, just past it, the black/yellow painted wall to which it ties at night. Tie to the jutting-out segment of sheer concrete wall directly on your bow, which is about one boat's length. Depth here is adequate but in most other locations of this small harbor it is not. No fees/officials. As is the case with so many islands, depopulation has been severe, and the village is very quiet. There is one shop, but it is often not open. Up the hill and over the top on the other (south) side of the island is a beautiful and clean sandy beach. The local specialty is octopus ("taco").

In settled conditions there is a very pleasant and quiet anchorage at **Kodomari Wan**, towards the eastern end of **Yasiro Sima** island, a few miles east of **Heigun Tō**. Protection is good from west through north to east, but you would not want to be here in a strong southerly. Our position: **33° 54.815' N, 132° 24.169' E**; depth 17 meters. There is a sandy beach at the head of the bay.

After Kodomari, the busy main shipping lane continues to the northeast towards Osaka, but a subsidiary route heads north and into the wide, island-studded Hiroshima Bay. There exists a variety of routes for smaller craft, but all are subject to tidal currents, between 3 and 6 knots in strength (see **Tidal Animations** above).

Yachts receive a warm welcome at the **Kaze No Ko** boatyard on a north-facing shore of the large **Kurahashi Shima**, in Hiroshima Bay. The boatyard is in a snug and well-protected cove that is partly encumbered by oyster farms and a number of moored yachts. Tie up to an irregular set of rickety floating docks at **34° 07.238' N, 132° 28.273' E**. Not in the Chartlet book; no officials/fees. The staff are very friendly; they are used to working on yachts and are specialized in fitting hybrid engines to sailboats. The only downside of this location is that, although the yard is on a small peninsula joined to the main island, there is no path or track; you must row 200 meters across the bay if you want to go anywhere. Shops are then some twenty minutes by bike. Kurahashi is linked by a bridge to "mainland" Honshu. Email kazenoko@sf6.so-net.ne.jp.

As you head north into Hiroshima Bay, you pass a number of high islands that have been defaced by massive limestone quarrying: a price Japan pays for its love affair with concrete. Strange-looking limestone-carrying barges can be found tied up in various quiet locations when not in use. Take care to avoid the increasing numbers of oyster farms that clutter protected bays. Although the areas in which these are moored are often marked in the Chartlet book (as red-hatched rectangles), their corners are only sometimes marked and lit with the regulation yellow beacons/lights on small rafts.

Approaching the marina on **Okinoshima Island** from the south, oyster farms dictate a particularly wide sweep to the north then east. The marina (Chartlet book H-804W, p. 67B) consists of four main fingers, totaling about 50 berths, of which about half were occupied when we visited. Our position: **34° 09.460' N, 132° 26.396' E**. This is a well-protected, picturesque location, with high mountains and greenery all around and, if you do not wish to proceed all the way to Hiroshima, it can be a good base for exploring the area. The marina has an excellent mechanic on staff. Haul-out by crane is possible. Water on the pontoons; there is a free open-air shower at the small beach, or coin-op hot showers. Free laundry, free ice, and free use of large freezer compartments. No officials. Rates nominally ¥50/USD0.70 per foot per day, but negotiable.

It is a 40-minute walk (initially up a steep hill, then across a bridge to the main island of Etajima) to the nearest village at **Fukae**, where there are two small shops. A further fifteen minutes takes you to two larger supermarkets.

The nearest bus stop is also at Fukae; from here there are regular buses to Koyo (30 minutes), whence you can catch ferries to Hiroshima or Kure (20 minutes/10 minutes). From the Hiroshima ferry terminal, trams (¥150/USD2) take you downtown; it costs the same to take the ferry from Koyo to Kure, then a suburban train to Hiroshima. With planning you can be in Hiroshima in about two and a half hours after leaving the marina. In Hiroshima there are also several marina options.

On Etajima Island (adjoining Okinoshima) an interesting visit is to the **Etajima Naval Academy**. There are several (free) guided tours a day which, although in Japanese, leave you forty minutes to look around the large and interesting naval museum.

In **Hiroshima** itself, the main sights are the various memorials to the victims of the first atomic bomb, and a large modern Peace Memorial Museum (with explanations in English) but the city is now a vibrant, modern place in its own right. Fifteen minutes by direct ferry from Hiroshima, also reachable by a cheaper tram/ferry combination, is **Miyajima Island**, which has hosted Buddhist and Shinto temples for over 1,000 years. It is famous worldwide for the spectacular and much photographed red wooden Tori (ceremonial gateway) that, at high tide, seems to float on the waters of Hiroshima Bay. You can take your yacht to Miyajima; there is a pontoon at the south end of the bay that contains the Tori.

Closer to Etajima, the large city of **Kure** (ten minutes by ferry from Koyo) has two museums of interest: one hosts a massive model of the World War II-vintage *Yamato*, the largest battleship ever built; the other (adjoining the ferry terminal; free admission) is run by the Japanese Self Defense Forces, who maintain a large naval base here. It has exhibits on minesweeping, but the main attraction is a decommissioned submarine of 1980's vintage, part of which can be toured.

G – Inland Sea: Central

Leaving Hiroshima Bay to head south and east once more, we revisited Kurahashi Shima. At **Katsuragahama**, on the south shore of Kurahashi, is a red pontoon reserved specially for yachts at **34° 06.169' N, 132° 30.549' E**. There are no officials; you are supposed to check in at the large spa/hotel to the right of the pontoon, but this was closed when we visited so we do not know if a fee is payable. The village is attractive, with small shops and a good sushi restaurant. On the shore close to the harbor is a large covered shed where you can view the full-sized replica of the kind of sailing ship that plied from here to Korea about 1,000 years ago. Ryusei Idehata is a local volunteer guide with very good English; he is also a yacht owner and Buddhist monk, with his own small 1,000-year-old temple on the hillside behind the village. Not in the Chartlet book.

Fifteen miles east on **Kamagari Shima** is a hotel complex with a fine sand beach and a large pontoon that is made available free for yachts. We visited overland and noted its position: **34° 09.965' N, 132°44.4217' E**. In calm conditions this would be fine, but it is open to the southwest. There is a nearby Onsen and a restaurant at the hotel, but no shops. Not in the Chartlet book.

In the waters near Katsuragahama we saw the rare Japanese murrelet, known locally as the Japanese penguin. Also in these waters you can sometimes see the finless porpoise, a beluga-like dolphin.

Mitarai (Chartlet book H-804W, p. 48). This historic village straggles along the western shore of a strait that separates Osaki Shima from Okamura Shima, and which allows for a good natural harbor, where anchoring is possible (current about 1.5 knots). **At 34° 11.313' N, 132° 51.160' E** is a tiny marina, just to the northwest of a large and under-used ferry pontoon. We entered the marina leaving to starboard a yellow, lit post. Inside, maneuvering room is tight; head straight in to one of the four pontoon berths, without making a large approach loop. Yachts over about 35 feet in length might be better off tying to the big ferry pontoon outside. There is no charge but check in at the shop/restaurant adjoining the marina; the ferry terminal also adjoins the marina. Water is available from a hose at the shop (ask). This would be very snug in heavy weather.

The main village is about fifteen minutes' walk away. This was an ancient stopping place on the route through the Inland Sea between Edo/Tokyo and Kyushu/Korea; in the quiet back streets are many houses that are several hundred years old. Today the main industry on the island is the growing of mandarin oranges; tiny funicular railways scale the steep hillsides and are busy in season (November/December); and in the harbor you can see a few of the old, specially designed, orange-carrying boats. There is a small tourist office through which you can request the services of a volunteer guide (free) in English; well worth it. Bicycles can be rented.

If you head under the bridges at the head of the Mitarai Inlet (of the three bridges only the easternmost two are high enough for a yacht to pass), the large island in front of you is **Osaki Kami Shima**. Here, on the south-facing shore at Okira, is a marina that we visited by ferry from Mitarai, position **34° 12.643' N, 132° 53.393' E**. The marina is expensive (¥3,200/USD $40 plus) and suitable for small to medium yachts only. The old town of Kenoe, on the east shore of the island, is a more run-down version of Mitarai. Shipbuilding is the main industry; yards are dotted around the shoreline, fabricating surprisingly large steel ships. There is a distinctive shipping museum, concrete but in the form of a ship, on a hillside south of Kenoe.

Miyaura, on Omishima Island. There are two pontoons in Miyaura Bay the approach to which is marked by two large green buoys. The largest pontoon, in the southeast corner of the bay, is nearly 100 meters long and covered; although this is only used for one small and occasional ferry, yachts are asked to go to the other, to its right as you enter the bay, our position: **34° 14.838' N, 132° 59.661' E** (Chartlet book H-804W, p. 95). Fee: ¥1 per ton per night (less than 2c US). There is a large village, at the inland end of which is a good-sized supermarket. Omishima is home to the third-most important Shinto shrine in Japan (Oyamazumi).

Working through the channels between the many islands hereabouts, it is important to calculate the tides/currents; in many places they run at up to 4 knots, but their direction is not always what you might expect. Using the excellent current animation available on the internet (see **Tidal Animations** above) we worked our way south and east to **Yuge Shima**.

Here there is a good natural harbor where it would be possible to anchor but where yachts are also welcome on a free pontoon, our position: **34° 15.482' N, 133° 12.201' E** (Chartlet book H-804W, p. 100). There is space for three yachts each side, but it might be flimsy in a big blow. On a hill behind the village is a modern hotel with a luxurious Onsen; enquire at the little log cabin/tourist shop on the waterfront and they will have the hotel pick you up/drop you off for free. On the east side of the island, only five minutes' away, is a beautiful sandy beach, popular for swimming in summer.

If a typhoon threatens, the gritty port town of **Onomichi** (Chartlet book H-804W, pp. 34-35) is an option. It lies on the north side of a narrow river-like channel between the big island of Honshu and a large offshore island, with houses tumbling down the hillside and a railway line running along the shore. The Chartlet provides good coverage of the entire channel and environs. Currents in the channel run at up to 2 knots and the waterway is busy with craft of all sorts; there are a number of shipyards in the area. On the north shore is a ten-berth marina, our position: **34° 24.484' N, 133° 12.185' E**. Inside, at its far end is a yellow pole light, which marks an underwater concrete mooring block that has 2 meters over it at low tide. While the marina is very secure from the weather (we hardly felt the passing typhoon) it is rocked by passing boats in the channel and, if occupancy allows, it is a good idea to tie up so as to hold yourself off the pontoon. Fee ¥1,600/USD20 per night, payable at the large Business Development office adjoining the marina.

Threading our way east through narrow channels bizarrely lined with shipyards in rustic settings, we stopped next at **Utsumi Marina** (http://www.setouchi-cruise.jp/en/visitor/detail.html?id=26) at **34° 22.243' N, 133° 20.047' E** (Chartlet Book H-803W, pp. 106-7). This is a modern, well-appointed marina in a beautiful quiet setting adjoining a fine swimming beach. There is a modern clubhouse with coin-op showers and a small restaurant; haul-out facilities and mechanic on hand; water and electricity; no village. ¥1575/USD20 per night. Visitor berths are at the inshore end of either of the two fingers of slips; the marina is securely locked at night (6:00 p.m.) with no easy means of ingress/egress after hours. It would be possible to anchor in this bay or the next bay to the west.

Four miles east is the quaint but touristy fishing port of **Tomo-no-Oura** (Chartlet book H-803W, p. 108), whose houses cluster on hillsides around an excellent natural harbor. It is possible to anchor here with adequate protection and swinging room: our position: **34° 22.830' N, 133° 22.755' E**, depth 5 meters. Although there are two pontoons in the harbor, one is constantly busy with ferry traffic, and we were told that yachts were not welcome at the other. There is a disappointing maritime museum (with a very few fragments from a recently retrieved wreck and not much else) but it is interesting to wander around the old, narrow streets and the colorful waterfront. For Tomo and neighboring islands it is useful to have Donald Richie's *The Inland Sea* on hand.

Japanese yachties often go to neighboring **Sensui Shima**, where there is a pontoon and from where you can cheaply ferry back to Tomo.

Ten miles further to the east is **Kitagi Shima**, an island long famous for its granite quarries and workshops where tombstones and carvings are produced. We Med-moored in seven meters at **34° 22.700' N, 133° 32.764' E**. Kitagi is not featured in the Chartlet book. The protection here is good but there is significant wash from the small local ferries as they buzz in and out of a pontoon on the other side of the harbor. There are two small shops in the adjoining village and a slightly larger one in a village on the north side of the island. There is a small Ramen restaurant here and two others on the island, one of which has a small adjoining Sento, useable if you take a meal there. There is a fine high-level biking/hiking track and a good path to the summit of the island, from where there are excellent views over the central Inland Sea. There are good swimming beaches on the west side of the island. Canadian sailor Colin Ferrel and his wife Mika no longer live on Kitagi; they now run a yacht chandlery and sail loft at Nishinomiya marina (Osaka).

Local ferries run to **Shiraishi Jima, Kasaoka** on the "mainland" (where there are much larger shops) and **Manabe Jima**, where the old wooden school is particularly interesting to visit.

Adjoining Kitagi to the north is **Shiraishi Jima**, also not in the Chartlet book. Here you can tie up (free) in the rectangular New Harbor, recognizable at a distance by its reddish exterior wall. There are some unmarked drying rocks about 100 meters due south of the harbor entrance, exactly on the approach path you might be tempted to take; beware. There is a conventional pontoon, and another runs one part way along the inner wall of the harbor; for longer stays we were advised that the pontoon parallel to the wall is preferred; no charge. Good protection. Our position: **34° 24.507' N, 133° 31.504' E**. It is a fifteen-minute walk over the hill to the main town, which depends largely on seasonal tourism. and which has one shop. On the town's main sandy beach, in season, expats Amy and Paul run the Moo Bar, which is a favorite hangout for expat teachers who come over here for some R & R on the weekend. There is a large temple complex on the island and some excellent hiking.

Heading east again, the gaps between the islands start to narrow down and it is advisable to pay heed to the current and tide. We made a stop at **Yo Shima**, which is a small island whose main function now is to serve as a base for one pier of the enormous multi-span bridge that here reaches from Honshu to Shikoku. The harbor is a small, square basin on the north side of the island; we tied up at **34° 23.645' N, 133° 49.083' E**. There are two large pontoons, neither of which is frequented by fishing boats, but tugs and fire boats occasionally call in, the harbor being very close to the most congested shipping area for the entire Inland Sea. The location is bizarre; there is an on/off ramp from the soaring suspension bridge, but on Yo Shima all that exists is a large car park, restaurant, gift shop, and games/tourism complex called Fisherman's Wharf—all abandoned. We were told there would be a fee of ¥500/USD6, but nobody came down to collect any money. Cars and trains rattle overhead, but the trains do not run at night.

Next stop to the east is the island of **Nao Shima** (Chartlet book H-803W, p. 87). Starting October 1st (through March 31st) beware of the large adjoining areas designated for seaweed farming; although they are usually well marked with lit yellow buoys at the corners, these often obstruct the obvious path to desirable havens. We tied to the southeast side of the roofed ferry pontoon at **34° 27.462' N, 133° 58.412' E**; the other side of the pontoon is in regular use by a local passenger ferry. Also adjoining is a terminal for larger car ferries; their arrival, so close, can be disconcerting—but wash is not a problem. Fee ¥1600/USD20, collected by staff at the ferry terminal.

Until fifteen years ago this island was suffering, like most in the Inland Sea, from depopulation and slow decay of the fishing industry. Then the Benesse Foundation (an arm of a large healthcare/education outfit) selected it as the site for locating a wide variety of contemporary art exhibits and happenings, as well as a luxury hotel that is decorated with Hockneys, On the other side of the island—about an hour's walk, or there is a free shuttle bus—six old houses in the village have been selected for "installations." There are many colorful outdoor sculptures, the most well-known of which is a giant yellow and black pumpkin by the famous sculptor Yayoi Kusama, sitting on an old stone jetty. Much of the art is free, and you can buy a single economical ticket to view all six art houses.

Not counting Awaji Shima, which forms the eastern "barrier" to the Inland Sea, the largest island is the next one to the east from **Nao Shima: Shodo Shima**. This is well-developed, but principally for tourism; there is little industry. We stayed in three locations on **Shodo Shima**.

In the west is **Tonnosho Higari** (Chartlet Book H-803W, p. 91); our position: **34° 28.588' N, 134° 10.941' E**. This a free pontoon, well-protected except for winds from due south (which seem to be rare); do not attempt to go on the inside (shore side) of the pontoon, it is rocky. It is a short walk through a tunnel to Tonnosho, the island's main town, which itself is a good natural harbor.

Protecting the pontoon to the east is a chain of three small islands, linked by drying strands; the walk between the islands is a tourist attraction called Angel Walk. There is a massive supermarket barely one hundred meters from the pontoon; this shopping complex includes a luxury Onsen but there is a cheaper and equally nice one on a hotel on the front, fifteen minutes' walk to the east. Small inter-island freighters often tie up for the night at the adjoining wharf, but the bay is quiet enough also to permit anchoring, if you are so inclined.

Ten miles further to the east a large hook forms a wide and extensive natural harbor called **Kusakabe Ko**; again, you could easily anchor if so desired, with 360-degree protection (Chartlet Book H-803W, p. 93A). In the extreme northwest of the bay is a small, three-finger marina. We tied up in the northeast of the bay to the southeast side of a nearby two-part covered pontoon, our position: **34° 28.744' N, 134° 17.896' E**; the north side is used by a local fast ferry. A fee of ¥2000/USD25 is payable at a small cafe at the head of the pontoon. As at Nao Shima, there is a terminal for much larger car ferries close by.

On the northeast tip of the island is a pretty bay with the village of **Yoshida**. Here you can tie to a flimsy pontoon off a small restaurant on a sandy beach, our position: **34° 33.403' N, 134° 20.855' E**, depth 2.5 meters but it looked shallower at the head of the pontoon. Beware an orange buoy forty meters out from the end of the pontoon; it marks the anchor chain for the pontoon. Fee of ¥1000/USD13 payable at the restaurant. The bay is open to the northeast and at certain tidal conditions (regardless of the wind) an uneasy chop comes in, which may give a few uncomfortable hours as the pontoon undulates up and down. There is a picturesque fishing village here, but no shops. If you walk fifteen minutes up the valley, in the shadow of an enormous hydro dam, there is a pleasant and cheap public Sento.

Crossing from Shodo Shima to the "mainland" of Honshu, in the first week of October, the waters were frenetic as small launches worked at laying out large seaweed-farming complexes. We had thought of stopping off at an interesting-looking group of islands at approximately **34° 40' N, 134° 32' E**, but every nook was occupied by a seaweed or fish farm. Some of the islands were being so heavily quarried that it looked as though they would soon disappear from sight. So, we continued northeast, towards a skyline filled with chimneys, petrochemical tanks and other paraphernalia of heavy industry.

The marina at **Kiba**, on the Honshu mainland, is in a well-protected inlet accessed through a relatively narrow channel (Chartlet Book H-803W, pp. 71, 70C); our position: **34° 46.391' N, 134° 43.402' E**. ¥1600/USD20, water & electricity; showers. There is a supermarket about 15 minutes' walk inland, and here you can also catch a suburban train to Himeji, the larger city of which Kiba is a suburb. **Himeji** is justly famous for its fabulous mediaeval castle, reputedly the best-preserved in Japan and featured in the movie *The Last Samurai*.

Almost blocking the east end of the Inland Sea, separating it from Osaka Bay to the east, is the large island of Awaji Shima. At the south tip, at Naruto, a set of narrows is characterized by whirlpools that tourists pay to see (and which are thus perhaps best avoided); in the north, the gap between Awaji and Honshu is wider and the current "only" reaches 7 knots (see **Tidal Animations** above). But this pass still demands respect and careful timing. The **Akashi Kaikyo**, as it is known, has been the scene of several maritime disasters; there have been fewer since a massive suspension bridge—with the second longest single span in the world, at 1,991 meters—obviated the need for local ferry services.

H – Inland Sea: Osaka area

Once through Akashi, you are into the wide expanse of Osaka Bay, with many mooring options; the Inland Sea is effectively behind you. Marinas in the area typically cost ¥40,000 to ¥70,000 per month/USD500 to USD875; rates negotiable, especially if you have a contact; hauling in and out is cheap by US standards but lay-days on land are expensive.

We began our stay with a free week at the well-protected and very modern Suma Yacht Harbor (http://www.suma-yh.jp/) in a suburb of Kobe, our position: **34° 38.497' N, 135° 07.857' E** (Chartlet Book H-803W, p. 51C). Note that the final entrance to the marina now has a couple more protective walls, necessitating a fairly sharp zig-zag; these do not appear on the chart but are clear on Google Earth/Maps. For the first time since we had left Kyushu, officials (Customs) visited us. Free water and electricity on the pontoons; coin-op showers; free laundry. Gas, diesel and haul-out (25-ton Travelift); very helpful staff. It is ten minutes' walk to the train station, the same to a Max Value supermarket, and a further fifteen minutes by train to downtown Kobe. Kyoto, Nara, and Osaka are also easily reached by train; it is four hours to Tokyo by bullet train.

Although ostensibly a modern suburb, with a fine beach, Suma has a very long history and features in Japanese literature as long as 1,000 years ago (*The Tale of Genji*).

We spent winter at Suma Yacht Harbor but reconnoitered the following 5 marinas with a Japanese sailing friend.

1 & 2) Moving clockwise from Suma (which is just west of Kobe, on the north shore of Osaka Bay), the next two berthing options are **Ashiya** and **Shin Nishinomiya**, which adjoin each other on the waterfront halfway between Kobe and Osaka. The tip of the entrance breakwater is at **34° 42.200' N, 135° 20.460' E** (Chartlet book H-803W, pp. 48, 50). Ashiya is smaller but a lot more expensive: essentially it serves a set of exclusive condos. Shin Nishinomiya is the largest marina in western Japan; see https://sinnisi-yh.co.jp/eng (site is in English and includes a good marina map). It is conveniently located (close to suburban train lines) for Kobe, Osaka, Kyoto, and Nara. Modern pontoons with electricity and water; showers; haul-out. There is a set of small yacht chandleries

in the main building, and a restaurant. Price: see website; no free time offered for foreigners. Safe and convenient but, for our taste, large and impersonal and the staff were not especially interested in discussing a concession for a long-term stay.

3) **Hokko Marina** (https://www.hokkomarina.com/) at **34º 40.432' N, 135º 24.4648' E** (Chartlet book H-803W, pp. 48-49, 47C), is the closest marina to Osaka proper. Smaller than Shin Nishinomiya it has all mod cons and welcomes foreigners, but local yachties do complain that it can be subject to the wake of passing ships, located as it is in the heart of Osaka's dockland.

4) **Dejima (Sakai) Marina** (Chartlet book H-803W, p. 43A) is in the extreme east of Osaka Bay, deep in the heart of semi-abandoned dockland at **34º 34.45' N, 135º 27.3565' E**. The location is not inspiring—a large highway flyover serves as the backdrop—and the pontoons are rickety, but the location is exceptionally well-protected and it may be possible to negotiate a much lower price here than at other marinas. No showers; Sento close by. Haul-out possible: a crane visits every two weeks or so. The marina is also a working boatyard and yacht dealership, run by Japanese yachting legend Katsuichi Nozaki and his son Kosuke, see http://www.op-yachts.com/ Email nozaki-k@op-yachts.com or kosuke@op-yachts.com. Very friendly, helpful people with good English.

5) On the southeast shore of Osaka Bay, sheltered by the artificial island of Kansai International Airport (KIX) is the **Aoki Yacht Club** (https://osaka-info.jp/en/spot/tajiri-ocean-community-center/), also known as **Tajiri**, at **34º 23.8981' N, 135º 17.2205' E** (Chartlet book H-803W, p. 39). If approaching from the northeast, a yacht can safely pass under the center span of the highway bridge that links the airport to the mainland. However, the clearance of the second, one-tower road bridge that spans the entrance to the yacht club is only 42 feet. The entrance is narrow, not easy to make out, and could be tricky in rough weather; inside, a long visitors' pontoon runs northwest to southeast, with the office at the head of the bay. Aoki San, who runs a sailing school here, is a well-known long-distance Japanese cruiser who sailed around the world in a 21-footer. There are convenient suburban trains to Osaka and a large "outlet" shopping complex a few minutes' walk away; this location is very convenient for the international airport, but the noise of the jets may deter from a long-term stay. Overnight stays cost ¥1600/USD20.

Southwest of Tajiri on the south shore of Osaka Bay, close to its exit into the Pacific, is **Tannowa Yacht Harbor** (https://tannowa-yh.jp/), our position: **34º 20.2855'N, 135º 10.72'E** (Chartlet book H-803W, p. 34A). It has lots of space, fair quality pontoons, haul-out; there is an active racing scene. The marina is convenient for trains to Osaka, a little less urban than most of the above choices but is on the approach to Kansai International Airport. Tannowa has a reputation for being exceptionally welcoming towards foreigners; monthly rate around ¥40,000/USD500, first week free. Closed Tuesdays (as are many marinas in the region). Email harbormaster Takeda Masayuki at tannowa.yh@nifty.com.

Exiting Osaka Bay to the Pacific, on the eastern shore of the "gap" and a few miles south of Wakayama proper, is **Wakayama Marina City** (https://www.marinacity.com/yacht/), our position: **34° 09.425' N, 135° 10.679' E** (Chartlet book H-802W, pp. 82, 85D). There are two adjacent marinas on this reclaimed island, which may not appear on older charts; Wakayama Marina City is the easternmost, the larger, and the cheaper. ¥1,000/USD12 on weekdays, double on the weekend. Free showers, but no water/electricity on the visitor docks (may be possible for longer stay). Laundry. Haul-out. It is one hour's walk to the station, whence it is four stops to Wakayama, where you can change for Osaka or Nara; this is a good place from which to visit the mountaintop Buddhist monastery at Koya San. The marina is very modern, well-maintained and well-protected, the staff very welcoming, but is in the middle of a modern leisure complex and some way from shops. An Onsen overlooks the visitor berths. Email yacht@marinacity.com.

There are more informal mooring options up the creek (approach from the southwest; the northwest approach, under the more modern of the two bridges, is shallow) behind the artificial island.

I – South/Central Honshu

Weather/current. In winter and spring, north through westerly winds predominate along this indented coastline, but as spring evolves into early summer, low pressure areas that start to pass through every three or four days bring periods of rain, increasing warmth, and easterly winds. Offshore, the Kurushio Current runs powerfully to the east but inshore we received no benefit from it, and probably were set back by counter currents. Its location can be tracked (https://www1.kaiho.mlit.go.jp/KANKYO/KAIYO/qboc/index_E.html).

Hazards. Heavy shipping (up to fifteen vessels per hour) may be encountered in the vicinity of the three major capes on this route (Shio No Mizaki, Omae Zaki, and Iro Zaki). Many coasters in the 700 to 1,500 ton range are not equipped with AIS transponders. Local fishing boats may also be numerous; their courses and vigilance can be erratic, and at night their displays of lights (e.g., all-around quick-flashing green and red, simultaneously) do not always conform to Collision Regulations. From October through May, large expanses of fixed nets may be encountered up to three miles offshore, often weakly lit and/or marked with tall bamboo poles; it is possible to obtain from the Coast Guard charts showing the likely location of such arrays.

Eastwards from the entrance to Ise Wan as far as Omae Zaki is a 60-mile stretch of coastline with no safe refuge. Provided you keep ten miles or so offshore—i.e., out of the normal range of the fishing boats—this stretch can safely be traversed at night.

Itinerary, west to east. Nineteen miles south from Wakayama, the quiet fishing port of **Ao** is a good refuge (Chartlet Book H-802W, p. 76A). Wall-tie to the east side of the center quay in the east pond (the west side is overhanging), or to the south wall in the same pool; our position: **33° 54.228' N, 135° 04.674' E**. There is one small shop in the village; fuel and water are available. No fees, no officials.

Twenty-five miles further to the southeast, on the Kii peninsula, is a large rock-studded bay that has **Tanabe** on its northern side. On account of the many rocks in the vicinity, the shallow underwater shelves off much of the coastline and a profusion of oyster rafts and fixed nets, many Japanese yachties are very leery of this area. However, there are adequate navigational markers and with care a very good refuge can be found deep inside an inlet on the south shore of the bay, at the resort town of **Shirahama**.

Approach as follows: a) **33° 42.420' N, 135° 19.100' E**; b) **33° 41.910' N, 135° 21.990' E**; c) **33° 41.570' N, 135° 21.980' E**; d) **33° 41.110' N, 135° 21.380' E**. There is a detailed two-page color chart, Chartlet book H-802W, pp. 72-73.

Tie either side of a pontoon with an arch at its head, with space for two yachts either side; our position: **33° 41.121' N, 135° 21.318' E**. Fee ¥2,000/USD25 per night but this may be negotiable. There is water and electricity on the pontoon; the closest Onsen is about 20 meters (there are many more in town). Shirahama is a resort town with a fine white sand beach on the seaward side; the season is July and August, and it seems to be quiet most of the rest of the year. There is a particularly fine open-air Onsen (Saki No Yu), with views over the Pacific from heated rock pools, west of the main beach. There are several supermarkets.

Just east of Shio No Mizaki (the cape at the tip of the Kii peninsula) and 40 miles on from Shirahama is the fine natural harbor of **Kushimoto** (Chartlet book H-802W, p. 66-67), protected from the west and south by the peninsula itself and from the east by an off-lying island, with a prominent arched bridge linking it to the mainland. If approaching from the west, you pass the Cape, then turn to port and under this bridge. There are various wall-tie options but we found a quiet stretch at **33° 28.162' N, 135° 47.151' E**. There is no water or electricity; no fees; no officials, although the Coast Guard moor one of their ships opposite this location. There are supermarkets in town, and a Sento. In stable conditions you could safely anchor in the bay outside the harbor walls, as coasters do, but (as elsewhere in Japan) this would likely puzzle the locals. This is a bonito and tuna fishing port.

Sixteen miles north and identifiable from seawards by a mega-hotel atop an island, is another fine natural harbor: **Katsuura**. The approach is from south to north with spectacular rocky islands—some with natural rock arches—to starboard, the mainland to port and the small town built around a set of pools at the head of the inlet. All of the islands to starboard are part of one vast spa resort.

Tie to a wall on the port side as the inlet reaches its final set of narrows and turns slightly to the starboard, our position: **33° 37.732' N, 135° 56.930' E** (Chartlet book H-802W, p. 60). No fees, no power, no water, no officials. Very well-sheltered. If there is no space here, you can tie to the wall of the artificial island you passed to port on the way in, on the opposite shore from the hotel—but it is the kind of wall (with hollows) where you need either a long fender board, or you must pay great attention to the positioning of your fenders. There is a public Sento (much cheaper than the many Onsens in the hotel) at the head of the inlet. At the colorful fish market the specialties are bonito and tuna. Good shopping. From the train/bus station you can easily visit the ancient shrine/temple complex of Nachi Katsuura, built around the highest waterfall in Japan. Close to Katsuura is the town/harbor of Taiji, infamous internationally for its annual massacre of dolphins and pilot whales.

Just north of Katsuura, in the next bay, is a small harbor that is home to several yachts and where a pontoon is made available to visitors: **Nachi Fisharina (33° 38.715' N, 135° 56.412' E)**. We looked at this from the mainland but were deterred by the absence of a detailed chart for the approaches, reports of a number of submerged and unmarked concrete tetrapods, and the presence of surfers just off the entrance.

Still further north is the large commercial harbor of **Shingu**, where logs and pulp from overseas are unloaded for local milling. In its northern extremity is the quiet and snug fishing harbor of **Miwasaki**. There are several basins but the quietest is the easternmost; tie to a wall topped with black and yellow paint, our position: **33° 41.047' N, 135° 59.454' E** (Chartlet book H-802W, p. 57). No fees, water or power but Customs may well pay a visit as they have an office that oversees Shingu. There is a foot Onsen in the fishing harbor and you can walk to the tiny shrines on the islands that have been joined together to form the harbor. A 30 to 40 minute walk to the south is a large modern mall with enormous supermarkets, a DIY store, and a McDonalds.

Twenty-two miles to the northeast is Miki Zaki (Cape Miki) and a pair of beautiful, steep, and tree-lined inlets: **Kata Ura** and **Kuki Ura**. These both afford excellent protection from the open ocean and, although they are studded with oyster farms and other fixed nets, it would be possible to find anchorage in either. In the southern (and larger) of the two inlets, **Kata**, there is a pontoon off a hotel (the Owase Seaside View), where yachts often tie up, for a fee of ¥1,500/USD20; we visited overland; position: **33° 58.088' N, 136° 11.789' E**. The pontoon is on the flimsy side: in a strong blow you would be better anchored away from it. There is a small walled harbor, but it would bear reconnaissance as much of it looks too shallow.

In nearby **Kuki** is a much more solid pontoon, identifiable from offshore by the Tori (shrine gate) at its head; use the south side; there is room for three yachts. Our position: **34° 00.814' N, 136° 15.220' E**. Electricity is available (if you have a long lead) and water from a hose 50 meters away; no fee; no officials. The location is picturesque and well-protected. The village is very small with one tiny shop; there is a train station but to go anywhere the route is largely through tunnels. Hal and Margaret Roth stayed here in the early seventies aboard *Whisper*.

Thirty miles to the northeast, with the shoreline now trending east-west, is a large, multi-armed inlet called **Gokasho Ura**. At its mouth, which is identifiable by an enormous steel yellow buoy, are several sets of fixed fishing nets. Heading up the inlet, you turn to port then starboard to reach the well-concealed **Shima Yacht Harbor**, also known as VOC (Vivre Ocean Club; http://www.vocshima.jp/; Email shima-yacht-harbor@vocshima.jp). For the last mile or so, particular care is needed as you wend your way around oyster and pearl farms, but on the occasion of our visit, large floating foam buoys marked in brilliant red and green indicated the final approach.

Choose a convenient outer finger for your initial berth—or head in as flagged by the marina staff—but only approach the inner bay by the office with caution: much of it is too shallow for a yacht. Our slip: **34° 20.148' N, 136° 41.123' E** (Chartlet Book H-802W, p. 44A, plus good area chart pp. 40-41). Very friendly English-speaking staff gave us an advantageous price. Free showers; there is water and power on the pontoons; haul-out possible; coin-op washing machine. This is a very beautiful, tranquil location where the only sound is birdsong. There is a restaurant/bar at the marina open on weekends/holidays, but it is 30-minute walk to Gokasho and the supermarket and bus station (no train). From Gokasho it is one hour by bus to the famous shrine complex of Ise Jingu. At nearby Hamajima there are good Onsens and some good fish restaurants, notably one called Yotto (Yacht). The Coast Guard visited us here.

Heading east from VOC, unless you turn into Ise Wan towards Nagoya, it is a long haul of over 60 miles to the next safe harbor, under Omae Zaki Cape. Much of the coastline is sandy beach; the one harbor charted (**Fukude**) is prone to silting on its approach and may often only have 1.5 meters of depth. Accordingly, it is best to undertake this passage at night, keeping eight or ten miles offshore so as to avoid fishing boats and nets. You can save a few miles, just after leaving VOC, by cutting through Fusude Strait (between the mainland and a set of pesky offshore islets/rocks) but this is best attempted while it is still light; although buoyed the strait is quite narrow and can be busy.

After Omae Zaki (many ships!) Suruga Wan opens up to port, with Mt. Fuji at its head. At **Shimizu** there is a good municipal marina that we visited overland: **35° 00.693' N, 138° 29.649' E** (Chartlet Book H-801, pp. 88-89—note new volume if heading east). This is in a redeveloped part of the harbor, with a restaurant/mall complex adjoining, but otherwise the surroundings are of an industrial kind. Good protection, with water and electricity on the pontoons. There is another marina in the south of the bay. It is two hours by local train to Tokyo, one by Shinkansen (bullet train). Haul-out by crane is possible. See https://www.portofshimizu-intl.com/overview-1/marinas/.

Shimoda, northeast of the southern tip of the Izu peninsula is an historic location that played a key role when American ships forced the "opening" of Japan in the nineteenth century. The excellent natural bay has been given extra protection by breakwaters, but things could still get choppy in the main bay in a strong southerly.

Shimoda Boat Services has two operations here. The first is a long pontoon and a set of yacht moorings in the quieter, less developed northeast corner of the bay (see English-language website, including prices, at https://en.riviera.co.jp/marina/shimoda/index.html). The second is a set of four pontoons in line, with room for one yacht on each pontoon on the "out" side only. It is on the port side as you make your way into the fishing harbor (which is inside a river mouth).

The second set of pontoons is better protected, more convenient for town, and happens to be at the exact location (marked with a statue and park) where Commodore Perry landed at the head of his squadron of Black Ships. Our position: **34° 40.290' N, 138° 56.777' E** (Chartlet book H-801, p. 74). Water and electricity. It is a five minute walk to the nearest Onsen, ten to Max Valu supermarket; there are two other large supermarkets. There is a book swap at Shelley's English School, in the north of Shimoda by the river. Gas and diesel are available on the waterfront where most of the fishing boats are tied up; they will deliver at no extra cost.

Pay at the office near the yacht moorings in the northeast corner of the bay. Itoh San, who runs the operation, is very friendly; he was associated with the 1992 Japan Americas' Cup challenge. Customs visit once a week (Wednesdays) and are happy to clear you out of the country; you do not need to leave the same day. In order to clear Immigration (a separate operation) you must travel to Shizuoka (three hours by train); they give you 24 hours to leave.

There are many interesting sights in and around Shimoda. Around the third weekend in May, the annual Black Ships Festivities takes place, with music, dancing, fireworks, and ceremonies; Shimoda is twinned with Perry's hometown, Newport, Rhode Island, and ties with the USA are strong. Tokyo can be reached by local train in three hours.

Acknowledgments

*I*n 70,000 miles of ocean cruising, *Bosun Bird* and her crew have never met with such kindness and hospitality as we did in Japan. In light of the overwhelming reception we were given—from fellow-sailors, from patient officials, from complete strangers who tolerated our faux pas with a smile—it seems invidious to single out individuals. But there must be a special thank you for Norimitsu Nishiyama who hosted us in Fukuoka and for Ishii Taizo of *Skal*, who greeted us in Hirado with a cold beer, then opened up his world (and his home) to us. Masami Nakamura of Shimoda deserves particular gratitude as well, not just for welcoming us to her city, but for helping with the translation of the title of this book into Japanese. Fellow Vancouver boat owners Andrew Dandridge (UK) and Martin Suo (Canada) were of great assistance in the design of the cover.

It goes (almost) without saying that neither this voyage nor the book would have been possible without the enthusiastic and unfailing support of *Bosun Bird's* admiral: Jenny Coghlan. She has been as attentive, supportive and careful an editor as she is a sailor.

Any and all errors of fact or interpretation concerning Japanese, the history and the culture of Japan are the author's alone, for which he apologizes without reserve.

About the Author

Educated in the UK, Nick Coghlan emigrated to Canada in 1981. He and his wife Jenny have sailed some 70,000 miles offshore, first in their Albin Vega 27, *Tarka the Otter*, then in *Bosun Bird*, a Vancouver 27. When not sailing, Nick has pursued a parallel career as a diplomat and was the first resident Canadian Ambassador posted to the Republic of South Sudan. Nick is the author of three books covering his diplomatic postings and a fourth on sailing: *Winter in Fireland—A Patagonian Sailing Adventure*. Nick and Jenny now live on Salt Spring Island, British Columbia. Their ongoing sailing adventures can be followed at www.bosunbird.com.

www.ingramcontent.com/pod-product-compliance
Lightning Source LLC
Chambersburg PA
CBHW050140170426
43197CB00011B/1903